Praise for *Who's the Favourite?*

'A moving, searching, deeply researched exploration of relationships so fundamental we sometimes stop noticing them altogether. Whether you're a sibling or an only child, Catherine Carr's book will leave you wiser and feeling more at home in the world.'

Oliver Burkeman

'Sibling relationships are one of the great unexplored human subjects. Catherine Carr writes about them with warmth, insight and intelligence, exploring everything from the funny private languages siblings share to the deep sadness of estrangement between brothers or sisters. Whether you are older, younger or middle, step or only, you will find pieces of yourself in this loving and informative book.'

Bee Wilson

'Eye-opening and true. I wouldn't be who I am today if it weren't for my brother.'

Gok Wan, MBE

'A seminal work on siblings. Authoritative, informative, calming, sense-making, inclusive and above all else immensely readable.'

Annalisa Barbieri, *Guardian* columnist

'Catherine Carr offers a vivid and insightful exploration of the complex relationships between siblings. With warmth and clarity, she examines how sibling relationships form and inform an individual's identity and life. Carr's engaging narrative style brings a fresh perspective to a topic often overlooked... A must-read for anyone interested in understanding the enduring bonds of siblings.'

Fern Schumer Chapman, author of *Brothers, Sisters, Strangers*

'It's so refreshing to read a book that explores the entire spectrum of sibling experiences. Thank you for dedicating a chapter to the complex journey of growing up with a disabled brother or sister – siblings sharing this experience will truly feel seen.'

Clare Kassa, CEO, Sibs

'The bond between siblings is unlike any other relationship. *Who's the Favourite?* reminds us so wonderfully how powerful, complicated and important siblings are, even when one of you is no longer here. Sibling grief can be overlooked and underappreciated, with many feeling like forgotten mourners. I'm delighted that this book shines a light on our stories and gives us a voice, too.'

Callum Fairhurst, Founder of Sibling Support

Who's the Favourite?

The Loving, Messy Realities of Sibling Relationships

Catherine Carr

A Oneworld book

First published in Great Britain, the Republic of Ireland
and Australia by Oneworld Publications Ltd 2026

Copyright © Catherine Carr, 2026

The moral right of Catherine Carr to be identified as the
Author of this work has been asserted by her in accordance
with the Copyright, Designs, and Patents Act 1988

All rights reserved
Copyright under Berne Convention
A CIP record for this title is available from the British Library

ISBN 978-1-83643-128-2
eISBN 978-1-83643-129-9

Typeset by Geethik Technologies Pvt Ltd
Printed and bound in Great Britain by Clays Ltd, Elcograf S.p.A.

No part of this publication may be reproduced, stored in a retrieval
system, or transmitted, in any form or by any means, electronic,
mechanical, photocopying, recording or otherwise, or used in any
manner for the purpose of training artificial intelligence technologies
or systems, without the prior permission of the publishers.

The authorised representative in the EEA is eucomply OU,
Pärnu mnt 139b–14, 11317 Tallinn, Estonia
(email: hello@eucompliancepartner.com / phone: +33757690241)

Oneworld Publications Ltd
10 Bloomsbury Street
London WC1B 3SR
England

Stay up to date with the latest books,
special offers, and exclusive content from
Oneworld with our newsletter

Sign up on our website
oneworld.co.uk

For Squidget and Bad Harry

Contents

	Introduction	1
1	Birth Order	17
2	Roles and Labels	45
3	Orphans of the Storm	77
4	Steps and Halves	103
5	Siblings as Friends	131
6	Sistren and Brethren	163
7	A Note on Only Children	181
8	Glass Siblings	207
9	Estrangement	235
10	Bereavement	275
	Afterword	309
	Acknowledgements	317
	Further Reading	325

Introduction

'Children of the same family, the same blood, with the same first associations and habits, have some means of enjoyment in their power, which no subsequent connexions can supply.'
JANE AUSTEN, *MANSFIELD PARK*

Couples who celebrate their diamond wedding anniversary are vanishingly rare. When spotted in their natural habitats – posing for pictures in the local paper, answering questions like 'Was it love at first sight, Beryl?' – I always wonder: who *are* these splendid individuals who have managed to sustain a relationship for sixty long years? All those Tuesday evenings, I think. All those baked potatoes. All those lazy conversations about overwatered house plants and unpaid bills. I marvel at their steady commitment and scour the scene for clues as to how it's achieved. But mostly, *mostly* I am touched by their ability to peer through varifocals and see the bride or groom of their youth. To behold at the same time the other person at twenty-two and to know what led from then to now. Likewise, I am undone by stories of friends who met over government-issue milk on day one of primary school and who remain inseparable today. It turns out I weep easily at the idea of being known and loved by someone for so long.

I am lucky to have old friends. Being in their company is one of my favourite things, precisely because I feel understood. If I'm feeling a bit lost, they know how to reach through time and summon up my younger self with all their determination and confidence. And I can do the same for them: reset their compass and give them a little nudge along the right course. We keep each other grounded. There is no pretending with old friends.

I have been married a long time, a child bride when it was not fashionable, and it goes without saying that I have indulged in fantasies of 2061 – my husband and I featuring on whatever form of media will replace regional TV news, clasping his dry, aged hand and telling whoever will listen about the young man I married and our secret to a long and happy marriage. 'All those Tuesday evenings,' I will say. 'All those baked potatoes.'

Then, of course, there are our parents. For most of us, our relationship with the people who raised us starts before we even enter the world. When I became a mum in 2007, I remember (high as a kite, naked in a tub) saying over and over to my little turtle-faced baby – in a voice raspy from gas and air – 'It was *you*. All that time, it was you... It was you...' The notion that he had been there all along – listening to the rhythms of my blood as it coursed through my veins during stressful work episodes; or to the rumble of my stomach as I sat on a fuggy train travelling home through the autumn rain – amazed me. So really, at the time of writing I have known

INTRODUCTION

both my boys for their age plus nine months… and, as with most parents, this knowledge of them is unbearably intimate.

Even as six-foot-plus adolescents – their giant flipper feet poking out of strewn duvets as they sleep – they are my babies. They still sleep the same way they did in their cots. Sometimes in the dusky dark, if I am still awake after they've gone to bed, I creep in to check on them. In that moment, the years contract to nothing. There is the older one, on his side, a ragged cuddly dog, both hands squirrelled under his chin. And his younger brother, looking like Hồ Chí Minh lying in state, with his open, peaceful expression.

And that is it, really. Enduring as the parent–child relationship might be, it is still – in the normal running of things – a process of letting go, of allowing your child to become who they are. Your job is to slowly prise them off you, ushering them out into the world, hoping against hope that you have done enough. And, of course, should the world turn as it ought to, you will shuffle off before them, leaving them with a chunk of their lives yet to live.

Magnificent as these relationships are, rewarding as these intimate and rich connections can be, and fortunate as I am to have them, they will probably not be the longest of my life, nor the most formative. That honour is reserved for the bonds I have with my siblings – my two sisters – bonds which have already lasted forty-seven and forty-one years. And should we all make it to old age (eighty-three is the average life expectancy for a woman in the UK), I could boast of knowing them for eighty-three and seventy-six years respectively. That is one hell of a long time.

WHO'S THE FAVOURITE?

It was a former colleague, Jane Garvey, who pointed this out to me during a phone chat filled with idle work gossip, family news and lockdown weariness. I can remember the moment: me slumped in the crook of the sofa mumbling 'yeah, I know' and 'mmm hmm, me too' and then suddenly shooting bolt upright, feeling as if I had been knocked over the head with The Truth. The relationship I have with my sisters could end up being the longest of my whole life. How had I failed to see this? And then almost immediately, I felt compelled to share this discovery with *everyone*.

One of the first things I found when I googled 'sister relationships' was an article by US psychology professor Victor Cicirelli, who has studied adult sibling relationships for years. He found that in older age, eighty-three per cent felt close to their siblings (a higher proportion than younger people had reported). He also noted that sister–sister siblings were most likely to remain close; brother–sisters next likely; and brother–brothers least likely. When I first read it, I remember the thrill that this body of research existed online, ready for me to discover.

The doyenne of sibling research, Dr Juliet Mitchell, wrote, 'When I came across sisters and brothers, "siblings", I had an experience common to many researchers in the field: One moment I hadn't noticed them; the next, they were *everywhere*.' It is true: once you start to consider the part that your brothers and sisters may have played or may still play in your life (even if the bond is frayed or fraught), it is hard to let it go, to ever unsee the ways that their lives are intertwined with your own.

INTRODUCTION

This book is the story of what I have found out between then and now. It is by no means an academic analysis of the sibling research literature. Instead, it is a hymn to my sisters, and to all siblings. It is an exploration of an area not quite convincingly addressed in the self-help space, though this appears to be shifting. Not only do I want to tell you what I have learned about sibling dynamics, I also want to make you long to spool back through the mental cine films of your own childhoods (or iCloud photo albums, if you must) and to reconsider your sibling story. Having spent so much time reading, thinking and – most revealingly – talking to people about their brothers and sisters, I have become more and more convinced of the value in looking carefully, as adults, at our sibling bonds.

If we can learn to understand (and maybe to forgive) our parents, we can gain useful insights into our upbringing and perhaps begin to understand how our shared history as siblings might have shaped the way that we see the world. I also think – if we are lucky enough – we can really benefit from investing in relationships that have the potential to be a refuge for the rest of our lives. I say all this as someone whose sibling story has been knotty at times, complicated by the lives our parents chose. But I do believe that, even if your sibling story can't ever really be *un*knotted, there is much to be gained in considering yourself in relation to them. Even if that is a more solitary quest for understanding and even if it is laced with heartache, it may bring a small sense of clarity or resolution.

Eighty per cent of us have a brother or a sister – and our relationships with them predate friendships, romances and usually outlast the parent–child relationship too. We spend decades alongside them. Research shows that even in adolescence we spend between ten and seventeen hours a day with our brothers and sisters. Obviously, we don't choose them in the way we choose a spouse or a friend but, if anything, this complicates things further. How do you navigate a relationship that is supposed to be close with someone you're meant to feel an affinity with, even when you don't?

> 'The advantage of growing up with siblings is that you become very good at fractions.'
>
> ROBERT BRAULT

Family is the arena in which we train for life. We experience love for the first time. We learn compromise and fairness (you cut, I choose) and, if we're lucky, we are taught kindness and empathy. We learn how to cope, to put up with each other, to plot, scheme and manipulate, united against the common foe (parental rules) and ideally, at the end of it all, we emerge as friends. A lot of this foundational developmental work takes place before we even step foot into formal education. And if we have built good relationships with our siblings, we may take those tentative steps towards our first classroom with a little more confidence.

Laurie Kramer, a clinical psychologist and co-author of a paper titled 'What We Learn from Our Sisters and Brothers', believes her research reveals the impact that good sibling

INTRODUCTION

bonds can have on us for the rest of our lives. I consistently found in my own research evidence of the profound effects of sibling relationships and how the influence of your brothers and sisters can be more significant than the influence of your parents.

Elsewhere, I noted that plenty of female friends, some now mothers themselves, were busy unpicking their own upbringings. A lot of reprocessing seems to happen naturally when you start to recognise parts of yourself in your own children. Often this is followed by a jolting realisation that you are starting to resemble the 'grown-ups' who parented you. Most likely they were also winging it, capriciously setting bedtimes and inventing consequences because they were tired or hanging on by a thread. It's not a new thought, but variations on this theme sure seem to take up a lot of emotional bandwidth at my stage of life – as people try to forgive their parents for making mistakes while (hopefully) doing their darnedest not to repeat them.

Of course, people analyse and vent about more than their mothers and their childhoods. They talk about marriages, friends and bosses, spend hours wondering and worrying about their own children's development and happiness. But I wanted to find out how often people were dissecting their sibling relationship(s) in discussions about immediate family. It seemed that as parents we are fascinated by things like the rivalry which exists between our own children, or the adoration a younger sister has for an older brother. We have all felt our hearts turn inside out watching a baby desperate to catch up with the toddles of her speedier older sister. But somehow, we don't tend to turn our attention back through our own history, to consider how perhaps our role as a frustrated baby or worshipped older brother *might* have shaped our identity. Yet from the moment we are displaced by the new car seat, filled with fresh blankets and a sleeping newborn, or first mimic our older sibling, something really, really significant is unfolding.

My research into sibling relationships began as I searched for books on the subject – the lack of these is telling. Those I could find were largely told from a parent's point of view, rather than interrogating the nature of the sibling bond itself. Understandably, parents are desperate to figure out how to stop the peace-shattering squabbles which plague many households. Of course they are – I know from experience that these are energy sapping and can leave the whole house on edge. But in quieter moments of reflection and introspection, we might look back at our 'family of origin' to learn more about *ourselves*. It seems that between untangling our romantic relationships, navigating friendships and wrangling children, we rarely take time to consider the rich relationships we share with our siblings.

THE PODCAST

As the Covid pandemic took over, I became obsessed, constantly thinking about the wonder of brothers and sisters. I looked online to see what podcasts there were on the subject, certain that I wouldn't be alone in thinking about this. To my

INTRODUCTION

surprise, there was little to choose from. The virtual shelves of audio offerings looked a lot like the real-life bookshop shelves: loads of excellent parenting podcasts, from pregnancy to the toddler years and teens, stuff on romantic relationships and on friendships. And so I began *Relatively*, a podcast about siblings.

It started to take shape in the summer of 2020, after the utter weirdness of the first lockdown when people were venturing outside a bit more (little did we know…). By that stage we had already learned some lessons: I learned that food was going to be very important, so I got better at cooking for my boys. I learned that nature – and walking – was an inestimable luxury. And I learned – during those terrifyingly dystopian times – how keenly I felt the bonds to my 'family of origin'. And I wasn't alone.

Lots of people told me that they had started Zooming their adult siblings in 2020, even if contact had previously been scant. We were frightened and something in our animal brains made us want to ensure our pack was OK. Launching the podcast around Christmas that year captured something of the joy in our connection to our siblings, amidst the uncontrollable drama of the pandemic. There is nostalgia baked into every episode, and that has a function, sometimes useful, sometimes not. Perhaps it was even more comforting to retreat to the familiar, albeit somewhat neglected, parts of ourselves, when the world was a frightening mess. As childhoods were being reshaped by the pandemic, *Relatively* recalled simpler times. As *The Times* put it, it reminded us of 'the forgotten textures of ordinary life in childhood'.

WHO'S THE FAVOURITE?

I wanted to create a show which drew upon the intimacy of siblinghood in order to allow for total honesty. Even someone very famous cannot pretend to be cool next to their brother or sister. The idea was simple: I would interview pairs of siblings separately and then together. That way, each one would have a chance to talk about the other privately and be able to tell the stories of their childhood from their own perspective. When I got the pair together again, I was able to report back what the other had said. The results were really worth the faff of organising and recording three separate interviews. I would sometimes be able to say things like: 'He really worries about you.' Or 'She has always admired your ability to persevere.' And then I could capture unmediated reactions, which were often very moving.

Occasionally, I would be roped into settling decades-old squabbles. Now and again, I would hear the exact same event from years ago – brought to life by two narrators – which I had the joy of piecing together. The creation of a winter wonderland using talcum powder as recounted by Member of Parliament Jess Phillips and her brother Luke was particularly hilarious. Actor and singer Johnny Flynn's memories of driving to Wales for the summer with his sister Lillie and singing in harmony as a family (to mitigate for broken speakers) was another memorable image. Each one of these appeared in my mind like time-worn family photos.

With less happy memories, I found that by interviewing siblings separately and then together, their different perspectives shed new light on the old stories each had come to view as gospel truth. To take part in this exercise, though, one has

INTRODUCTION

to accept that ours is not the only perspective and that all memories are imperfect. Once you do that, you might slowly twig that what you have previously treasured as absolute, impartial facts in your past are always only one part of a much richer reality. Everyone's perspective counts.

Drag queen and LGBTQ+ activist Divina de Campo, for example, tearfully remembered his parents loudly arguing downstairs as he lay in his childhood bedroom. 'It was like World War Three at home,' he said, while his sister Carys, falling asleep in the room down the landing, was completely oblivious. In the same episode, he described the way he dealt with homophobic bullying at school during the dark days of Section 28 (which prohibited the 'promotion of homosexuality') and had no idea that Carys – sitting in the same dining hall at break time – was fully aware of the abuse and felt guiltily powerless to stop it. In these moments of revelation between siblings, they would each come to see the other as the main character in a story about their past.

Since starting to interrogate my own history, I have found that bringing all the versions of one event together tends to be painful. It's usually because the stories we cling to most Gollum-like are the ones where we were either innocent or victimised: I was the *most* hurt, the *least* understood, the *most* unkindly treated. I think there is that tendency in us all (although I also know I'm particularly guilty of this). So to then hear another person's version of events provokes a strange kind of recalibration. You might just start to see the whole of the moon. Or at the very least consider a good hard edit on your own starring role in history.

WHO'S THE FAVOURITE?

Perhaps a more consistently cheering exercise – and one which I did with every pair of siblings – is to find out how each sibling would describe the other. Just as with the stories we hold on to from childhood, we also hold on to quite a fixed idea about our function within the family unit. The labels assigned in childhood tend to stick.

MY OWN SIBLING STORY

I am the middle of three girls, twenty-two months younger than my older sister Bex and a whopping six years older than the baby, CJ. Growing up, we definitely did not swim in the same waters. In 1984, when I was six, our family moved to the Netherlands. Bex was nine and CJ ('Squidget') was just a few months old. For five or so years, we all lived together near the sea in Scheveningen. Bex and I (and eventually CJ) went to the nearby British school. But when I was eleven, my mum moved out, going to live in a nearby town – with a man she had fallen in love with. She took my little sister – then six – with her. Bex and I stayed with my dad in our family home for another year or so before moving back to the UK. Some of those years are blurry in my memory, the chronology still shaky today. But I know my mum remarried quite quickly, and my dad later. Both stepparents already had two children of their own, so we ended up as a separated trio of sisters, with stepsiblings in two countries: seven kids in the mix. I am not for a minute suggesting that our childhood was the strangest or hardest set-up. I have talked to enough people to

INTRODUCTION

know that. But I am sure that the complications in the way we were brought up forced me to think more about siblings than many.

Having the same parents but living apart meant that we became a very small uncontrolled nature/nurture experiment. It also meant that in an instant our unit of three was forever changed. My older sister and I became a pair and the baby became a de facto only child: the hierarchies were realigned. On top of that, because we lived apart, we had to make the effort to keep our relationship going. As children in the 1990s, we didn't do that very well: there was no internet, no email or Zoom, no WhatsApp. Photos still had to be developed on the high street and then stuffed into envelopes and posted across the North Sea, so keeping up with each other's lives wasn't easy. And childhood moves quickly.

That story of sibling separation is *the* seismic variable of my childhood. To understand its effects fully will be the work of a lifetime, I suspect. Interviewing so many other siblings has helped me make more sense of our story. I have learned from other siblings' tales of separation, divorce, pain and enduring sibling bonds – and I want to share some of these with you, in the hope that reading other people's stories might prompt you to reconsider your own history.

Experts on siblinghood say that even in the most cookie-cutter families with 2.4 children and little upset along the way, it is natural for siblings to grow closer as older adults. It doesn't take a pandemic for that to happen. We see the same pattern in people's mid-life tendency to hunt down old friends from schooldays and university. I believe it is because of the deep comfort of being in the company of someone who sees all those versions of you: the child, the teen, the football obsessive, the rebel, the exhausted mum.

It wasn't until I was twenty-one that my mum moved back to the UK. My little sister, having spent her whole life in Holland, came to the UK to do her GCSEs. I had been back for almost ten years and could just about empathise with her bewilderment. We bonded a little over the strangeness of English schools (gym knickers? Lift-up wooden desks?). But ours was still a fledgling relationship, not natural or truly familiar. There was a lot to catch up on, and as teenagers we barely understood what we had to fill in.

Now in our forties, we have done a lot of work, taking time to sketch out our pasts for the other – to make sure we understand each other as fully as possible. But I still find there are things which are impossible to express. In 2020, a friend from school died in a terrible accident. It was someone CJ had never met. All she understands is my sadness about it – she doesn't know how he fitted in with my other friends, my school, the neighbourhood, the town we were teenagers in, so she will only appreciate the fact of the loss, without being able to travel back there with me.

Our separation was exacerbated by the fact that two years after CJ arrived back in the UK, I married my university boyfriend. Six months later, my older sister also walked down the aisle and moved to New Zealand. This period of living on the same soil as both of my sisters ended almost as soon as it had begun.

INTRODUCTION

Though the three of us were pulled apart again, our story is ongoing and (I hope) has decades-long chapters left to write. After all, I would love to fulfil the ambition of sustaining a ninety-year-plus relationship, with all its ups and downs.

My hope is that this book will nudge siblings to think and talk more about what they shared and still share. Because who we grow up with is profoundly important and can tell us so much about ourselves in the present. To get to the truth about who we are, we usually have to start from the beginning, when roles were assigned by birth order and parental whim. And then figure out if these still hold true, because, chances are, we are not exactly who our parents assumed.

1

Birth Order

Or Middle Child Syndrome

'I am the third oldest and I think it would have been a good idea if I was the youngest too. I am not quite sure why my mum and dad wanted to have more children after me.'
LAUREN CHILD, *UTTERLY ME, CLARICE BEAN*

In any family with more than one child, there will be an 'oldest' and there will be a 'baby': a first- and last-born. Add another sibling and you create a middle child: and the scene for so many familiar dramas – both fictional and not – is set. Our places on the roll call will never change. And, as such, a part of our identity will always reside in what position we have held – relative to our brothers and sisters – *from birth*. The tension or puzzle in all of this is just how much of our identity 'birth order' accounts for. Or, more specifically, perhaps – as we mature – how much we allow ideas about our position in the family to dictate the way we act, relate to our siblings and think about ourselves out in the real world.

WHO'S THE FAVOURITE?

What we know (or think we know) about birth order is largely down to an early-twentieth-century Austrian psychotherapist called Alfred Adler. A contemporary of Freud's, Adler was fascinated by the idea that our position in the family might have a direct effect on our character development. He wasn't the first to come up with such theories, but his are some of the stickiest – and will probably sound quite familiar.

Broadly, Adler considered firstborns to be 'privileged, but also burdened by feelings of excessive responsibility... thus prone to score high on neuroticism'. They are 'dutiful and sometimes conservative, mature and high-achieving'. Their neurosis, Adler concluded, stems from having once held the undivided attention of their parents, before being dramatically 'dethroned' by a new baby. Youngest children, he said, were usually the most ambitious, as well as being more likely than their siblings to be 'charming, outgoing, free spirited, manipulative, immature *and* open to taking risks'. He also noted that they could be rather spoiled: after all they are forever the baby and their position in the family constellation is never usurped.

Adler came from a big family, the second of seven siblings. I find myself wondering whether he saw himself as a middle child. He describes these as optimally positioned in the family and characterised by emotional stability, but also – less cheeringly – to have more negative feelings about themselves. Lacking the distinction of being either the firstborn or the baby, middle children can feel bereft of 'significance' (giving rise to behaviour more recently typified by the term 'Middle Child Syndrome'). Middles, notes Adler, tend to be 'people-pleasers, jealous, insecure, outgoing and adaptable'. As a middle myself, reading the birth order research makes me feel a bit torn: on one hand I resent the way that tropes about middle children tend to focus on the negative and home in on our feelings of neglect. On the other, I do sometimes feel overlooked and have joked that I created a podcast to 'finally get some attention' – thereby fulfilling my role to a T.

That Adler's categorisations of birth order attributes remain popular is perhaps because they feel so intuitive. If you look for them, you can easily find examples in your own lives. Just recently, I watched a mother walking down the tube platform, more or less dangling a chubby toddler from her left hand. He was doing a kind of weightless twirling and hopping dance, small shoes barely scuffing the concrete. His mother was visibly anxious: after all, trains come in quickly and the station was crowded. But then I noticed a small girl following about three feet behind. She was swinging a book bag and wearing a too-big blazer, navigating the people and the platform alone. She can't have been more than eighteen months older than her brother. In that moment, Adler popped into my mind. There has to be some truth in it... at least some of the time, I thought, as I watched this vignette of 'the cosseted baby and the responsible firstborn' play out before my eyes.

ANYTHING TO BE NOTICED, AKA NICHE THEORY

After Adler, studies into birth order continued apace. *Born to Rebel: Birth Order, Family Dynamics, and Creative Lives*, written by the American psychologist Frank J. Sulloway in the mid-1990s, is a standout example. In it, Sulloway coined the term 'niche theory', which asserts that birth order *materially* impacts personality development because of our constant need for parental attention and approval. Once the firstborn has cornered the market with, let's say, conscientious and perhaps conformist behaviour, the subsequent children must work hard to hone their personal brand – or niche – which is distinctive enough to pique their parents' interest. Hence those charming and free-spirited last-borns, tap dancing (metaphorically or literally) in front of their parents' faces, twirling harder and harder for any morsel of attention.

Naturally, we all want to be unique and special but, within the family constellation, it's all relative. We're in it together while at the same time running our own little race. Whether you are the doted-on firstborn, supposedly conditioned for an organised life of duty and fulfilling expectations, or the charming baby – used to every indulgence and some seriously relaxed parenting (Coco Pops on tap, in our case) – your experience of childhood will always be somewhat the same but actually *different* to your siblings. So yes, the firstborn gets the parents' undivided attention for a while – something the siblings will never experience. But the fourth child will have the adoration of five people from the get-go. This is identity-shaping stuff.

As a child, I was a bookworm and there were certain books I read and reread, until their covers were tattered and it didn't particularly matter if I lost my place from one night to the next, since I knew the stories so well. One of these

BIRTH ORDER

was the *Little House on the Prairie* series by Laura Ingalls Wilder. From watermelon-borne illness, to Ma making molasses in the snow at Christmas and Pa building their log cabin from scratch, I loved these stories. (I never seemed to clock the extreme peril involved in Frontier life, which lurked on every page.) What hooked me – aside from the intricate domestic details of life as a pioneer – were the sisters. They are an Adlerian dream. In the eldest, Mary, was an exemplar of sensible, upstanding behaviour; in Carrie, the carefree spirit of third-born babies everywhere; and in Laura – the middle child – well, there is rebellion in spades as you see her struggle endlessly to be as 'good' as her older sister. I loved Laura.

> The beads were even prettier than they had been in the Indian camp. Laura stirred her beads with her finger and watched them sparkle and shine. 'These are mine,' she said. Then Mary said, 'Carrie can have mine.'
>
> Ma waited to hear what Laura would say. Laura didn't want to say anything. She wanted to keep those pretty beads. Her chest felt all hot inside, and she wished with all her might that Mary wouldn't always be such a good little girl. But she couldn't let Mary be better than she was.
>
> So she said, slowly, 'Carrie can have mine, too.'
>
> 'That's my unselfish, good little girls,' said Ma.
>
> She poured Mary's beads into Mary's hands, and Laura's into Laura's hands, and she said she would give them a thread to string them on. The beads would make a pretty necklace for Carrie to wear around her neck.

WHO'S THE FAVOURITE?

Mary and Laura sat side by side on their bed, and they strung those pretty beads on the thread that Ma gave them. Each wet her end of the thread in her mouth and twisted it tightly. Then Mary put her end of the thread through the small hole in each of the beads, and Laura put her end through her beads, one by one.

They didn't say anything. Perhaps Mary felt sweet and good inside, but Laura didn't. When she looked at Mary she wanted to slap her.

Birth order springs up all over the place. It is very useful grist for writers and producers, providing recognisable archetypes that eighty per cent of us have some kind of personal insight into. From C. S. Lewis's *The Lion, the Witch and the Wardrobe* with brave Peter as the de facto 'head of the family', peacekeeping middle Susan (and 'something to prove' middle Edmund) and baby Lucy. To Sharon Horgan's recent award-winning show *Bad Sisters*, in which Sharon plays the responsible eldest Eva, while Grace, Ursula, Bibi and Becka slot neatly into versions of prescribed birth order roles like ducklings following behind her.

And like a call and response from popular culture to our own lives – and back again – we watch and read stories about feckless younger brothers or spoiled baby sisters, and then keep adding our own. When showing people our new house, I have (more than once) heard myself say 'strong firstborn energy here' when sweeping an arm over the meticulously tidy scene that is my older son Max's bedroom. By comparison, his younger brother Theo's room often resembles a bin fire. A primary school teacher I know revealed that colleagues in the privacy of a staff room sometimes triangulate a child in terms of sex, birthday and birth order to explain classroom challenges or triumphs. For example:

> Teacher A: Alfie is really struggling with sitting on the mat.
> Teacher B: Alfie… remind me…
> Teacher A: Summer baby, youngest of three boys.
> Teacher B: Ahhhh. That explains it.

When recording the podcast, I also found that in almost every single instance, these (Western) tropes about birth order seemed to have been thoroughly internalised, often used as shorthand by siblings to privately describe one another to me: 'Oh, he is every inch the baby' or 'She was such a goodie-goodie big sister.' It's fascinating that stereotypes are offered up as ways to explain the dynamics in people's specific sibling relationship. Perhaps that's because they provide a comfort of 'knowing your place' in the family and feeling you belong to each other, in a system which only really makes sense when you are together. Or maybe it is because it is inescapably true that you are – and always will be – the baby or a middle, even if you occasionally deviate from the accompanying scripts.

All the brothers and sisters I interviewed wanted to demonstrate just how intimately they understood each other. It was sometimes through private jokes, shared language (which we will come to) or stories. But at some point, these tropes were invariably wheeled out to articulate something about each other's dispositions. Birth order provides an affectionate, sweet and, crucially, easy way to do that. 'She *would* say that, as the youngest.' For that reason, I usually started each interview with a question like 'Who came first?' It's the perfect warm-up. Starting with the birth order 'icebreaker' (just as I have here) prepares people to go further into more idiosyncratic aspects of the sibling dynamic, into details which might be harder to capture, messier, funnier and ultimately more revealing than the familiar stereotypes of 'big sister/little brother'.

> 'A very long time ago, when I was a little girl, I didn't have a naughty little sister at all. I was a child all on my own. I had a father and a mother of course, but I hadn't any other little brothers or sisters – I was quite alone.'
>
> DOROTHY STYLES, *MY NAUGHTY LITTLE SISTER AND BAD HARRY*

Lewis Goodall, a political broadcaster in the UK, told me that his world was rocked with the arrival of his little sister Meg when he was four. He distinctly remembers wondering what on earth his parents could want with another child. After all, he had spent four years being a very happy little funnel for absolutely all of their love and attention. He took his disappointment with Meg's arrival out on, well, Meg. 'I remember very much the world when she wasn't there,' said Lewis. 'In the whole of the family, I was the only kid and I kind of loved that and I didn't feel that we needed another one.' I asked him if he had a nickname for her as a child, and he replied, 'Yeah: "Go Away!" I just didn't want anything to do with her.' Their relationship matured as adults. And when Meg helped Lewis through a tricky patch in his life, he finally stopped seeing her as merely a willing prop to his elaborate and slightly exploitative imaginative childhood games of *Crystal Maze*, pub landlord or (more tellingly) radio DJ, and valued her more as a confidante instead. She said, 'For so many years he thought of me as his tiny sister whereas I am a fully grown woman. I have children. I can deal with issues and I can help.'

It was the conversations that flowed from the familiar premise of birth order theory that were always the most interesting, when siblings left that well-worn territory behind and plotted the course of their lives together afresh. How brothers and sisters became friends as teens, for example, how they interact as adults, or negotiate, care for and depend on one another over decades proved the richest territory. I loved hearing how the so-called annoying baby of the family grew up to be the coolest of the bunch, showing the older kids the way, or how the dominant older sibling and the rebellious middle child worked out their differences as middle-aged women. It's the evolution of this fascinating and long-lived relationship and our ability to reflect on it as we age together that provides the most fertile ground for analysis.

One of the most honest and self-reflective sibling pairs I talked to were the singer, actor and author Johnny Flynn and his little sister Lillie, also a singer and actor. They came on the show merrily expecting to talk just about nicknames and nostalgia. But what 'Stumblebum' and 'Squirtface' ended up sharing was that Johnny's life didn't mean much BL (Before Lillie) and that he was so in love with her as a kid, he wanted to marry her. They were inseparable and, when he left to go to boarding school on a choral scholarship, he was devastated. 'It was quite bleak,' Johnny said. 'I find it hard to talk about, and have since wrestled with a lot of sadness around it.' When his own son reached the age he had been when sent away to school, Johnny found himself holding him closer. Their sibling rapport has proved fundamental to subsequent relationships. I could relate: when my eldest reached the age I was when things collapsed in my childhood, I was overwhelmed. In that little boy, I saw my small self, and I was finally able to grieve, for the first time, for everything that had been broken. That grief encompassed the temporary loss of my little sister.

Both Adler's and Sulloway's work on birth order has informed research the world over. Many of the studies test a version of their theories asking: 'Does a person's position in their sibling group determine certain personality traits or outcomes?' The more of these I read, however, the more I found flaws. Studies involving children don't really account for the ages of the children participating. So the firstborn may exhibit more maturity at the time of participating by virtue of simply being older. This risks confusing the effects of birth order with the effects of age. And they don't always factor in the size of the family – which is key. So when articles about high achievers make a fuss about them being the eldest, they may neglect to point out that the majority of these success stories come from small families, where they have benefited from more parental attention anyway. All these things matter.

It also became apparent that many of the studies ask people to evaluate their own personalities. And I wonder how accurate anyone's description of themselves can be. If you're asked about your character for a sibling study and you're well aware of the assumptions about your position, it might be tricky to see yourself through any other lens. You might find yourself leaning into or consciously away from these assumptions. A problem which doesn't just present itself in responding to academic studies – but also often in life. The American Psychological Association points out that the very belief that the 'hypothetical condition' Middle Child Syndrome exists, may have something to do with how assumptions about the personality characteristics of 'middles' are endlessly recycled (I always think of Elliott in *E.T.*, but many more modern examples abound). The creation of an annual Middle Child Day, which takes place in mid-August – for example – does little to help. I also know from personal experience that I am more likely to be ribbed for behaviour that matches the Middle Child Syndrome stereotype and that instances of me taking risks or being creative (like the youngest) or conscientious and uber-responsible (like the eldest) are more often allowed to slide past without comment. Confirmation bias is strong in this field.

Dr Julia Rohrer works at the University of Leipzig in Germany. On a podcast about her work, she said she only really heard about birth order stereotypes later in life and has been fascinated by their cultural purchase ever since. She believes they resonate as strongly as they do, simply 'because people are endlessly interested in trying to understand why we are the way we are'. Looking at where you are placed in the family provides a neat starting point.

Dr Rohrer's research is distinguished by the sheer volume of data she has accumulated. With her team, she has evaluated over 400,000 people from America, the UK and Germany, comparing the personality profiles of same-family siblings but also same-position children from different families and who had never met – so comparing firstborn brothers from several families, for example. She was (broadly) trying to assess if a child's position in the family maps on to the Big Five Personality Traits, widely used in psychology.

- Openness – are you open to new ideas and experiences or do you prefer routine?
- Conscientiousness – are you organised and dutiful or more impulsive?
- Extroversion – are you more outgoing or reserved?
- Agreeableness – are you naturally trusting, empathetic or more suspicious?
- Emotional Stability – are you even-tempered, calm or prone to anxiety?

Throughout her research, nothing confirmed that a person's position in the family would engender a pattern of personality traits: simply being the older brother or sister will not *make* you more conscientious and nothing about being the baby *equals* an easy-going extroversion. There are simply too many other variables at play.

I discovered, however, that Dr Rohrer did find that the firstborns tended to score very slightly higher in questions to do with 'self-reported intellect'. For example, they more readily agreed with the statement 'that they enjoy thinking about complicated ideas'. On that basis, the study found that there is a sixty per cent chance that the firstborn will be a teeny bit smarter – but that is not *determined* by the fact that they are the eldest. Because, of course, that would mean that 100 per cent of firstborns scored higher on these questions, when, in fact, in four out of ten cases, the children born later did. Something that Rohrer says really pleases her younger sister.

Rohrer's research chimes with the work done by Petter Kristensen and Tor Bjerkedal, whose 2007 study looked at 60,000 pairs of Norwegian brothers. They found that, on average, firstborns enjoy a slightly higher IQ than their younger siblings, by about three points. Those born first also tend to complete their education with a higher-level degree and opt for traditionally prestigious careers, such as medicine or engineering. Interestingly, the research also included some families where the eldest child had died. In those instances they found that second-borns who then grew up as the oldest (living) child in the family had average IQ scores equivalent to firstborns. This was designed to illustrate how family environment and expectations can also account for 'markers of intelligence' alongside genetics.

WHO'S THE FAVOURITE?

After all, the firstborn is likely to benefit from the funnelling of 100 per cent of the parental attention until the next child arrives – which might just set them up for a smidge more of a chance at academic or career success than their younger siblings. Although the picture will vary a little from family to family – depending on things like the age gaps between children and how much *total* time the parents have at their disposal – broadly, with more siblings the attention pie must be divided into a greater number of slices. This is known as 'resource dilution theory' and might well explain why there is a perfectly filled-out baby progress book for many firstborn children, complete with locks of hair, footprints and fingerpainting samples. And why – if you are child number two or three or beyond – your arrival and first steps are probably documented by little more than a few creased snaps stuffed into a scrapbook somewhere; your parents were just too busy.

A NOTE ON AGE GAPS

Dr Cara Goodwin, a child psychologist and bestselling author, has analysed dozens of academic studies on the subject. She suggests that, from the parents' point of view, the ideal gap between siblings is around two and a half years (a conclusion based overwhelmingly on the physical effects of pregnancy and birth). From the point of view of the children, however, a wider age gap seems to be more beneficial – particularly in terms of achievement. Partly due to that resource question again: time as well as money.

A larger gap, I might add, can have a positive effect on the siblings' relationship, as well as on their schooling. Children with more years between them are less likely to have intense rivalries and are more likely to listen to each other. That's according to Professor Victor Cicirelli, author of *Sibling Relationships Across the Life Span*, whose research also shows that younger siblings are more likely to take the advice of a sibling who is four years older, than one who is just two years their senior.

Drew Law is a psychotherapist who is fascinated by birth order and always asks clients about their relationships with their brothers and sisters. He says, 'When I was studying, I was always saying to myself, "Why aren't we making more use of this dynamic? Why did we give up this as a resource?" Now working in practice I realise that it always provides a useful perspective.' Through the work he did with classical musicians early on in his career, he found that in orchestras, the first violinists were usually oldest children and the percussion sections tended to be heavily stacked with middle children ('You'd want to go for a drink with them,' he laughs). Those violinists were generally bad at negotiating with each other, creating a fraught working environment as a result. Drew knows a lot about resource dilution theory and realises there are possible sociological explanations for the tricky dynamics caused by the strong personalities in the string section (perhaps canny parents pumped money into making sure *one* child 'made it', for example). He also understands that simply being the first-born does not ensure that you will automatically be a more talented or ambitious musician, or struggle more with compromise.

But he has also worked with enough siblings to conclude that you ignore birth order and the relationships between brothers and sisters at your peril. 'It's rare,' he remarks, 'for patients to acknowledge that it [the sibling relationship] is going to have the weight and value that it eventually can have.' He continues, 'Of course, birth order is not deterministic. But whether or not it's any more or any less non-deterministic than, say, [child psychoanalyst] Melanie Klein and what eventually became attachment theory, or Freud and conflict between fathers and sons... is hard to say. But if a story that an individual patient brings to you has a sibling element, it's *never* incidental.'

NATURE, NURTURE, CULTURE

Much of what I have discussed so far as received wisdom or cliché is, of course, largely culturally based and should not be extrapolated to imply that any such thing as the 'universal family' exists. I mean, even in my own postcode I know that there is no such thing. And if there was a universal family then it would follow – argues Dr Rohrer – that if you researched siblings born in countries where 'families are large and resources are scarce', you would see even more pronounced effects from the dilution of resources on the younger born siblings. But this is not the case. Looking at the effects of birth order on personality types in Indonesia, for example, she found the second-born was more likely to be more 'intelligent' – not the first. And the reason? It's still traditional, in some parts of the country, to take the older sibling out of education early and send them to work to start helping to support the family.

Similar findings were reported in a study by researcher Michel Tenikue, whose work looked at families from across twelve sub-Saharan African countries, and it showed just what a crucial role household income plays. Poorer families, he found, tend to send the older kids out to work as soon as possible – to increase the household income immediately – meaning their education suffers. Whereas in more financially robust households, parents invest more in the firstborn's education than the second-borns, because they will 'age out' first, becoming responsible for the parents' welfare in older age. Equipping them for better-paid long-term employment is sensible.

The financial security of a family can interfere with any 'traditional' birth order stereotypes in both developing and developed countries. The results of that Norwegian study were breathlessly written up in the *New York Times*: 'a cumulative effect that could mean the difference between admission to an elite private liberal-arts college and a less exclusive public one.' But dig deeper and you'll find a 1989 study of more than 100,000 people, published in the journal *Science*, which found that in small and medium-sized families, birth order had no effect at all on how far children went in school. And in some really big families, the seventh- and eighth-born kids were *more* likely to continue their schooling, often because their slightly older parents had more money by the time they arrived.

Likewise, psychology professor Joe Rodgers has pointed out that what might at first glance 'look like a difference in IQ based on birth order and family size' could actually be related to 'parents with low IQs having larger numbers of children'. As he concludes, 'Have parents with lower IQs in the United States been making larger families? Yes. Do larger U.S. families make low-IQ children? No.' It's hard to completely untangle birth order effects, it seems, from the kaleidoscope of other forces at play.

> 'I looked at him and thought about having to go through it all over again. The kicking and the screaming and the messes and more – much more. I felt so angry that I kicked the wall.'
> JUDY BLUME, *SUPERFUDGE*

Drew Law is firm on one thing when it comes to brothers and sisters: the precise moment the younger sibling joins the family. He believes that regardless of how siblings evolve and mature, the way their stories start matters. The first baby is born into an adult world. 'That is their brand,' says Drew. 'It is what marks them forever. They are bathed in adult behaviour and adult speaking patterns... and the longer the period of time that they spend by themselves in that adult world, the more fixed that experience of relationships becomes.' It also means, he says, 'they have quite a long psychological journey to make' if, after three or four years, a sibling turns up.

When my own second child was born, his older brother was only twenty months old and he had not yet acquired much language. One evening, however, shortly after the baby arrived, he found the motivation to try. We were all in the sitting room, and he was enjoying a bottle of milk and a bit of TV while I fed his little brother on the sofa. After a minute or two of side-eyeing us, he pointed to the baby and said, 'Put that,' and then gestured to the bassinet on the carpet and added darkly, 'in there.' I was proud of his verbal development even though the moment felt quite ominous.

By contrast, says Law, what distinguishes the second-born child 'is that they are born into a family. They're not born into an adult world with adult values.' Their role models are often two-year-olds. Plus, according to a 2017 study from MIT, second-born children tend to have less maternal attention than their older siblings overall. Because while they enjoy the attention of their mother (or father) on family leave when they are born, their older sibling is also often around during that period, cheerfully lapping up an extra share of the available input. The latter, in effect, gets two bites at that particular cherry. So, argues Law, when second kids become rebellious, it is understandable that it is a rebellion 'against the conservative adult focus of the firstborn child. But they do that in a kind of non-verbal way' from when they're tiny. Anyone with two children will relate to the dynamic of facing the flailing fury of the 'baby' who cannot tell you that they do not want to leave the park/go to the shops/turn off the telly, alongside an oddly rational older toddler who has understood the brief. Sometimes they even try to intervene – to reason with their younger sibling, in a strange little sing-song voice you recognise as a version of your own. 'Mummy says you can have a biscuit if you stop.' It makes you feel like weird co-conspirators and must be doubly maddening for the tantrum-er, who not only isn't getting their way but is now being ganged up on: by people who can *speak*.

It is with the arrival of a third child, says Law, when the trouble can *really* start. 'The middles will look at the third-born and think, "OK, maybe I've got an ally here to challenge the conservative dominance of the firstborn child", or maybe they'll realise that Mother is giving all her love to the baby.' This, he thinks, is where the middles get their practice in manipulating and negotiating. Put out at the unceasing funnelling of love to the baby (who will be the subject of a much stronger maternal focus forever if they are the lastborn), middles then often sidle on over to the oldest and start to forge an alternative alliance. 'They'll say, look: what you and I share is that we've been usurped by that!' They have, he explains, both been dethroned. But what Drew Law says he likes about middles is that they maintain this ability to 'drift' through life. They are naturally adaptable.

While eldest and middles might feel put out by the baby's arrival, the process does help to toughen them up, Law believes. Last-borns, so secure in their mother's affection, might end up being the most vulnerable of all. The first time they experience an emotional abandonment like their siblings have might well be the death of a parent: 'When they do have their first crisis in adult life it is both traumatic and unfamiliar.' It is something he sees in his work. 'I have sat with barristers and fund managers who found redundancy or replacement almost impossible to bear, and who would have previously told me they were "the baby of their family". For all their competence and confidence, they hadn't yet developed the requisite resilience their siblings had.'

After listening to Drew, I returned to Sulloway's niche theory – the premise that we all fight (consciously or not) for the parental limelight, by differentiating ourselves in their eyes. The next chapter is all about the roles and responsibilities that siblings assume (or are given) in the family and how they might shape our experience of sibling relationships both as children and adults. But the more I read about birth order and personality, the more I believe these areas are inextricable from one another. That there is a smudgy crossover between the idea that it is birth order that determines which identity we develop (when of course it cannot genetically *really* be true), and how the roles we choose to play – or are assigned – when we are with our parents, our brothers and our sisters go on to shape us. I think it comes down to this: how closely we identify (or have been encouraged to identify) with the stereotypical ideas about our birth order influences which labels we go on to accumulate.

Perhaps a good example is the way that (incredibly) twins repeat the birth order/personality clichés, when obviously the age difference is normally measured in minutes. But ask any set of twins in your life, and I bet you they will be able to tell you who is the older twin and by precisely how long. I would even wager another few quid that the twins will talk in terms of 'older/more responsible/protective'. It's endearing. (A note that in some countries, the older twin is considered to be the one who is born last, staying behind to push the younger one out... their first demonstration of 'big brother or sister energy', perhaps.)

TV doctors and food policy campaigners Chris and Xand van Tulleken talk a lot about their entertaining and often fractious twin relationship. They have even discussed about it in their award-winning BBC podcast. When we initially spoke, they explained that they firmly adhere to the notion of one twin being the oldest (Xand) and the other (Chris) being the youngest.

We ended up talking at some length about the ways that siblings (in general) can be so different from one another. I told them that I like to think of families being formed along rivers: when we are born, we are placed – Moses-like – on to the rolling stream and away we float. If we have a twin, they are likely bobbing along beside us (give or take a few minutes) and the water surrounding us is largely the same. It is just as cool or fast-flowing, muddy and swirling or benign and chuckling. We have the same experience.

However, if we are not twins, we are never in the same body of water together. The conditions we arrive in will have changed, just like the weather... and the water has moved along. When I think of siblings, this image really helps me, because it illustrates how implausible it is that a child would have the same experience in their family as their sibling. It's so improbable.

The parents are invariably older, maybe richer, poorer, more tired, separated or remarried. Studies like the one in Indonesia do much to convince me that there are a great many forces on us. Quite aside from money, the family may have relocated and the environment is kinder or harsher. The school in the new place is better or worse, more nurturing or less. There's a new dog, a hamster dies… a grandparent becomes sick or a sibling leaves home. They are the firstborn, who created their 'parents', or they are the final addition to a gaggle of kids – the one who 'completes' the family. And the river flows.

A version of this 'shared environment theory' comes up when a family experiences trauma. This week I chatted to a woman who walks her dog in the same park as me. She told me about a friend of hers who had died suddenly over Christmas. The friend was young, her children only nineteen and seventeen. The lightning bolt of their mother's death has struck them at different ages and stages and so their experience of loss will not be the same. They will be united by their loss in many ways, of course, but when their mum died, one was in their first year at university, the other was at home with his dad, managing his school exams. Over time, this difference in experience will be part of the story they tell about the most awful Christmas ever – and part of the way they come to accommodate the enormous sadness of their loss.

'A sibling is the lens through which you see your childhood.'

ANN HOOD

WHO'S THE FAVOURITE?

And I suppose that's why it makes sense to me that the existing research into the effects of birth order demonstrates that it cannot categorise us all neatly. In some ways, thanks to my own childhood, I understand this very well. As adults, my sisters and I have talked at length about the way that the break-up of our family affected us. CJ was six, I was eleven and Bex was thirteen. There is comfort in the shared trauma – and at the same time a huge amount of loneliness in the bits that hit us uniquely hard. Even at the time, the ways in which we felt permitted to grieve the situation was dictated by our birth order. The baby was to be protected as she was so young. But really, eleven is not so old. It just happens to be older than six. And thirteen is tough for a host of reasons. Everything is relative.

Since starting the podcast, I have read academic papers describing the role that siblings play in one another's lives as potentially the 'missing piece' of psychoanalysis, neglected in the endless study of the parent–child dynamic. I find myself sympathetic to this theory, particularly because it is 'live'. Parenting in the sense of raising or educating children does tend to end. And there is a sort of role reversal that can gradually take place. But siblinghood is an ever-changing enigma, pushing us closer and pulling us apart according to age and circumstance, altering our sense of self at times dramatically, at times imperceptibly along the way.

One grim evening ten years ago, during an overwhelming week of solo-parenting, house renovations and work, I suddenly realised that I might have to cancel a longed-for day with old friends. After putting the boys to bed, I perched on a dusty sofa bed and sobbed about it on the phone to my little sister. She soothed my hiccupping pity party and came up with a calm and practical plan. It felt like she granted me permission to have the fun she knew I needed. The relief I felt – and still feel – when I lean on her and find she is strong enough to prop *me* up, is enormous.

Jess Phillips MP and her brother Luke Trainor came on the podcast in its infancy. Their sibling story has stayed with me ever since. As a teen, after a harrowing incident which left him angry, Luke began to take drugs and spin out of control and, eventually, out of the family house. Jess, the older sister, felt immensely protective towards her little brother, instincts which were tempered at times with anger, sadness and grief. As adults, the roles have significantly switched. Luke is an academic at Birmingham University and Jess is a member of the Labour government. Following the murder of the MP Jo Cox (and I would bet even more so after the nastiness of the 2024 election campaign) Luke was worried and frightened for his big sister, who these days inhabits a world full of real danger. Nothing about the order of their birth comes into it. Nothing about the fact that she is the oldest prevents her baby brother from worrying about and protecting her. Circumstances change and, if we are lucky, our relationships with our siblings can bend and flex to accommodate them.

THE FAMILY AS A CONSTELLATION

Dr Rachel Watson is the director of the Institute of Family Therapy, and her work is based on the idea of the family as a system in which everyone influences everyone else. 'Think of it like one of those mobiles which hangs above a baby's cot,' she told me. 'If you move one bit, all the other bits of it change.' When she sees a patient, she always considers their place in that system or 'constellation'. This kind of therapy which can involve talking to the whole family 'has the strongest evidence base of any psychotherapeutic modality', Rachel explains. Getting accounts from mum, dad, brother and sister means that all perspectives are covered and hopefully the truest and most detailed account of what is going on can be formed. In practice, she says that could mean that if she's working with a teenager who is not willing to speak, she might be able 'to change their experience of themselves' by working with – and talking to – their parents. Change one thing in the interconnected system and every other piece of the system will respond. When I spoke to her about birth order effects specifically, she told me that it is something she definitely bears in mind (along with a host of other factors) but that she 'does not hold with any static ideas of what it means to be an older, middle or baby'. It plays a role along with all kinds of other contextual influences.

However, one way that birth order can have a material effect is in dictating how the siblings in a family – sometimes called a 'Sibset' – operate as a group. 'It functions,' she explains, 'within the bigger family, but also works separately. It has its own unique hierarchy and discrete "rules", for example about who has a right to have a voice, and when.' As children in that sub-system, your siblings are not really your peers – there are power structures at play. That might be because of birth order – being the eldest and dominating the younger ones. It may also depend on innate personality traits, environment or emotional maturity.

Dr Watson says she always finds particular value in involving the brothers and sisters of a patient in sessions, because they know so much about what is going on in the sibling sub-system – much more than the parents do. She finds siblings are often the 'most generous with their ability to say, "this is what's *really* happening"'. She adds, 'In my experience they're very able to say, "I think this is not *just* about you"... They have a bird's eye view that nobody else has.' It can be both humbling and reassuring.

When I was very small, I was introduced – via a jumble sale book stall – to the series of children's novels by Beverly Cleary about Ramona Quimby and her big sister Beezus (Ramona's mispronunciation of 'Beatrice'). The books are a treasure trove of big sister/little sister truths and I have been rereading them while writing this book. Beezus and Ramona fight, fall out, get angry, claim not to love each other, and make up. The books are written from Ramona's point of view, so even when you see her tactically deploying a tantrum to get what she wants, she is given a voice to explain herself, and you can't help but sympathise. After talking to Dr Watson about who has a chance to speak in the Sibset and why, I now see this as a very clever device. By contrast, Ramona's sister Beezus is the well-behaved, quiet older sister, who is exasperated at Ramona's antics, calling her a 'pest': 'Pest was a fighting word to Ramona, because it was unfair. She was not a pest, at least not all the time. She was only littler than everyone else in the family, and no matter how hard she tried, she could not catch up.' I think about that last sentence a lot.

In a later book in the series, Beezus is driven mad by her younger sister who spoils her birthday cake. 'Beezus felt very gloomy indeed as she dried her face. She was a terrible girl who did not love her little sister. Like a wicked sister in a fairy tale. And on her birthday, too, a day that was supposed to be happy.' But a few pages later, her mum Dorothy and her aunt Beatrice tell Beezus about all the terrible and awful things they inflicted on each other as children. Beezus is amazed. 'Why, thought Beezus, Aunt Beatrice used to be every bit as awful as Ramona. And yet look how nice she is now. Beezus could scarcely believe it... A lovely feeling of relief came over Beezus. What if she didn't love Ramona all the time? It didn't matter at all. She was just like any other sister.' As with both Beatrice and Dorothy, it is generally not until and *unless* we spend some time talking as adults – when we are on a more equal footing perhaps – about the dynamics which shaped our shared childhoods, that we might be able to see exactly where and how things started.

2

Roles and Labels

'Go out more, keep cheerful as well as busy, for you are the sunshine-maker of the family, and if you get dismal there is no fair weather.'

LOUISA MAY ALCOTT, *LITTLE WOMEN*

Dr Avidan Milevsky is a research scientist at the Department of Behavioural Sciences and Psychology at Ariel University in Israel. He's convinced that the sibling dynamics forged in childhood can last our entire adult lives. 'When I speak to American audiences,' he told me, 'I often say, unlike Vegas, what happens in childhood does *not* stay there.' Alongside his academic research into siblinghood, Dr Milevsky also works as a therapist, asking clients to think about the labels they were given (or took) as kids, how that shaped the roles they played in the family and how both might be affecting them now. 'So much of our adult self, from mental health, family dynamics, marital issues, success at work… once we kind of peel away at it, the raw element is a sibling dynamic,' he says. 'And there's some very good research about that. It's the power of the sibling dynamic together with the power of childhood: that this is your label, and this is *you*. Now, fifty years later, you're still kind of burdened by it.'

WHO'S THE FAVOURITE?

Birth order automatically generates a few labels – the conscientious older child, neglected middle or rebellious baby – and these might go a long way towards describing your role. But there are myriad other labels which we are assigned (or assign to ourselves) in our nuclear universe. We might be the worrier, the sensitive one, the careless one or the kind one, for instance. We might develop a reputation for being helpful in the kitchen, hopeless with homework or great at entertaining younger relatives. All of these labels add up to describing our function in the family. It's not hard to imagine a significant crossover: instances where a child's role in the family is informed by their birth order position. The eldest daughter, for instance, with her dutiful attitude, might slide into the role of Chief Organiser of Family Events or, later in life, Co-ordinator of Elderly Parental Care.

The labels from childhood can endure, lasting well into adult lives. But while they may be obvious to our families, they are not always that clear to others, lurking below the surface and ready to pop out whenever you are back together with your siblings. You may be amazed to discover that your party animal friend from university is actually known as the 'quiet one' when at home with her rowdier brothers. This phenomenon is probably not that unfamiliar – those of us who have visited their partner's family for Christmas or a birthday celebration may well have witnessed the weird transformation that takes place, the person we know as independent but reserved morphing into someone helpless or a little bit bossy.

One explanation for this process can be, says Dr Milevsky, the parents: there is something about the 'force of parents, who helped shape the sibling dynamic in the first place. So, for example, the siblings might be fine until the parents walk into the room, and then? They kind of revert to those old ways of doing things.' Parents are usually the ones who first attach labels to their children, by commenting on their habits, talents or shortfalls. It stands to reason that their very presence serves as a reminder of a dynamic they had a hand in creating. Without the parents (and perhaps away from home), siblings may feel more able to express their grown-up identities, as they do in the real world. With them there, the old patterns re-emerge: everyone knows their place, and the family slots back to 'how it always was'. It can be a comfortable and worn-smooth groove that we slide back into as brothers and sisters, remembering old jokes, stories and behaviours. 'He is acting like that and so it "makes" me act like this.' We play our relative part.

Perhaps you have felt the shift as you settle into a weekend with your siblings? Expressing your new grown-up self with a pension, a new hobby or even professional expertise can feel awkward and can get promptly squashed. You may be ridiculed for thinking you could be outdoorsy – 'You hated getting muddy as a kid!' Or patronised for your new personal finance enthusiasms. The fact that you once threw away a Christmas cheque with the scrunched-up wrapping paper in 1987 will be wheeled out as evidence of your total hopelessness with money: *forever*.

'Siblings: children of the same parents, each of whom is perfectly normal until they get together.'

SAM LEVENSON

WHO'S THE FAVOURITE?

Professor Susan McHale's work on childhood labelling stands out in this field. She takes the idea of our identities out in the world, 'smart or sporty or caring', and points out that we often only see that success measured in relative terms against our brothers or sisters. 'You can be the smartest kid in your class,' she observes, 'but if you have a brother or sister who's smarter, it doesn't matter.' In other words, your self-image out in the world is shaped, at least in part, by how you compare to your siblings, potentially forever. Sibling researcher Dr Laurie Kramer agrees and thinks the deep-rooted tendency to compare ourselves to our siblings can affect what we try to achieve even as adults. 'Asked to give a speech or do a challenging job, a less accomplished younger sibling might decline, thinking, "If they knew my older brother, they wouldn't think I was so great."'

Flashes of insecurity like these, Dr Milevsky explains, can be destabilising, because they mentally return us to childhood: 'Let's say a co-worker minimises me at work, and I spiral into depression. Once you start digging into it, there's a guy who has a story of an older brother who's more successful. As a child, he was told, "Why can't you be like him?", and so now he's *very* sensitive to being seen as "less than". The sibling dynamic is at the core.' He believes that using the 'sibling lens' with his clients can 'open up' all kinds of different issues, which are still driven by unresolved tensions between siblings. These unresolved and unhappy dynamics cast a shadow over relationships you build as an adult. If someone close to you acts a familiar part – perhaps bullies you in the way your older sibling used to – you may instinctively revert to old sibling behaviours to cope, reflexively finding yourself playing a well-practised role.

DIFFERENTIATION

In 1976, American psychologist Frances Fuchs Schachter investigated the labels that siblings choose for themselves. She found that the strong desire to be 'known' as an individual fuels the need for separate roles in a family. Her paper 'Sibling Deidentification' (a concept now usually referred to as sibling differentiation) proposes that brothers and sisters share out the traits among themselves to limit competition for parents' attention and increase their own status within the family group. It's an idea which chimes with the niche theory set out by Frank Sulloway from the previous chapter.

Schachter's theory is roughly this: to be loved for who you are you must be seen as truly distinct from your siblings. So, to try to resolve sibling rivalry (also known as the 'Cain Complex'), children *deidentify* with their brothers and sisters, claiming different labels and creating individual roles. This usually happens during adolescence – the stage of 'Identity Development'. For example, if your older sister is known for being organised and studious, there is greater value, Schachter argues, in 'deciding' (perhaps subconsciously) to be creative and a little messy. There is then a little list of things which you, and you alone, can be uniquely loved for. I found this beautifully illustrated in an interview by Simon Hattenstone in the *Guardian*, who spoke to the tennis star Serena Williams about her siblings. 'We sisters all fit into particular roles,' says Serena. 'Tunde was the forgiver; she had a heart of gold. Isha was the caretaker; she looked after each of us. Lyn was our play pal; she was everyone's favourite knockabout buddy. Venus was my protector... And me, I was the princess; I was everyone's pet.' I read this quote to Professor McHale, who immediately asked if Serena was the baby of the family. She is.

In my own family this kind of labelling was tricky. In common with lots of families who live between different homes and not always together, it is simply harder to keep track of who is supposed to be what. When my little sister CJ was still in Holland and I lived back in the UK, I didn't know much of what she was up to, and vice versa. The effect of that disconnect was twofold. It removed the competitive element of claiming roles, as the family structure was scrambled and parental attention was fairly low down the hierarchy of needs. And, because we were not plugged into the day-to-day of one another's lives, we made do with pretty scant headline updates.

I honestly could not have told you how academic my sisters were compared to me. Or whether I was the sporty one or whether that title belonged to another. Before mobile phones and the internet, it was hard to get a handle on the ups and downs taking place in someone else's life. For those reasons, some of my ideas about my little sister were frozen at a particular point of her development – in my mind she was six years old for a *very* long time. She certainly remained the 'baby' for longer than perhaps she should have done. The moniker 'Little One' which my dad used lasted well into her adult life.

This matters because when you gather with your siblings and settle back into the familiar patterns of your shared childhood, these identities can provide a rich sense of belonging and intimacy. While it may be annoying to be teased for always being the person with the messiest bedroom or accused of attention-seeking even when you're not even speaking, there is comfort even in the irritation. You can reminisce and poke fun. The stories might be tired, but they feature you all. The jokes might be well worn, but they get funnier over time because everyone is in on them – there's a tenderness to anticipating the punchline. For children who don't have that reservoir to go fishing in together, it can – believe me – feel like a loss.

As adult sisters, we have made the effort to understand each other, to celebrate our individual strengths and to paint new pictures about what we are like now. At times we have told the others about who we were, filling in the blanks from the past. 'I was such a goodie two shoes at secondary school.' 'I used to skive every single cross-country run ever. HATED it. And now I love to run.' Each of these little nuggets of information help to colour in the pictures I have of my sisters in my head, but I will never – with confidence – be able to say to them, 'You've *always* been so stubborn/bossy/spoiled.' Because I'm just not quite sure.

Schachter found deidentification to be particularly pronounced in same-sex siblings and those close in age. After all, on the surface, so much is similar. I know I am not the first younger sister or brother to be treated with some surprise by teachers who, having taught my older sister, assumed I would be a 'mark 2' version of them. I was not. It was annoying for assumptions to be made based on my sibling and to disappoint simply by not being her.

This theory may also help answer the big question that sibling researchers are always circling around: 'How can it be that two siblings who share genetics and a home end up being so different?' It's a phenomenon partly explained by the 'non-shared environment theory'. That's the idea that while siblings may live together, many other things about their specific experience are different: they had parents interacting with them differently, usually relaxing into their parenting style over time, and they had their own set of teachers and friends. And it is also partly explained by birth order: how many children were in the family before them, and how many came after. But another key part of the puzzle, researchers believe, is siblings *actively* deciding to craft a different identity than the one their siblings already have: hence, deidentification.

Psychologists – and the siblings themselves – seem to agree that the labels and roles 'up for grabs' are usually not used twice. Once one child has claimed the title of 'funny' or 'peacekeeper', it is unavailable for anyone else. My own two boys are close in age, and perfect candidates (according to Schachter) for deidentification. They haven't ever been particularly jealous of one another, but by the ages of eleven and nine there was evidence of the younger one trying to assert his individuality in opposition to his sibling. The oldest was (and is) very keen on football. Being almost two years older, he had learned to play – and developed the necessary strength and coordination – first. By the time his little brother started to catch up physically, there was a sense that the 'sporty' label had been swiped. It was demotivating. He started to give in a little too easily (I thought) to his brother's perceived prowess. The solution? Semantics. When we started calling him 'athletic', things changed for the better and his competitive spirit kicked in. We were basically saying the same thing but using different words to do it, allowing them to *feel* different enough to claim their space and separate identities even though they were both focused on sport.

'I'll never forget the family with two sisters,' Susan McHale told me. 'They were not too far apart in age and played football. And I asked them how similar or different they were, and they said, "Oh, we're completely different. She plays offence, I play defence!" And the parents collaborated in that differentiation.' What feels touching in these examples – the footy-mad girls or my own two boys – is how to the outside world, the differences are likely imperceptible and immaterial; they won't affect how they're seen or treated at all. What matters hugely within the family, where the quest for individuality and need for attention is heightened by the proximity of brothers and sisters, all jostling in the same arena and fighting for distinction, is of negligible importance anywhere else.

'In families, children tend to take on stock roles, as if there were hats hung up in some secret place, visible only to the children. Each succeeding child selects a hat and takes on that role: the good child, the black sheep, the clown, and so forth.'

ELLEN GALINSKY

Although these are sweet stories, there is a note of caution about the temptation for parents or carers to get involved in labelling their children or divvying up the roles at all – no matter how carefully. It's easy to see how and why it might happen, by trying to demonstrate that you see and value your children for being individuals. 'You're so creative. You're the family's little artist.' It's the kind of scenario which usually arises when you're trying to settle a sibling squabble by soothing hurt feelings caused by something painful like failure. A noble enough impulse, but – if done thoughtlessly – it can create real pitfalls, says Dr Watson from the Institute of Family Therapy. 'It can influence how people are thought about. What attributions siblings are given by others impacts on the ways in which they have room to grow, develop and thrive.'

For over thirty years, Laurie Kramer has run a programme in the US called 'More Fun with Sisters and Brothers', working with children aged four to eight. The aim is to build strong sibling relationships by improving social and emotional competencies. When it comes to the parents' role in all that – especially when thinking about labelling – she told me, 'We're looking for equity. We're not looking for equality. It's not like every time you tell one child "you're really good at art", that you have to say [to the other sibling] "you're really good at spelling". But over time, you know that the kids will definitely keep track. They're taking counts of who is favoured at whatever moment, and they're wondering why… and is it fair? Or accurate?'

In his clinical work, Dr Milevsky says there is often a tendency to ignore the impact of the parents and to 'blame' our sibling for the relationship we have. 'We say, "My brother was such and such, or my sister was such and such, and therefore xyz." But we have to be honest. Is it really your sister's fault that this happened? Or did your parents compare you, or set unhealthy boundaries, which then helped to *shape* that relationship?'

It all goes back to the idea of the family as a system, where one moving part will have an effect on all the rest. He explains, 'In the [sibling] literature it's called the parental context. It speaks to the power that parents have.' The firm glueing of rigid labels on to developing kids by their parents is not the only way that sibling dynamics can be spoiled, of course, but it is a significant example. Another, arguably more toxic one, Dr Milevsky continues, is when parents cling unwaveringly to a whole 'family narrative' which requires absolutely everyone to toe the line: 'In the United States, the pressure might be about going to an Ivy League university. "All our kids go to Harvard; all our kids go to Cornell." It's not a healthy definition of "family" and it creates sibling dynamics that can be vitriolic.'

I never intended for this book to act as a manual for parents. But I do think it is helpful to acknowledge the role they play in creating family culture. More often than not, the effects are fairly benign, but in dysfunctional families the story is different. The categories that professionals use to describe family roles (in children and adults) are eye-opening and I bet that once you learn to identify them, versions of them will seem to pop up everywhere: in film, literature and maybe closer to home. The most common categories are: the Clown, the Invisible Child (sometimes called the Lost Child), the Enabler or Caretaker, the Golden Child and, finally, the Black Sheep/Scapegoat.

> 'Lydia was the first daughter, the first child, the one who had to be everything her parents wanted, the one who had to be perfect.'
> CELESTE NG, *EVERYTHING I NEVER TOLD YOU*

I have recently rewatched the TV adaptation of Celeste Ng's novel *Little Fires Everywhere*. Having read and loved all her books, I could suddenly see just how much of the narrative drama is created by siblings wrestling with the childhood labels they carry. In her work, there is also often the overlay of cultural expectation, which adds a sharpness to everything. In *Everything I Never Told You*, which deals with child death, the sadness is unbearable. In it, Hannah is a textbook Invisible Child, tiptoeing through the family, desperate not to disrupt the fragile equilibrium: 'Hannah, as if she understood her place in the cosmos, grew from quiet infant to watchful child: a child fond of nooks and corners, who curled up in closets, behind sofas, under dangling tablecloths, staying out of sight as well as out of mind, to ensure the terrain of the family did not change.' 'Invisible' children like her can have low self-esteem, feeling their opinions aren't heard or valued. They may also find it hard to express emotion. They can, however, become precociously wise about human behaviour, having quietly watched people from 'under dangling tablecloths' for so long.

In the same book, Hannah's older sister Lydia (who dies as a teenager) is the perfect Golden Girl, 'the reluctant centre of their universe – every day, she held the world together. She absorbed her parents' dreams, quieting the reluctance that bubbled up within.' The weight of parental expectation on Lydia is crushing, as any success she enjoys is closely chased by the twin fears of failure and rejection.

Golden Children in families often feel burdened like this: shackled to expectation, condemned to conform and perform, sometimes driven to succeed by parents who cannot see the toll that being 'perfect' can take. Lydia bears a double burden: her mother is vicariously academically ambitious for her – pushing her towards a career in medicine that was never available to women of her generation. Her father is desperate for Lydia to flourish socially; fearful she may replicate his lonely experiences as a child of Chinese immigrants. Children like Lydia, tottering under such impossible weight, but nonetheless 'delivering', can easily start to feel as though any affection or attention is dependent on achievement, rather than because of who they are. It is miserable and unsustainable, as Lydia's mother eventually realises:

WHO'S THE FAVOURITE?

Lydia tugging a heavy book from the shelf, saying, 'Show me again, show me another.' Lydia, touching the stethoscope, ever so gently, to her mother's heart. Tears blur Marilyn's sight. It had not been science that Lydia had loved. And then, as if the tears are telescopes, she begins to see more clearly: the shredded posters and pictures, the rubble of books, the shelf prostrate at her feet. Everything that she had wanted for Lydia, which Lydia had never wanted but had embraced anyway. A dull chill creeps over her. Perhaps – and this thought chokes her – that had dragged Lydia underwater at last.

Before I learned about all of the different roles, I had only really heard about the idea of the Black Sheep, which I thought simply referred to a wayward uncle or rebellious cousin, used to mean 'someone who is less keen than us to play by the unspoken rules of the clan'. What I hadn't realised was how the Black Sheep might function in the family system, where very often they are the yin to the Golden Child's yang. The glare of attention on the Golden Child can create a vacuum of sorts: a space for the family's Black Sheep to be painted into being.

In English, the 'black sheep' was originally, well, a sheep. Darker than the rest of the herd, its wool was less valuable at market. From the eighteenth century, it has been used to describe people and usually implies a degree of rebellion, an uncomfortable feeling of 'not fitting the mould'. While there's no agreed clinical definition, psychologists use the term in family therapy to mean things like 'the sibling who has looked on in horror at the curse of the Golden Child and chosen to reject it'. Or the sibling 'who steps off the path' prescribed by that whole 'family narrative'. Psychologists report that Black Sheep can be left angry and impotent, with little motivation to try to succeed, saddled with the label of 'failure' simply for not wanting to conform.

In truly unhappy families, 'Black Sheep' can be used interchangeably with the term 'Scapegoat', which suggests something altogether more troubling. After all, its biblical roots describe a creature forced to carry the sins of others, before ultimately being sacrificed. And sometimes that scapegoat, says psychologist Annie Wright, a specialist in family trauma, is treated like 'the person that everyone in the family thinks "needs fixing" (or the "identified patient")'. 'A family unable to face up to the fact that the whole system is *collectively* responsible for the happiness or unhappiness of the family unit,' she explains, 'will instead simply pick on the scapegoat,' essentially deferring and outsourcing the pain, tension and anxiety felt within their dysfunctional system on to just one person. That person then psychologically, and sometimes physically, 'holds' the emotional energy of the family, manifesting it in symptoms and behaviours that the other members of the group can point to and say, 'There's the problem. It's her, not us.' It's an uncomfortable thought.

The Enablers and Clowns hold very different functions, although both try to deflect attention away from what is really wrong in a family. Enablers will try to 'keep up appearances' by endlessly trying to sort and fix every slight problem. Their tendency is to empty their own tanks while attempting to rescue the person struggling. Jess Phillips spoke on the podcast about sitting on the phone to her brother 'for hours' every day during the height of his drug addiction. 'I was scared,' she said. She described how she had 'been picking Luke up out of the gutter since I was a child'. No one can criticise her instincts, but there is a risk that in those kinds of binds we begin to believe that if we could only try harder to help (lend more money, listen more), the issue would resolve.

Ironically, the message this sends to the sibling is that their deplorable behaviour is somehow... acceptable. It is usually better (but much more difficult) to step back and allow the natural consequences to play out. If not, you risk creating an intense and often doomed sibling dynamic. In families where the parents have enabled the behaviour of one sibling, to the dismay and frustration of the other children, therapists agree the resentment lasts well into adulthood.

Clowns are also working hard to avoid confronting the root cause of the family's problems. But, instead of setting themselves up as self-appointed 'fixers', they take on the mantle of court jester, greeting any tension with a joke. It can appear fun, but the cumulative effect is to deny other family members the opportunity to express themselves fully: to open up, have difficult conversations or resolve conflicts.

And that one gets to the crux of it all. If we feel somehow forced to 'stay in our lanes' – performing the same role ad infinitum – we don't give ourselves or our siblings room to develop. At the more harmless end of the scale – in average families full of their unique foibles and oddities – it might just have a kind of mild stifling effect, making the family dynamic feel superficial and stale, like a wind-up toy, only able to do the same trick over and over again. At the other end of the scale, in families with serious issues, being confined to performing the same unhealthy roles on a loop can fuel real unhappiness. If you have ever watched *The Bear*, the excruciatingly painful Christmas episode 'Fishes', featuring Carmy's mum Donna (played exquisitely by Jamie Lee Curtis), will be burnt into your brain. Her monstrous behaviour is endlessly enabled by the practised choreography of her damaged children. It's so easy to see the slow-motion car crashes of family upset when shown to us on screen, and so hard to imagine ourselves escaping the part we play in our own real-life family dramas.

Though it may be a stretch to describe the family in Louisa May Alcott's *Little Women* as dysfunctional, it is another book where the 'parental context' – the influence parents exert on the sibling system – is defining. Published in 1868, it traces the four March sisters on their journey out of childhood during the American Civil War and under the guidance of their 'Marmee' (their mother). The girls have very distinct roles. The eldest, Meg, assumes a second mother role to the others, which continues in later life. Jo, the second eldest, is passionate and rebellious, determined to pursue a career; Beth is pure, 'a conscience' to the others. And Amy is the spoiled baby through and through. A decent helping of 'Christian struggle' narrative underpins Marmee's attempts to shape her daughters into four ideal 'little women', urging them to modest virtue, humility, self-sacrifice and sisterly love, the better to build characters 'fit for heaven'. It is their own version of *The Pilgrim's Progress*. 'Our burdens are here, our road is before us, and the longing for goodness and happiness is the guide that leads us through many troubles and mistakes to the peace which is a true Celestial City.' Rereading the book as an adult interested in siblings, and with new-found understanding of identity development, I find the idea that all the girls are measured against just one character ideal even more challenging than I did as a little girl who identified strongly with Jo and all her rebellious ways.

> 'I'll try and be what he loves to call me, "a little woman," and not be rough and wild; but do my duty here instead of wanting to be somewhere else.'
>
> Jo March in *Little Women*

It is worth noting two key aspects of role making and taking. One: the size of the family can affect the precision of the identities. If there are two or three siblings, it is easier to hand out unique badges (and most sibling research is carried out on sibling pairs). But in Israel, for example, where Dr Milevsky lives and works, he knows many families with lots more children. He jokes, 'The labels run out if you have twelve kids!' There aren't really enough adjectives to go around, so it all becomes much more muddled.

The second is cultural context. For more individualistic (Western) cultures, the idea, for example, that the older sister takes on a significant caring role for the younger siblings 'like a semi parent' may be considered unhealthy. But, says Dr Milevsky, 'in samples from Eastern cultures, it's a given that the older sibling is going to take on a parental role for cultural reasons, for socio-economic reasons. There is a whole other angle to how these labels and definitions play different roles in other places.' Likewise the role of older brother can mean you might have to assume the role of breadwinner, working to support the rest of the family. 'In that example,' says Professor McHale, 'you have this status because of the accident of your birth order, then – what is so interesting – is what comes *with it* in terms of how your family treats you.'

Award-winning author, critic and journalist Lucy Mangan came on the podcast with her little sister Emily. They ended up talking overwhelmingly about their differences as siblings: they are chalk and cheese. Lucy said that if she and Emily didn't resemble one parent each, people would 'really assume that one of them was adopted'. Lucy described how they grew into good little citizens of 'Mini North Korea', in a household where her mum's iron grip rarely loosened. Lucy mainly spent hours and hours reading while Emily was always on the go, out on her bike or building with Lego.

The Mangans neatly illustrate another very specific way that siblings carve out identities for themselves, which is by modelling themselves on one parent or the other (or 'split-parent identification'). It is – maybe obviously – most common with pairs of siblings. While it was previously thought to be more common in mixed-sex sibling pairs, with the girl identifying with the mother and the boy with the father, the evidence for that is shaky. The process lessens any rivalry because, by identifying with a parent each, neither child feels that the other sibling is favoured: win-win.

In the Mangan family, Lucy was an introverted, fairly anxious child – 'overthinky', as she puts it. Her mother would despair at her shyness and wail that she was 'just like your father.' Lucy and her father (who she nicknamed 'The Potato') simply never felt the need to talk unless asked a direct question. Emily, by contrast, is a positive extrovert and much more like her mother. They are both driven, says Lucy, to fill 'the unforgiving minute'. But parents are not the only people we model. As we grow and develop, we look to everyone close to us as examples of how to interact with the world, as well as to establish our role and position in our environment, and that includes our siblings. It's only natural.

SIBLINGS AS ROLE MODELS

Until now, I have talked a lot about labels and sibling rivalry – and for good reason. As children it causes upset and possibly domestic stress, and as adults, there will be episodes when old hurts from sibling competition will be made to sting again. We are also culturally primed for the idea, says academic Mark Feinberg, who writes that 'the power of sibling relationships in shaping life course development was demonstrated in the founding document of the Jewish, Christian, and Muslim religions – the book of

Genesis'. These stories are hard to shake: look at Eve and the apple. Feinberg sees echoes of Cain and Abel, Joseph and his brothers thrum through to family life in the present day.

When I started reading about the roles and labels that siblings have and how they acquire them, it did feel as if there was always an assumption that brothers and sisters are engaged in near constant (albeit not murderous) rivalry and that the only reason they develop their own identities is to distance themselves from their siblings to try to minimise the conflict. But that's not the case. Sibling strife is real, but there is a lot more to the relationship. Across the life span of our sibling relationships, we can be many things to each other. We are often, for example, both rivals *and* role models. 'Siblings can have direct effects on one another's development when they serve as social partners, role models and foils,' explains Professor McHale. 'They can also influence one another indirectly by virtue of their impact on larger family dynamics – such as by serving as building blocks of the family structure, holding a favoured family niche, or diluting family resources.' I will talk more about resources in the chapter on brothers and sisters with additional needs, but in every single family striving to meet the members' needs, the question of how parental resources (energy, time, money and attention) are shared out will leave all siblings with lasting stories and occasionally grudges.

Jordan Blazo, a sports psychology professor at Louisiana Tech University, has studied the younger siblings of serious athletes in the US. In his research, he found some younger children 'delighted' in their sibling's success and found the family focus on sport 'an agent of cohesion'. Travelling to watch their brother or sister compete allowed the family to find new adventures and bond. However, he also heard from plenty of younger siblings, full of resentment, fed up with tailing their sporty sister or brother, angry at being compared with the family star, and feeling neglected by the parents, all of which damaged their relationship with the older sibling. 'It kind of ate me up because of all the attention that she would get,' one younger sibling reflected.

In the US, support for the families of profoundly gifted young people is provided by places like the Davidson Institute, which also recognises the needs that the 'neglected' siblings may have. Dr Sylvia Rimm, from the institute, believes 'these children should be encouraged to admit their feelings of jealousy. Most children have them. They learn to handle these feelings better by accepting the challenge of openly admiring their sisters or brothers.' A tough ask, when a particular talent may require a considerable slice of the available resources. She counsels against treating the talented sibling too much like a 'prince or princess'. After all, if you put them on too high a pedestal, the risk is they have further to fall. 'Gifted children who are first in the family often get the most opportunities for attention,' she warns, 'but also suffer the greatest risks for dethronement... First gifted children are, after all, usually experiments. Whether they come earlier than expected, or later than hoped for, they are often over-welcomed.' Finally, she advises parents to appreciate honestly the individuality of every sibling, including their weaknesses or idiosyncrasies. 'You must emphasise that everyone in the family needs to work on all their skills – emotional, social, physical and academic – to create a whole smart family.' Gently pointing out that a sporting superstar sister or brainiac brother may need to brush up on their *emotional* intelligence, for example, seems like a good way to remind everyone that they have feet of clay.

After dividing up the roles and labels, and apportioning resources between siblings, there is another – obvious – way that brothers and sisters can influence each other – and that is by how they behave. A study by the University of Toronto looking at siblings as role models focused specifically on sibling pairs who were pre-school age – often found tooling around and playing on the carpet together. In the results, academic Rona Abramovitch recorded younger brothers and sisters as 'more likely to watch, approach and imitate their older sibling', and also more likely to take over toys that they 'abandon' (that idea of a pecking order). One small detail I found particularly sweet about this kind of modelling is that, by copying, the younger sibling is trying to create a shared meaning, a place where they can show that they understand what the older sibling is doing.

It seems common sense that – to start with at least – an older sibling will have more influence on any younger ones, especially if they are close in age. They are each other's first companions, playmates and guides. Brothers and sisters born close together might spend the majority of their early lives in each other's pockets: it's an intimate set-up.

The Canadian research also points out something I had always taken as read: the process rarely works the other way round, with older siblings looking up to their younger counterparts. I know it seems self-evident, but then so does much about the sibling relationship, in part because it is so often taken for granted and therefore left unexamined. We might be tempted to think 'so what?' But as an adult reading this now, I invite you to remember playing together with your siblings, building dens or making Barbie houses, playing schools or rampaging through the garden. Can you remember who was copying whom and how it felt? I wonder what patterns were being set down and how they may have shaped the role you have ended up playing in the family. 'It's not surprising that siblings copy each other,' says Susan McHale. 'It's just: what are the implications?'

Does the accepted 'role model' dynamic help to explain, for instance, the strange feeling that occurs the first time your older sibling leans on you for emotional support, recognising that you have somehow 'caught up' with them, and you are both just... people? Or the experience of seeing your 'baby' brother or sister being congratulated for their professional achievements? I know I found both of these experiences weird. They broke the moulds of our relationships. Dr Kramer describes it as the feeling 'of a vertical relationship becoming more horizontal over time'. Things can shift back and forth depending upon the context and the activities that siblings are engaged in. She uses a visual example to express what she means. 'So, a second-born child grows taller than the first-born, and they both like to play basketball. You know... it's like everything is off kilter for them. It's becoming more peer-like, rather than hierarchical and vertical.'

When the Ang Lee film version of Jane Austen's *Sense and Sensibility* was released in 1995, I was seventeen. My teenage heart was primed to despair over Marianne's jilting by Willoughby and desperate for Edward and Elinor to get together. I still watch it multiple times a year and can quote great chunks by heart. Yet it took me some time to see that the most significant part of the story is the relationship between the sisters: prudent older sister Elinor and passionate younger sister Marianne. Throughout the course of the novel they learn from one another, to express their feelings fully while retaining dignity and self-control, although Austen wants us, I believe, to end up erring more on the side of decorum as the more desirable default. It's certainly the lesson Marianne admits to learning:

> Your example was before me; but to what avail? – Was I more considerate of you and your comfort? Did I imitate your forbearance, or lessen your restraints, by taking any part in those offices of general complaisance or particular gratitude which you had hitherto been left to discharge alone? – No; – not less when I knew you to be unhappy, than when I had believed you at ease, did I turn away from every exertion of duty or friendship; scarcely allowing sorrow to exist but with me, regretting only that heart which had deserted and wronged me, and leaving you, for whom I

professed an unbounded affection, to be miserable for my sake.

It is a reciprocal story – the sisterly relationship between the women tilts away from the purely hierarchical. It is not all older to younger, the traffic is not all one way. Elinor sometimes allows herself to see Marianne as a peer, whose passions have something to teach her too. I am not the first to suppose that Jane Austen's own close relationship with her elder sister Cassandra might be the reason she writes siblings (sisters) so well. Jane was described by Cassandra as 'the sun of my life, the gilder of every pleasure, the soother of every sorrow, I had not a thought concealed from her'. If that is not a love story, I do not know what is.

The idea that we learn from other people (not just siblings) is called 'social learning theory', and Canadian psychologist Albert Bandura is likely the best-known name in that field. Born in 1925 to farming parents who had emigrated from Eastern Europe, he had a tragic sibling story. One of his sisters died during a flu pandemic, and a brother was killed in a hunting accident. What Bandura said about how we learn generally is this: 'Learning would be exceedingly laborious, not to mention hazardous, if people had to rely solely on the effects of their own actions to inform them what to do. Fortunately, most human behaviour is learned observationally through modelling: from observing others, one forms an idea of how new behaviours are performed, and on later occasions, this coded information serves as a guide for action.'

One of Bandura's conclusions is that we are more likely to model ourselves on people who are like us. Perhaps because it is easier to identify with them, their behaviours seem more relevant and attainable. It's not a stretch, therefore, to suggest that might mean it is, in fact, more natural for us to copy our siblings than our parents. 'I think the influence of siblings on each other is an area in psychology that has not nearly received the attention it deserves,' says Lisa Damour, a psychologist and author, in a recent *New York Times* article. 'When we look at child development, our main frameworks have been around the influence of parents on children, and that's the established tradition that we've had a hard time moving past.' And yet, how many times have you heard a parent implore a child not to do something rude, silly, dangerous or violent because their younger sibling 'will just copy you'? Behavioural psychologists would add that if a younger sibling sees the positive results of good or desirable behaviour (praise, sticker on a chart, biscuit from the tin), they are even more likely to model their action on the older sibling's behaviour.

> 'I think the best thing about having siblings is that you always have someone to fight with, and the worst thing is that you always have someone to fight with.'
>
> CARMY IN *THE BEAR*

At the Human Development and Family Studies faculty of the University of Utah, Dr Shawn Whiteman studies the way that teenage siblings influence each other, focusing on 'rebellious' behaviours. These are not toddlers who can be cajoled into behaving via a star chart. In adolescence, he says, there is a whole range of ways from imitating each other's 'good' (or bad) behaviour to learning from others' mistakes. In his own family, he believes it was the latter: he strove *not* to emulate his sister, who was 'not asked to return to college' after her first year. The incident inspired him to work extremely hard, eventually leading him into an academic career. 'It put me on a track which took me to a place I never thought I would be,' he said. 'When I went to college I thought I was going to be a radio DJ.'

By speaking to both siblings and their parents, Dr Whiteman has concluded that how the age and gender of the siblings intersect is key. 'Brother–brother relationships tend to be more conflictual and physical. Sister–sister relationships tend to be more intimate. And mixed gender siblings tend to be less intimate and warm overall – especially during adolescence.' Understanding this, he assumed that in sibling pairs of the same gender, 'the influence would be stronger as there is a more salient model to copy'. But what he found was – more than age or gender – it was puberty which mattered most. 'The timing of puberty varies quite a bit, person to person, but girls mature earlier than boys. Therefore, if the age gap between the younger sister and the older brother is within the normal range of two to three years, there will be a period during which they are developmentally equal.' And, according to Dr Whiteman's work, that is the time when sibling influence is shown to be strongest. In fact, after carrying out surveys with six hundred families over three years, Dr Whiteman has noticed something even more interesting – that those sibling pairs whose behaviours were also more similar reported having better relationships than if their answers to the survey showed that they behaved very differently to one another. They express 'less rivalry and less jealousy'. He wondered about the reason for his surprising finding. 'As younger siblings,' he says, 'maybe we elect to differentiate ourselves from people we don't get along with, as opposed to elect to be different in order to get along with them better.'

In the families he spoke to it means that if you think your older brother is really cool for smoking cannabis, for example, you may do the same – happy to embrace the idea that you will be lumped together under one banner. But if you think he is a bit of a loser for his habits, you might double down on your studies or athletic training to make sure everyone knows you are nothing alike – and that your role in the family is different. Either way, you may end up with the same result: less sibling conflict.

HORIZONTAL TO VERTICAL

Birth order, labels, differentiation and modelling all help to explain how we find our sibling roles. But they are not enough to explain the process. Put simply, sibling relationships are in a category of their own, as identified by academic Judy Dunn in 1983 – and which I have touched on already. Susan McHale summarised Dunn's findings thus: 'sibling relationships are unique in that they encompass both the complementary interactions typical of adult–child relationships and the reciprocal and mutually influential interactions of peers'. It was an idea which stopped me in my tracks when I first came across it as it goes to the heart of what can make finding our identity as siblings so endlessly interesting and complicated.

Our brothers and sisters are people we do not choose to be in a relationship with, but who are (potentially) our peers for life. In many ways it is an equal relationship. We share a lot (including genetics). Socially we are often lumped together and treated the same, under the banner 'the [insert surname] children'. But the hierarchical dynamic between siblings is real. The relationship has both egalitarian and complementary elements. Needless to say, it's very complex.

In times of stress and crisis this tangle between the horizontal and the vertical is laid bare, and can sideswipe siblings who have not made progress towards that more horizontal and honest peer relationship. If the tendency is always to revert or cling to the habits of hierarchy, then just like birth order, the other familial roles we play (the clown, the clumsy one, the smart one) become unhelpfully rigid. If 'baby' brothers, say, continue to conform to type and shirk responsibility, it will more than likely create fresh rows and new resentments which are laid on top of very old foundations.

Avidan Milevsky is keen to stress that although these roles can become like 'core beliefs' we have about ourselves, it is possible to 'reconfigure or challenge' them, especially if their persistence makes us miserable or robs our confidence. If we manage it, he says, the benefits – particularly to our sibling relationships – are profound. 'I often bring siblings together in therapy,' he explains, 'to talk about the labels they received in childhood. I ask them, "How accurate are they now?" When siblings do this work together, and they describe how their personal labels were destructive, it's a very healing process which can result in a very, very powerful supportive sibling dynamic.'

That is not to say he thinks we should automatically throw out the baby with the bathwater. Instead, his practice is rooted in the twin idea that the sibling relationship must evolve as the years pass, to be strong enough to help you all to cope. But while that (maybe lifelong) process is taking place, there will be moments along the way when we slip into a more familiar dance with our brothers and sisters (or feel our hearts tugged with envy or old resentments). Dr Milevsky told me he first started thinking about this when he came across two small boys fighting.

'I ran up to try to help them out. And someone said, "Well, they're siblings. They're just beating each other up, it's OK." And then the older one really injured the younger one. And the four-year-old was bleeding from his nose from the beating he was getting from his five-year-old brother. So I separate them and I give a bottle of water to the four-year-old. He takes a sip, he wipes his bloody nose with a sleeve, and he hands the bottle to his five-year-old brother to share the water. So literally, like moments after his older brother tried to kill him, he's sharing this water bottle with him. And I said, "This is an amazing thing to witness. There is such intense love in that relationship, and sharing, but with it so much rivalry.'" The scene was still so vivid to him – twenty-five years later.

That idea that our sibling relationship contains multitudes is why Dr Milevsky and other experts in the field focus not only on the idea of allowing or creating space for your brothers and sisters to mature beyond their childhood labels but also the permission to honour the precious, sustaining pieces of a shared past, where your identities were formed. After all, you are allowed to return to the comfort of the years which first shaped you, if you do it in a way which is not stunting or squashing. If you manage it, you will hopefully find a much more expansive way to relate, free from the constriction of constantly rehearsing the same tired old routines. It's the only way to create a mature relationship strong enough for the challenges which most adult siblings need to work together to face. The energy required to do that – and to help reconfigure a whole new way for the family system to function around it – is considerable. But nobody ought to feel they need to be one-dimensional. It is worth breaking character. The trick is to strive for that, while knowing when it's OK to rest in the cradle of the sibling dynamic, allowing its familiarity to soothe or bolster you and when to face the world together as equals.

3

Orphans of the Storm

The stories we (think we) share as siblings

'To the outside world, we all grow old. But not to brothers and sisters. We know each other as we always were, we know each other's hearts, we share private family jokes. We remember family feuds and secrets, family griefs and joys.'

Clara Ortega

Professor Charles Fernyhough is a developmental psychologist with a special interest in memories and how they're made. 'A cliché that always comes up,' he says, 'is the idea that memory is a sort of object that can be taken out of one person's brain and put into someone else's brain. Everything from Arnie Schwarzenegger in *Total Recall* to *Harry Potter* uses some version of that myth.' Yet the facts about memory are far more interesting than the fiction: the process of making memories is collaborative and never completed – and it's a process which feels central to evolving sibling relationships. 'Memories are not files,' explains Fernyhough. 'They're active, dynamic constructions, always being negotiated, fought over and shaped by the memories of others.'

Learning to tell the story of our own lives by talking is an essential developmental skill, but it's tricky to master at first. Until they are about five, children have little meaningful concept of time and consequently 'struggle to do the kind of time-travelling that makes autobiographical memory possible', outlines Fernyhough. It doesn't stop them trying, though, as anyone who has been bewildered by a toddler earnestly explaining that 'yesterday we will go to Grandma's house' will recognise. Keen to practise the art of making and sharing memories and lacking the ability to do so properly, small children pair up with others (usually a parent or carer) to make a 'remembering team'. These adults are metaphorically in the wings, like very enthusiastic theatre prompters, mouthing the words or providing clues to help the child fill in the blanks. Parents of small children might relate. 'Parents draw children into conversations about the past that are initially very heavily structured, with the adult providing much of the detail and the toddler mostly tagging along,' says Fernyhough. 'Over time, children become more involved in filling in the details, until they can come up with their own autobiographical narratives.'

Research carried out by Professor Robyn Fivush, who runs the Family Narratives Lab at Emory University which studies how families talk about memories, shows that even the style of reminiscing provided to children by their mothers (usually) – as part of the remembering team – is significant. She writes that 'children of more elaborative mothers develop better narrative skills, earlier theory of mind, a stronger self-concept, and better emotional regulation'. A 'highly elaborative' mother would, for example, ask more open-ended questions. So instead of 'Did you see giraffes at the zoo?' the child would be nudged with a question like 'What did we do at the zoo?', a question which allows more 'avenues of reminiscence' to open up. It's amazing to think that the way the other members of your remembering team colour in the outlines of your memories – carefully, with detail and flourish, or haphazardly, leaving areas unshaded or carelessly scribbled – might really impact the way that memory is stored in your mind. Simply: the better the other members of your remembering squad are at co-authoring the tale, the more vivid the memory might be. 'Autobiographical memory functions through the medium of language,' says Professor Fernyhough. 'Talking about the past, to ourselves as well as to others, helps us to create richer representations of it, and these support richer memories.'

What I especially loved discovering from the literature was just how much this varies from culture to culture – depending on what each considers to be important. Professor Fivush's recent work about 'elaborative' mothers was purposely carried out among a fairly homogeneous group of American women to demonstrate that any differences were down to styles of communication and nothing else. But elsewhere I read about the children of Māori parents, who not only consistently report having the earliest memories (from when they are two and a half, compared to four or six in other parts of the world) but also place a special emphasis on the stories around a child's birth and Māori ancestry more generally. There is a broad and deep tradition of storytelling in that culture, in which the individual's personal stories are woven by their parents into a more intricate tapestry.

The idea that building memory with children might be part of a population-wide 'culturally constructive process' was the subject of a study carried out by Professor Qi Wang at Cornell University. She found that memories and stories made in Chinese families, for example, are shown to be less about encouraging the child to 'have and tell one's autobiography' – a skill which is valued in more individualist cultures – and more an opportunity for underlining moral principles: a learning opportunity. For example, 'Chinese mothers seem not to focus on personal storytelling but more on reinforcing the position of the mother as an authority figure.' The children she interviewed – as young as three – demonstrated culturally very varied styles of remembering. For example, all the children talked about birthday parties, but the Euro-American pre-schoolers relayed their memories rich in preferences, feelings and opinions – i.e. 'I liked the birthday cake' and what presents they received – all quite main character energy. Meanwhile, their Chinese counterparts 'more often spoke of other people relative to themselves', focusing on describing who came to the party, how the guests interacted and who gave them the presents, not what they got. This highlights just how malleable memory is: like any narrative, it varies in terms of inclusions, omissions, intention and style. And crucially it is always a collaboration, to varying ends. It made me realise that our memories are tender things indeed.

Of course, mother–baby remembering teams are not the only relevant combination. There are fathers, stepparents, aunties, uncles, godparents, grandparents, friends and siblings, all surrounding us as we grow, stepping in and out of our timelines – influencing the many ways we remember. This web of relationships contains a multitude of ways to knit together shared memories and to canonise family lore. But even sticking within the confines of a 'traditional' nuclear family set-up, once there is more than one child, new combinations of teams emerge – and the siblings will start the process of co-creating, shaping and adopting each other's perspectives. If there are three or more children involved, there are so many various configurations that it makes pinning down any kind of universal version of events nigh on impossible.

> 'My brother and I recall our childhoods differently. But who can say which of us is right? Memory is not a precise art.'
> Tim Lott, *The Scent of Dried Roses*

Psychologist and siblings researcher Professor Alison Pike says she finds talking with her brothers and sisters about their '*supposedly*' shared childhood completely fascinating. 'There is a tension,' she comments, 'between what was real and our perception and... I wonder: does the reality matter? I think that what matters much more is how we experience it. I am constantly amazed by the differences we have perceived as well as the shared history.' A researcher who has interviewed countless sibling pairs, she is familiar with the idea of the 'non-shared environment' we encountered in the previous chapter, which describes how each child in a family is born into a separate reality, and will go on to have necessarily different experiences of childhood; carried on their own unique tide. It is an idea that I heard child development expert Dr Gabor Maté take even further on a podcast about sibling relationships, arguing that no two children in the same family have the same parents. He explains: 'Temperamentally every child is unique and that means they evoke a different part of the parent… so even if a parent loves their kids equally – which I'm not questioning – they will not respond to the child in the same way. The child will not evoke the same responses from the parent, one child or the other. So no children have the same two parents.'

And yet there is a paradox, a tension right at the heart of what it is to be a sibling – and it's the reason why Professor Pike emphasised the word 'supposedly'. On the one hand, there's the fact that we are separate and alone, experiencing our childhood from our unique vantage point: as the baby, the middle or the oldest of five. Who else in our sibling subset could understand exactly what that looks and feels like? And, on the other hand, we are, at the same time, together as members of the same family – even in those families which don't fit into a neat mould. We share so much. Even if we have distinctive relationships with our parents, we still have them in common, with the personalities they have, the careers, the friends, and the environment they create in the home. So, yes, what Gabor Maté and others have touched upon is insightful and relevant but it is not to be overstated.

As sibling therapist Erin Runt explains, 'No one else has that really intimate knowledge of those early years of your life, nobody else understands the nuance of it. They're the only person who can go back and be like, "Was Dad always cranky?" "Were you always the golden child in this family?"... And even if they had an alternate experience or interpretation they were still *there*. So if you're trying to figure out your reality and the reality of your childhood, there are so few people in this world who can help you do that.'

Yet, as Alison Pike explains, your siblings can only ever do it imperfectly. And that is, I have come to believe, one of the central tensions in sibling relationships. On the one hand, there is a kind of desperate wish to be thoroughly known, seen and understood. The people you grew up with seem like such obvious candidates to fulfil this need. And yet for so many reasons, it is impossible for them to do the job completely. Their perspective is not *your* perspective. It's as if they were videoing the scene from another part of the room, picking up certain audio and visual cues but missing some of the bits you might be zoomed in on. The result is a distortion of what you have long replayed in your own mind as a faithful record of events. You might yearn for people to understand, for example, why you are terrified beyond belief of the ocean, remembering the horror of a wild and wavy day at the beach. Your siblings were there; they would back you up, surely? And yet – let's say – you were three years old, and the waves that threatened to sweep you off your feet barely lapped at your older brother's shins. On the same beach, on the same sunny day – *you* were panicking and afraid and *he* was happily paddling in the shallows. Both can be true at the same time.

When it comes to reporting what 'actually happened', the natural hierarchy granted by birth order may well mean that your memory is disregarded. More often than not, author rights seem to be automatically conferred to the older sibling, meaning that their memory, their version of the trip to the shore is given more weight. Those of us who have experienced the authority that eighteen months' worth of maturity is somehow granted know it can be maddening and almost impossible to fight against. 'My (older) sister still tries to convince me how much fun I had on a roller coaster,' remembers Fivush, 'when I recall it as one of the most traumatic experiences of my life.'

In her book *The Myth of Sanity*, Martha Stout argues that trauma in childhood is much more commonplace than you might think – and is often connected to recollection. She writes, 'It can be anything that leaves behind a memory of fear and helplessness, anything that overwhelms a child's ability to cope.' Childhood memories suffused by such frightening feelings are ripe to be disputed or misunderstood by grown-ups (or older siblings, perhaps). Trauma, writes Stout, doesn't just mean the obvious: divorce, death, abuse or family addiction. Seemingly minor experiences can leave a mark. 'It may be as subtle as a mother who is chronically late to pick up her child from school, leaving the child anxious and wondering if she has been abandoned. If this happens often enough, it can leave an imprint on the child's psyche, shaping the way she experiences relationships and trust in the future.' Stout goes on to explain that one of the reasons that fairly subtle or small events loom so large in a child's emotional landscape is precisely because they have no prior experiences to assure them that things will turn out all right: this is the very first time they have experienced it. (Professor Fivush had no reason to trust that she would survive her terrifying ride on that roller coaster, for example.)

It made me think of the classic toddler memory of losing your mother in a busy shop – grasping the wrong skirt at the checkout and looking up to find, with utter horror, unfamiliar eyes peering down. It may only be for a moment, but who can forget that icy fear of feeling completely alone in among a sea of legs, none of which you recognised? You didn't know in that moment that your mother was near and it would all be OK. No wonder if someone else tries either to diminish or recategorise a memory like that as 'not so bad' it can feel like an affront.

In her book *The Sister Knot*, psychologist Dr Terri Apter quotes a woman incensed by her sister's narrative version of their 'shared' past. 'Her memories are so twisted… It's outrageous how unfair she can be.' The reason we get so cross when our memory is not believed, she explained to me, is that the function of memory is complex. It is not just a record of what (you think) happened, it is a reconstruction that reflects how you see yourself and how you want to be seen. 'Our memories become part of our identity. If they are challenged, it's a challenge to the entire sense of who we are and how we stand in relation to other people. The person who's making a claim on my family story is telling me that I'm not who I think I am. It can be very disconcerting.'

MEMORY AND MEANING MAKING

A study conducted in 2016 by Professor William Dunlop about the kinds of stories we collect and retell as young adults shows that those gathered in our memory during emotional periods or which are particularly tied to a developmental stage are the most fiercely guarded. As Dr Apter pointed out, these are the memories which we believe say something significant about who we are. For example: holding on to a memory about learning to ride your bike at the precocious age of two and a half might be part of the evidence you present for your identity as someone who has always been physically brave. It would be maddening to have such a significant story (of yours) co-opted or disputed by a sibling, whose supporting role in the story (as you see it) barely merits a mention. They say you were actually three because the bike had been a birthday present. Surely this isn't something you would have forgotten! It's not only destabilising because it messes with the sense of yourself that you've constructed in your memories, but is also very likely to be infuriating. It can act like a lightning rod to a tinderbox filled with many other painful sibling grievances in which you might have felt powerless as the youngest, perhaps, or the only one of your gender in the mix.

Professor Fivush points out that family storytelling as a way of remembering becomes increasingly important during our teenage years. That's when children are working hard to create their identities as they prise themselves away from the family and start to explore their independence. Stories about who they are, what they were like when they were smaller, and (crucially) why they are not the same as their brothers and sisters are integral to their sense of self. It's not hard to see what a tricky and emotionally fraught experience it might become when an individual tries to untangle themselves from the web of well-worn family stories, some of which are about them.

We all have a library of agreed-upon memories about the family's past which repeated and collaborative telling have cemented into received gospel. But, explains Professor Fernyhough, these are just family 'fictions', 'created so many times over that they come to have a special kind of constancy. It's not that we're laying them down in some permanent store and repeatedly accessing their immutable truths. Rather, we make memories in the present tense, according to the needs of the present. If they tell the same story each time, it's because they are more like habits.' And yet, if there is an often-repeated funny family (fictional) tale, in which a child's forgetfulness or laziness is the punchline, for example, it could easily start to feel stifling to an adolescent, desperate to shrug off old ideas about who they are, as they stretch towards a more mature version of themselves. They may never even have internalised that particular version of themselves in the first place. Their memory might be poles apart.

WHO'S THE FAVOURITE?

In the case of disputed family memories, the facts (like what someone wore to a party, who cooked you breakfast on your birthday or drove you to school last Friday) are always much less important than contesting the emotions you recall around it. And in the case of significant or traumatic events, where feelings dominate, the stakes are higher. 'Disputing emotional perspectives over family tragedies and difficulties may lead to family rupture,' warns Fivush. Perspective is key – and it's why it is so important not to automatically take the older child's or parents' version of memory as the indisputable truth about 'what happened'. After all, the adults' viewpoint will always differ from the children's.

As a child, I knew that my parents were not privy to half of what was going on between me and my sisters, and that means we have completely contrasting memories of the same events. I expect, for example, that my mother's stand-out memory from my aunty's wedding – at which I was a three-year-old bridesmaid – is the moment my sister Bex and I got so hot that we discarded our Laura Ashley gowns for a spontaneous swim in the hotel's outdoor pool, wearing only knickers and our fresh flower crowns. I have no real memory of that (although I have seen the photos often) or anything else from that day, except the taste of cold chicken legs from the buffet, eaten sitting on a doorstep shoulder to shoulder with an equally tiny pageboy. Plus, our perceptions of time and other important ingredients are completely at odds with one another and will inevitably skew our memories in weird ways. As a parent myself, I have to remind myself constantly that there are multiple realities happening in our little family of four, and that the version created and shared by my boys is one I will never fully understand or share. For example, they still complain about a hated babysitter who looked after them 'all the time' during primary school. I know I used her perhaps twice, and then never again. But the intensity of their feelings is what matters, not the dates in the diary. She made her mark and it is important to them that I understand.

WHO OWNS THE STORY?

As well as holding on to contrasting versions of past events, siblings have also been found to fight over authorship of the same memory. A study of twenty twins by a team in New Zealand led by Mercedes Sheen asked each to independently produce autobiographical memories in response to cue words. Fourteen of the pairs produced at least one memory that was claimed by both twins. 'One pair of 52-year-old twins,' says the study, 'disagreed about which of them had made a dramatic attempt at running away from home at the age of six. Both recalled sitting in the back of the car while the mother frantically searched the streets for the missing twin.' This made me laugh. The study also noted that in cases of disputed memories and siblings, we are more likely to 'remember' ourselves playing the more heroic role. (The twin driving around with the grown-ups and searching for their poor lost sibling, perhaps.) As I have said before, when recounting stories involving our siblings, we have persistent main character energy – and it seems this is entrenched for stories we have co-opted as our own.

Personality and disposition also play a role in the memories we gather as children of the same family. Those who are attuned to the mood music, who loiter on the landing during dinner parties, or who listen in to adult phone calls, may be busy gleaning a wealth of intelligence in which to triangulate family memories. They will be the ones gleefully reporting the 'real reason' that Aunty Beth left Uncle Jack in the 1980s, or that the guinea pigs you had as children were not, in fact, sent off to 'enjoy their retirement' in Spain. One older sister I spoke to anonymously for this book told me she spent a portion of her wedding day avoiding her younger brother, who had somehow never twigged that their mother had left their father to pursue an affair with a family friend. She had figured it out thirty-five years ago, when the events took place. So her brother was caught in a roller-coaster ride of memory reconfiguration, all during the heightened emotional setting of a massive family wedding.

In Professor Fivush's Family Narratives Lab, she has hit upon a solution to particularly fraught cases of disputed memory. She encourages open and honest conversation between family members (sometimes easier said than done) where everyone's perceptions are taken into account during a process of 'explaining, negotiating, consulting each other's memories, and ultimately agreeing on a shared story... although the agreed upon memory may deviate in some details from what may have actually happened, all family members' perspectives are honoured.' Because the chasms between the memories held by different individuals in the same family can be so vast, it is easy to misunderstand and upset each other. When we share the stories of our lives, we make ourselves vulnerable. It is deeply personal and always suffused with emotion. We should try to be gentle and, as Alison Pike suggests, ask ourselves, 'Does the reality matter?'

KEEPERS OF HISTORY

For all these reasons, post-production is never complete on the home movies of collective memories. They can't be tidied away and then replayed uncontroversially as and when we feel like it. There is no final cut. 'We edit our memories all the time,' reminds Professor Fernyhough. 'Memories are shaped by the self who is doing the remembering, and when the person's beliefs and emotions change, so does the story.'

In an interview with the bestselling authors Manni and Reuben Coe (who are two of four brothers), Manni told me through laughter about the 'yoghurt throwing years', during which their (exhausted) mother had been known to lob the occasional tub around the kitchen at dinner time. A somewhat shocking spectacle for a bunch of young boys, confused by the outbursts; at the time, they may have felt upset or even angry at the scene. Now, as middle-aged men, they know well the havoc that a clash between perimenopausal and adolescent hormones can wreak in a household. The 'blame' has shifted and the picture is brought into a much clearer, more mature focus. Sharp edges have softened and the 'villain' can now be understood as more of a victim. All in all, it is much funnier now. Even for their mum.

'In *Harry Potter and the Half-Blood Prince*,' adds Fernyhough, 'Professor Slughorn has tinkered with one of his memories, editing out the parts he doesn't want to be known. It's a brilliant metaphor for how memory works: we are all, in a sense, editors of our own pasts.' He counsels, however, that memory editing is not always driving us closer to the truth and that, in fact, the things we think we remember are always vulnerable to being kind of 'infected' by others: 'The term "social contagion" describes how we sometimes wrongly incorporate information that has been provided by other people into our own psyches. We often feel pressure to fall in line with the memories of family, friends and colleagues. Much of the time we can resist it, but occasionally we accept other people's mistaken recollections of the past.' The idea that there is one true version of events which we might accurately remember if only we tried hard enough or gathered more evidence including all the alternative perspectives feels fanciful.

'Do you think it's possible to ever see the past as it actually was?'

Ann Patchett, *The Dutch House*

But the tension remains; despite the fact that perspective, age, disposition, hierarchy and time materially affect our recollections, we can't help ourselves. In her beautiful novel *The Dutch House*, Ann Patchett tells the (fraternal love) story between siblings Danny and Maeve who try, over many decades, to come to terms with the fact that when they were three and ten years old respectively, their mother left them (in their lavish home) to go and help the needy in India. 'The best part of a story,' says narrator Danny, 'is the part where someone tells you something you already know.' Their mother leaving is an understandably pivotal event for the children, who are forever bound in the shared misery of their abandonment, despite their vastly disparate perspectives on the events as adults, and the book constantly skates over and around this idea – of being together and yet totally alone. Yet, any solace Danny and Maeve find is in their ability to physically go back together: to revisit their childhood home. It serves as the perfect metaphor for their shared memory – a stage on which the drama they lived through played out. Physical places and things are fundamental to childhood rememberings: nothing will yank you back to your past as quickly as the texture of an old sofa, the scuff mark on a skirting board which looked like a wonky face, or the heavy gravy jug brought out on Sundays. But a house and its objects are merely a stage and its props. The *story*, how it unfolds, what role you play and how long you get to occupy the stage, provide the lifeblood. In this story, the siblings grow up with completely opposing ideas about what relationship they would like to have with their (now returned to them) mother. Danny is angry and incredulous that Maeve can forgive: 'After all these years of hating her, you just drop it because she walks through the door?'

In families where there has been some significant upset like this, there is a push and pull. On the one hand, there is the intimacy of surviving a terrible thing together; on the other, the isolated nature of trauma. It is a stark rift to navigate. And yet, when there is a central flame of past trauma around which you can gather, despite your differing perspectives and memories, there is still this *thing* that definitely happened. It might have affected you in contrasting ways, and your individual recollections will be patchy, but you were all 'there'. There is, then, some comfort in drawing on what your siblings can (or choose to) remember, in order that you might stitch their versions of events on to yours, to create a fuller picture of what 'really' went on. It can be the work of a lifetime.

The novelist Gill Hornby told me that she sometimes pities her children whose functional upbringings meant they are nowhere near as close to each other as she is to her big brother Nick. 'Not getting on with your siblings is the great benefit you can draw from coming from an over-secure home,' she said. 'If you're from a dysfunctional background you cling together like orphans in the storm.' While children, Gill and Nick's father left their family home to go and raise his other family in France. This 'new' family was well under way before he left, so that by the time Gill and Nick found out about it, there was a little boy and a little girl, waiting for their father to come and raise them. It was devastating and clearly affected them for life. The pair tenderly consider themselves the keepers of each other's difficult memories. 'Gill is the only person who knows my reality,' Nick said. Heartbreak and loss brought them closer.

In the US, half of all children will witness the break-up of their parents' relationship, an experience which continues to have a significant psychological impact, even if the divorce or split is amicable. 'After the period of divorce, which is a terribly stressful time for everybody, siblings in some cases actually become closer,' says siblings researcher Nina Howe, 'because they become a team, especially if they're going back and forth between the parents.' Who else could possibly get close to understanding the transition that Gill and Nick made, between the guilty and 'seductive' fun (and pain) of France, where there was sunshine, a swimming pool, a fridge with fizzy drinks in it and a father they longed for... and the UK, where they had to hide all that from their lovely mum and where there was nothing 'flashy'. Instead they made a note to 'moan a lot' to their mum, to console her. While writing this book, I heard the legendary interviewer and writer Lynn Barber on the radio, talking about families. She said with characteristic pith, 'No one else understands the mess you came from.' It is not a closeness that is to be desired, no matter what Gill jokes... but if you have been through hard times as children, it is of the deepest comfort to have even unreliable witnesses to your past pain.

Of course, it is not as simple as childhood trauma equals sibling bonding. In fact, the coping mechanisms children rely on will – in most instances – vary vastly, meaning they are more likely to remember hard things through very distorted lenses. Broadly speaking, how much someone understood about what was happening at the time, how close they were to it and how they responded in the moment will colour their memories. Perhaps they rebelled (stood up to whoever was causing the harm), joined in (complied with the dominant family dynamic, even if wildly dysfunctional and damaging) or froze (which looks like shutting down or dissociating). Trauma therapist Annie Wright also points out that how a child reacts while the trauma is unfolding can be wildly at odds with how they might choose to or manage to cope later on in life. What stories they tell themselves afterwards, therefore, and what memories they feel able to keep will be just as varied again. 'After-the-fact coping mechanisms can look like having gaps in their memory, rewriting or revisioning the family history, conflating the abuses and abusers, diminishing the abuse and abusers, aligning with one parent and demonizing the other,' she writes, 'denying the reality of anyone who thinks alternately than them, and so much more.' Establishing any kind of consensus is harder than cleaning up an oil spill.

My sisters and I were together for six years before our parents separated. After that, we shared very few experiences. It's true that we often got together for Christmas or summer holidays but we missed out on the mundane glue of arguing over the TV remote or who finished the nice cereal. We skipped the chance to nurture the true sibling familiarity that comes from spending lots of unremarkable Sunday afternoons mooching around the house together. But more than that, there was just such a vast space between our realities. At one end of the scale, the cupboards in each other's houses were full of biscuit brands which we did not really recognise, and the washing powder smelled wrong. At the other end of the scale, we only had one parent each and lived in different countries. We couldn't easily chat about our teachers, friends or schools when we were visiting our other parent and other sister. They didn't know what we were talking about. And that meant that so many stitches in what it usually takes to knit siblings together in their shared memories were missing. And yet, for all the separation we endured and all the ways we experienced the fallout from the break-up of our family, the unique set of ingredients which went into the events of those years are ingredients which only we understand. There is a mishmash of wider family context, recent (and not so recent) family history, geography, personalities and psychologies which all came together to produce that event, and we know it. When we bring our unique perspectives to bear on the divorce and the events which followed, even if we're standing in vantage points which feel miles apart, holding on to stories which are almost unrecognisable to one another, we are still contemplating the same mess.

It is only recently that we have started slowly telling each other about the years spent apart from our own points of view, and it's a strange experience to hear one of your childhood memories retold by a sister who (naturally) casts herself as the main character. At eleven, my mum left *me* and that has been a defining experience in my life. But at exactly the same time, when my little sister CJ was six, she lost her siblings, her family home and her dad. Revisiting these events with her and Bex has sometimes made the pictures in my mind warp and the feelings that have been so tightly woven around them unravel. I have felt dizzy with the realisation that these parallel histories exist just as vividly in my sisters' minds. We find ourselves saying to each other, 'I had no idea. I'm so sorry, I never knew.'

> 'But what if, even at a late stage, your emotions relating to those long-ago events and people change?... I don't know if there's a scientific explanation for this… All I can say is that it happened, and that it astonished me.'
> JULIAN BARNES, *THE SENSE OF AN ENDING*

Secret families and sibling separation are dramatic examples of childhood trauma, but the theory holds for upsets on a lesser scale. If you think about your own experiences as children, there may not be such remarkable tumult, but there will be episodes which can provide a similar kind of emotional glue, laid down somewhere as memories to share. It may be something like the death of a grandparent, moving house, the loss of a parent's job or navigating a new school. Perhaps the new school was easy for one sibling and impossibly hard for another. Maybe it was universally disliked. Revisiting these challenging memories as adults, with our more mature perspectives, is so valuable, and understanding how your brothers and sisters were shaped by an experience you shared is a profoundly revealing exercise. It is also a process which can elevate your relationship with your sibling, help nudge it towards a more equitable friendship, perhaps.

When I spoke to Professor Fernyhough, he explained that with adults who choose to enter into a relationship as friends or maybe lovers, one of the first things they do is start to form a shared representation of the past. 'Pretty much without that,' he says, 'a relationship, a marriage, whatever it is, will be quite difficult in all sorts of ways, unless you agree on that first date, the first kiss, the moving into your first house, all that kind of stuff.' There is a strong pressure from society to do it, attached as we are to coherent narratives.

And one of the things that you *lose* if your relationship breaks down – as it does in cases of divorce – is that shared past. Everything which you remembered with an overlay of trust and romance is brutally edited, now seen through a lens of betrayal or heartbreak. 'One of the things that's most painful about break-ups can be things that you used to agree on about the past you no longer agree on.' So even the good times are forever tainted in the unending process of looking back with acquired knowledge. The memories – such as they were – are 'gone' and a lot of the happiness associated with them can vanish too. It is a trope of many romance-gone-wrong movies and novels, an eruption of grief which comes with the loss of a past you thought you understood, but which you now need to reconfigure completely. 'He is not the man I thought he was' and 'our marriage was a lie' are all laments to do with the sanctity of our shared memories being shattered, and, of course, with that, the sense of who we thought we were within them.

Brothers and sisters never enter into the kind of social contract that married people or adult friends do. They are never pressured to negotiate a shared version of the past. In fact, it is more likely that siblings will disagree or dispute each other's versions of the past, because there is a tendency to disagree with your brothers and sisters full stop.

Exploring their individual recollections of a shared past is a process that activist, author and founder of parent-focused website Mother Pukka, Anna Whitehouse, and her sister Karen talked really movingly about on the podcast. Karen reminisced that when Anna left home, 'it was like a limb was missing... I felt so lost.' Both got tearful, hearing about how the other had experienced that chapter. As Anna was swept up in the fast-moving currents of university life, downing two-for-one drinks in nightclubs and making a reasonable fist of studying law, her sister was still in the shallows. By middle age, we have some distance from our younger selves and can hopefully sit and talk about these memories in a slightly more clear-eyed manner. Perhaps some of the emotions around them even hang a little looser. We might feel able to embark on a little light collaborative pruning or editing, without creating more upset. Or we could have a go at practising what Professor Fivush preaches, by forming a collaborative version of events which allows everyone's 'truth' to be honoured, so that we can start to move on. As adult siblings I imagine that the memories created by our shared pasts are all pinned to a messy corkboard: a bunch of contested, muddled, overlapping and misappropriated rememberings to be stared at for clues. What incoherent collage hangs there, created by the sibling team(s) we belong to, will certainly not be the *truth*, but it will certainly be the best we have to try to make sense of what we all went through together-apart.

4

Steps and Halves

'The modern family is a dark and twisted river.'
                                    ANN PATCHETT

So far, I have made some assumptions about siblings. I know that. While it is true that sibling relationships can be long-lasting and enjoyable, they are often anything but straightforward – dependent as they are on the shape of the family around them. When I started planning my siblings podcast, I had thought a bit about the common or garden exceptions to the two or more children plus two parents 'rule'. I'll admit I had expected to kind of tick them off as I recorded and published the episodes: 'Steps'? Done. 'Halves'? Done. And so on, as if they were remarkable. What I hadn't anticipated when I started the project was just how many configurations there are for the family unit in the first place. Not to mention when it's shaken up, ripped apart, blended and put back together again. At the end of the interview I did with TV chef Briony May Williams, whom I interviewed flanked by her brothers Max and Ben, the three of them stopped laughing and teasing long enough to casually mention that they were actually three of seven: 'Oh yeah, Catherine, our dad likes him some wedding cake.'

WHO'S THE FAVOURITE?

In an essay for the *New York Times*, novelist Ann Patchett describes the slightly unorthodox annual family Christmas party she used to throw. 'I have a very loose definition of family,' she explains, 'and anyone who could fit beneath that wide umbrella was welcome, including, but in no way limited to, my mother's third husband's first wife, their grown children, and the spouses and children of those grown children. My stepsister's husband's parents came.' I have read that sentence over and over, mentally sketching a family tree, but I am still confused. Our family has thrown similar parties, where the exes mingle with their 'replacements' and the other (non-related) guests are baffled by it all (and when they find out, horrified that they may have inadvertently put their foot in it). But reading the description of Ann's labyrinthine family tree has given me fresh sympathy for those I have watched get puzzled, then bored and eventually sometimes irritated as I try to explain the dynamics of my own step situations. Other people's complex families are so hard to get straight in your mind.

Eventually, Ann's family called time on the annual party that 'everyone hated'. Reflecting on it afterwards, she writes with some relief that 'by continuing to throw the Christmas Eve party, I was interacting with this endlessly extended family as if I were still a child, brightly rolling up my sleeves and getting along. When you're a kid someone else deals you a hand and you have to play it. As adults we're free to fold.' From what I can work out, she still gets along cheerfully with everyone who has come her way, but recognises that she will inevitably like some of them more than others. But her observation about the lack of choice she had as a child in a blended, bonus or stepfamily sprang off the page: gaining new siblings as a child, simply because an adult in your life has fallen in love, is a challenge.

A little bit on definitions. A stepfamily can be just two adults and one child, where the child is biologically related to only one of the adults. For example, a man who lives with his son and a new partner. For the purposes of this book, however, I am obviously interested in those stepfamilies which also have stepsiblings. For example, a woman and her daughter, who now live in a house with the woman's new partner and *her* son. (I hope this isn't turning into the written version of Ann Patchett's festive drinks.)

And then, if the adults in a stepfamily go on to have a new baby of their own, that baby will be a half sibling to the existing children in the family (because they share blood with both sides) and, magically, the family is transformed from a stepfamily into a 'blended' one.

I will spare you the endless Venn diagrams which can result from just these two kinds of families. But it is helpful to bear in mind a couple of points. Firstly, children could easily end up having *three* different kinds of sibling relationships. For example, after their parents' divorce, they could come with their full sibling into a new household where they gain stepsiblings, before going on to gain a new half sibling as well. (This is without delving into the sibling relationships involved in families who adopt or foster.) And secondly, these kids may also regularly move between this house and another house, where the sibling relationships are just as nuanced.

> 'Family isn't about whose blood you have. It's about who you care about.'
>
> *Yours, Mine & Ours* (2005)

Katherine Walker is a psychotherapist and author of *Step Up*, an excellent book about creating happy step and blended families. She is quick to acknowledge the confusion. 'I would put money on the fact that ninety-five per cent of people wouldn't know what the difference is between stepfamilies, half siblings and blended families.' She also points out that steps, halves and full siblings often make a point of using the labels, or pointedly *not* using the labels to 'say something' about the level of intimacy they feel.

In stepfamilies which turn into a blended family, for example, the family often feels so integrated that they give up on the 'steps' and 'halves' and 'full', and just say 'my sister or my brother' for everyone. 'They can be so established, and so proud of the new family they have created,' Walker says, 'that they have reidentified as a nuclear family.'

There are other reasons, says Walker, why families might not use all the different labels: the still prevalent stigma around 'broken families'. In her clinical work, she has come across many families who say things like 'I'm with a long-term partner, and she's got children' but will refute 'being a stepfather', distancing themselves from that identity.

It doesn't help that there are only a very modest number of studies about step and half siblings, and the few which exist are generally muddled. For example, until 2020, all research in the USA carried out by the Pew Research Center put half, step and sometimes even adopted siblings in the same category, with only one box for families to tick – making the data very difficult for academics to decipher. It is a shame when 'all the siblings are tossed in there together', says family therapist and stepfamily expert Dr Patricia Papernow, because in her experience, the ways that each of these kinds of children experience family life can be very different, and she would love more evidence to back up her clinical observations.

In spite of this, according to the 2021 census, there are 780,885 recorded stepfamilies in England and Wales (out of 16.9 million total families). Poking a little further into the statistics, it shows that 8.8 per cent of all dependent children – or 1.1 million children – live in a stepfamily. In the US the numbers are sixteen per cent of all children – or 11.6 million. (You can't tell from the data how many children are stepsiblings, I am afraid.) Even if the data is fuzzy, these are not insignificant numbers, says Katherine Walker, who is frustrated that the issue 'is still in the shadows'.

Before I go any further, it would be worth reminding ourselves why we call families 'broken' in the first place. Then we can assess the stigma which might skew what data we have.

The notion of an 'ideal', nuclear family – complete with mother, father, a boy, a girl and a golden retriever – stems from a very specific kind of conservative nostalgia, says historian Stephanie Coontz. It harks back to a very short period in the 1950s when this family arrangement flourished. But overall, the nuclear family is an anomaly, the result of some very particular economic and social conditions in the post-war period. If you take the long view of families, there is no 'traditional' or 'natural' shape for the family at all. In her book *The Way We Never Were*, Coontz takes great pains to argue against any notion of the 'white picket fence stay-at-home-mom and working-dad-in-a-tie version' of Western family life which people seem to collectively conjure up when thinking about The Past™.

Instead, Coontz shows that during some periods around the world, single-parent families, stepfamilies and half siblings were more common than they are now, even if the causes were different. 'Even though marriages today are more likely to be interrupted by divorce,' she writes, 'they are much less likely to be interrupted by death, so that about the same number of children spend their youth in single-parent households today as at the turn of the century.' When marriage was merely an economic proposition, she explains – and life expectancy much lower – it made sense for a widow or widower to quickly find a new partner to ensure that the family survived.

This tendency to remarry for financial security likely gave rise to the wicked stepmother trope and the idea of competition between non-blood siblings, most famously depicted in

Cinderella. That fairy story is 'a legend with its basis in fact', says Coontz, because in the past, stepparents may well have tried to 'get rid' of their stepchildren to ensure that property or wealth was passed to their own biological offspring instead. These days, she notes, most of the dramas in stepfamilies are because the stepparent wants the 'love to develop faster than is comfortable' between them and the stepchild. 'Cinderella would have settled for that,' she quipped during a US college address.

Her book also considers how divorce – the main impetus for modern stepfamilies – has been managed in various cultures. 'No-fault' divorce arrived in the UK in 1969, and unsurprisingly prompted a sharp rise in the number of divorces, from 50,000 in 1971 to 150,000 a decade later. Before this, couples would have to prove one party had violated the marital contract, usually due to adultery or abuse. Needless to say, women were often held to a much higher standard.

All of that is to say that, if you took a short view of history, starting in the 1950s and ending today, you could – as Margaret Thatcher, Donald Trump and others have – declare the nuclear family the moral default. Something which has been 'dismantled' or broken. And you could handily make those who 'do' the dismantling feel rotten about themselves for not conforming to some Norman Rockwell-esque ideal.

The political right has had that position bolstered by the fact that, until recently, much of the research into divorce and stepfamilies has been 'framed from deficit perspectives, that position family complexity as bad for children and society', explains Dr Caroline Sanner, an expert on post-divorce families. Assumptions are even baked into the language used: 'two-married-biological-parent families were called *intact families*,' she writes in her 2023 paper on stepfamilies, 'families with separated or divorced parents were called *broken families*, and stepfamilies were called *reconstituted families*, suggesting that marriages represented (or should represent) an attempt to restore the family back to the nuclear ideal.' But, says Coontz, this language is misleading. 'Both contemporary studies and historical experience show that children are resilient enough to adapt to many different innovations in family patterns: When they cannot adapt, this is caused more often by the economic and social context than by their parents' "wrong turns" away from traditional family patterns.' I think it is worthwhile to take a longer view of step and blended families, but also to set aside any ambition to cover every variable surrounding them – like geography, race, income, educational standards, etc. There simply isn't enough research.

LOVE AND MARRIAGE

Because stepfamilies and blended families are now much more likely to be created because of divorce rather than death, they tend to come with more baggage – adults may have made quite selfish choices to get to this point and that might be hard for the children to accept. Rather than losing one parent, you will gain one or two new ones. Having four parents is very obviously more complicated in a practical sense. (Think about all the people you know who agonised over table plans at their wedding or have an unwieldy number of family WhatsApp groups to manage.) It also requires a particular emotional dexterity and sensitivity to foster and invest in all those overlapping relationships.

But I also think modern stepfamilies can be hard for the children involved for the very reason that our whole Western idea of marriage centres around a love match, which means the divorce or separation is now about that love somehow failing. (Or if your spouse dies, of losing that love in a way which is tragic.) 'What we have created is a marriage that – when it works – is fairer and more fulfilling than any time in history,' explains Coontz, while also being 'more optional, more fragile and less bearable when it doesn't live up to that potential'. We don't stay together any more because of our adjoining land, for social status or political influence: everything else being equal, if we are unhappy in a marriage, we are free to leave it. It means there is a greater need to understand and not judge. Children in step and blended families tend to need more support and empathy because, as Dr Sanner so beautifully explains, 'stepfamilies have – baked into their very being – histories, memories, and the scars of wounds healed, or the scabs of wounds still healing'. These make a huge difference to the stories which the stepsiblings might tell about their 'old families', and about how they might start to make sense of their new ones.

In the 1970s, Brenda Maddox wrote a book called *Step-Parenting* in which she describes how hard it can be to unite 'families with a past'. When you create a stepfamily, she explains, you are bringing together two sets of people, each with their values, traditions, identities and stories. The children from each of those families are well versed in the subtleties of it all. Even though the family they have 'lost' wasn't perfect or even particularly happy, it was *theirs*. Furthermore, if you were born into a family with either a real memory or just a lingering notion that your parents once loved one another and that you were born because of that love, that can be hard to let go. The romantic love between parents is part of the child's history as well as the family's shared identity. When it ends, the child mourns too.

My own parents' divorce was not unforeseeable and yet it was still a massive shock. By the time we were assembled at the dining table for the announcement, my dad on a rare day off work (to build a guinea pig enclosure, I had been led to believe), my parents weren't happy at all. But they weren't happy in a way that I was fine with. Children can be self-absorbed and thankfully unaware of the extent of the misery which surrounds them. Plus, my parents must have been doing a good job of masking the worst of it, so our family still made sense to eleven-year-old me, and I wanted it to continue. As far as I was concerned it was 'working' just fine and I didn't want to imagine an alternative. Looking back now, through the lens of everything which unfolded since, I can see so many more signs that The End was inevitable. I have a memory from that very afternoon of hugging my mum and only later realising that she was so thin that she was wearing one of my jumpers and her corduroys were held up with a large safety pin.

'You're not my brother. You're just some weird kid my dad met at a resort.'

BLENDED (2014)

In 1966, Sherwood Schwartz came up with the idea for *The Brady Bunch* TV show after reading in the *LA Times* that '20–30% of marriages [in the United States] have a child or children from a previous marriage'. In the show, widow Carol Ann Martin marries widower Michael Brady, and their families unite with six kids (three boys and three girls), a dog, a cat and their housekeeper. It's a sunshine-filled, usually funny programme, in which the children are definitely *not* encouraged to acknowledge the emotional complexity of their situation. In one episode, Bobby, the youngest boy, feels neglected and considers running away. His stepmum's response is to say to him, 'The only steps in this house are the ones that lead up to your room'; i.e. 'we don't talk about the fact we aren't biologically related: family unity above all else.' In other words, says Caroline Sanner, it is not very realistic about the challenge of merging families. 'It did not help us when it comes to what to do in stepfamilies. It sets a lot of folks up for disappointment at best.' The reality of the kind of careful, honest and thoughtful work that she believes is necessary to foster good stepsibling relationships just wouldn't translate to good TV. Then again, says Canadian author Susin Nielsen, whose Young Adult novels tackle the issues of divorce, parental dating and stepfamilies head on, 'Where's the drama in a happy family?'

Nielsen writes about what she knows: she grew up with a single parent and acquired a stepfather, before discovering she had a second family. 'You can't choose your family,' she says, 'and families are what shape us, for better or for worse.' She maintains she is thankful that she had left home before her mother remarried a man who had four kids of his own. 'I remember selfishly thinking, "Thank God!!"' she writes in a blog about her book *We Are All Made of Molecules*, which asks, 'What would it be like for two very, very different kids to be suddenly thrust together under one roof?' Having finished writing the book, she acknowledged that she would have found the experience of living with her stepsiblings 'awful'. 'It really is a huge upheaval for kids,' she concludes.

To successfully build a new family bringing together two sets of siblings, you have to navigate enormous amounts of change. And, says therapist Patricia Papernow, 'one of the things that we know is that as the rate of change goes up in a family, kids' wellbeing goes down'. After a divorce, separation or bereavement, forming a new family is a choice made by the adults, who are often 'eager to move forward... and they're often moving forward much too fast for kids'. For the children, she says, the new romance represents a loss. Not only of 'the ways things were' but of their parent, who may now be less available, 'caught up in this fantasy' of creating a new life and preoccupied with their new partner. It is definitely a kind of bereavement, says Dr Bailey Oliver Blackburn, who specialises in stepfamily conflicts. 'They're grieving the loss of a parent, who now lives elsewhere, and the loss of their "old" family.'

Papernow observes that in 'study after study', children in stepfamilies are shown to 'lose parental time and attention, and the "regulating connection"' which is so important for their wellbeing and happiness. Stepsiblings navigating a new family will feel this pinch on their valuable resources acutely. Not only are they with just one biological parent at a time, but they may also have to accommodate that parent's new infatuated behaviour, as well as their interest and investment in relationships with the new stepsiblings (who are their stepchildren). All of which draws them away from the primary 'parent–child interaction,' i.e. *you*. It is a theme, says Dr Blackburn, which has cropped up continually in research on children in stepfamilies since the 1980s.

On top of this, children will be trying to get their head around the idea of a new family (or even two), possibly a new home (for all or some of the time), and maybe even a new school. There will be a change in routine, unfamiliar food, maybe a shared bedroom for the first time and different rules. That is a lot of change for anyone. But the biggest change of all, of course, will be the acquisition of new family members.

In our case, the loss of our original family was swiftly followed with the announcement of two new ones: a new stepdad, a new stepmum, two stepsisters on one side and a stepsister and stepbrother on the other. 'There's just so much change,' reiterates Papernow, 'and the adults are often not that tuned into it.' The children, on the other hand, are all too aware. 'As a child of divorced parents, you've seen your parents in pain, with the break-up of the marriage, and I think you become hypervigilant. You don't want to add to the upset.'

How children adjust to all this change, including their new siblings, is shaped by so many factors, including age, gender and willingness – or not – to 'make a fuss'. (Stepsiblings who are close in age and of the same gender fare better, with – ironically for Cinderella – stepsisters at the top of the tree.) But most crucial, as Melinda Baham and her co-authors point out in a book chapter entitled 'Sibling Relationships in Blended Families', is whether the child 'accepts' that their new stepsiblings are family in the first place. It is more likely that older children – adolescents and beyond – will struggle to fully accept stepsiblings as family, for the obvious reasons that they have lived much of their life without them, and they are busy trying to establish their 'grown-up' identity, which is separate from the family, anyway. It follows that stepsiblings are more likely to end up 'getting on' better the younger they become stepsiblings *and* the more time they spend together under the same roof, creating shared experiences.

In an episode of the BBC World Service's award-winning podcast *Dear Daughter*, Rehman shares a letter he wrote to his three daughters: one from his first marriage and two stepdaughters he gained from his second marriage. They now all call him 'Baba'. But after praising all three girls individually, he is honest about the challenges of bringing two sets of siblings together. 'It's a tightrope,' he says wearily, reflecting on the difficulties of sharing himself between his three biological kids, three stepchildren and a new wife. 'It was much easier when it was just the normal nuclear family.' Rehman was introduced to his new wife during a family holiday to Pakistan. His first wife had died suddenly and his potential new partner was a widow. 'I am not built to be alone,' he told podcast host Namulanta Kombo. But 'now everyone wants a piece of dad... I am remembering how hard I have worked, the WhatsApp messages I have written, the voice notes I have sent, the awkward meetings I have had, to try and get my kids to accept this situation... It has not been plain sailing.'

For Rehman, his three children were all older than his new stepchildren, which may have made the process of gelling more difficult, as the opportunities to spend time together as peers were limited. The shape of the new family also meant that most of the children (except the very oldest and very youngest) had new places in the pecking order of the new super-sized sibling group to adapt to. His youngest biological child suddenly became the middle of six. His middle lost his 'special status' and his oldest stepchild suddenly found there was a new queen of the castle. It is really common when adults try to knit their families together that the birth order of all the new siblings is scrambled and shuffled like this, children dovetailing in between one another, sometimes begrudgingly budging up to make space. It's not easy and can result in the loss of the children's established identities, partly shaped by their place in their original hierarchy.

In my family's case, we ended up with two 'oldests' instead of one, and a new stepbrother – the family's first boy. My little sister 'lost' her siblings and, for the majority of the year, felt a lot like an only child. It was quite a shift for someone used to toddling after two much older sisters, who led the way and showed her the ropes. For Patricia Papernow – whose interest in stepfamilies was (as is so often the case) born out of her own experience – when she married her second husband, her only child instantly became the youngest of four. 'Yeah. Wow,' she deadpans, wide-eyed.

As well as rearranging the sibling order, the creation of a stepfamily can also disrupt the niches children have carved out for themselves. If they are suddenly no longer the indulged baby or their new stepsister is better at 'their' favourite hobby, what is their USP? Deidentifying from their siblings, for example, will now involve all the new step or half ones, as well as the old ones. Continuing to emulate or identify with their mum or dad might be harder, simply because they're with them less of the time. Overnight, stepsiblings gain more brothers and sisters to watch and copy, new characters to chafe against. The household is busier with all the comings and goings of various family members and there is an overall increase in the intricacy of family relationships. There are simply many more players in the game.

A SENSE OF BELONGING

In 2003, Professor Glenn Weisfeld and his team published the results of a fascinating experiment designed to (among other things) measure how close step and half siblings were, compared to full siblings. Instead of using traditional measures like 'how often they saw each other' or 'what levels of support' they offered one another, they used the sense of smell. The paper published in the *Journal of Experimental Child Psychology* reported that pre-adolescent children could identify their full siblings by scent, but they could not identify the odours of their half and stepsiblings. The authors concluded, 'These findings support the possibility of an evolved basis for discrimination among different types of siblings.' The study also found that mothers could identify their biological children by smell, but not their stepchildren.

It's an approach to predicting sibling closeness which Dr Blackburn is familiar with. 'There are lots of theorists,' she comments, 'who say we're more likely to invest in and maintain relationships that have biological connections, because we see them as "involuntary", we have no other choice, so "we might as well".' It's an interesting idea (hampered by murky data) and not one she subscribes to, as some of her research contradicts the premise entirely. However, she does accept that there has been some work which shows that the intimacy of your sibling relationship is affected by the genes you share. On average you share something like fifty per cent of genetic material with a full sibling and twenty-seven per cent with a half sibling (and zero with a stepsibling). 'The findings indicate you show affection differently, based on those differences in genetics,' she says. 'So twins show each other more affection than full biological siblings, who show more than halves, who show more than steps, who show more than adopted siblings. There is that research out there and I can't ignore that.'

However, counter-intuitively, it is also true that if you don't share blood because you are 'just' stepsiblings (and maybe can't sniff each other out in a line-up), you might actually have a more harmonious relationship and more 'positive interactions'. Simply put, researchers at Java University found you might end up better pals with a stepbrother or stepsister because you lack the intense familiarity of full siblings, and so may approach building a voluntary connection with them in much the same way that you do with your friends.

It's a phenomenon that Patricia Papernow recognises. 'There is simply sometimes less rubbish to navigate, less friction in stepsibling relationships,' she says. She describes working with one family where a new stepbrother arrived and quickly bonded with the youngest of two full brothers. The younger boys were a similar age and became great playmates, much to the dismay of the older boy, for whom it was a kind of double grief, as he was already navigating the loss of his 'original' family.

I found the 'smell' study strangely evocative of the years our family broke apart and reformed into new ones. Because it gets close to describing my disorientation at losing the almost primal feeling of belonging in our little pack, that physical familiarity which begins with all the senses. Our homes have a particular smell, our clothes, our shampoo, hair and skin are all so recognisable. When my mum (and little sister) moved out, I remember searching the house for something she might have left behind, to comfort me. Finding only an unfamiliar scarf in the bottom of an empty drawer – which used to be full of her clothes – I slept with it on top of my pillow, next to my skin, until any traces of her smell faded away. Decades later, when I used to kiss my youngest goodnight, he would often combine a cuddle with the unwinding of a scarf I wore from round my neck, so he could snuggle it as he slept.

As a stepsibling, you might well have to learn to feel at home in a place which will not only smell different but look different and eat food which tastes different. There is no comfort in being served a familiar dish – like Bolognese – if it tastes completely unlike the one you grew up with, and which used to be a shorthand for 'home'. One stepchild I spoke to remembers trying to explain this sense of dislocation in a note to her mum after they moved into their stepfather's house. 'I don't like the smell of the washing powder we get,' she wrote, 'or the kind of biscuits in the tin. And the house feels cold.' Of course, to her stepsiblings, the smell of the washing powder was normal, the biscuits familiar and the house felt 'just right'. 'A good metaphor,' says Papernow, 'is we've got Japanese and Italians trying to live together, and you can't make everybody eat pasta with chopsticks. That's going to be miserable, you know? A lot of the sense of how "we do things" doesn't have language until somebody does something that breaks an expectation. And then there's a spike of arousal, of irritation or upset.'

'You and your mom are hillbillies. This is a house of learned doctors.'

Step Brothers (2008)

Arguments increase between stepsiblings around holidays, like Christmas. Changing the established rituals and traditions about things such as when the presents are opened or what time the turkey is served is a very clear example of how the children in each of the 'old families' will have to let go of some of the stories of their past, and it can be tough. (As can dividing the holidays up awkwardly or celebrating on pretend days.) For other stepsiblings, moving constantly between houses (one week here and one there), the emotional adjustment is constant. The creation of stepfamilies makes 'insiders and outsiders' of the children involved, says Papernow. 'The insiders may live in the house most of the time, and other stepsiblings may be outsiders. They're coming and going. They come in as the outsider to this already up and running family and feel left out. And the insider kid feels invaded. You know, "This weird kid comes every half week or every other week, and I have to share my mom with him, plus he likes TV programmes that I hate."'

An old friend whose parents divorced during his teenage years remembers a cardboard fruit crate which he would move from one car boot to another, depending on where he would sleep that night. Insider or outsider. It contained a washbag, some pyjamas, a change of clothes and some other bits and pieces he wanted – or needed – to always have with him. Thinking of this kid trying to find his place in two households, with two sets of rules, siblings, parents, expectations and norms, I found the idea of this little box of familiar and constant items very poignant.

The challenges of merging two families, the insiders with the outsiders, were clearly seen in our own post-divorce holidays. While these trips, with my dad and sisters, my stepmum and her children, were generally good fun – because all the kids really got on – they weren't all smooth sailing. There was some bickering, usually caused by different approaches to the whole concept of a holiday. In *our* family, we had an almost relentless 'make the most of the day' mentality, which meant that lie-ins were generally frowned upon and breakfast was punctual. (Even in Italy, in August.) If you want to look for the root causes of this 'productivity mania', you might find them in the lives of my two sets of military grandparents. I don't know. Whatever the reasons, the upshot was that our ideas about what constituted a good time were almost hilariously at odds with the 'others'. They preferred to kick back and relax, favouring long lie-ins over early morning breakfasts in the garden, and felt no shame about it.

We can laugh about things like this now, as we are all older and settled in ourselves. (And as an adult I can definitely see value in resting and relaxing.) But at the time it just felt like an awkward mismatch between one set of expectations and another. One which highlighted all kinds of strange loyalties to the parents who had created the value system (one of whom wasn't even there) and to the people who lived by it (me and my sisters). As a child, it is very hard to contain your feelings of defensiveness, upset and sense of being 'right' when the way you have always done things is questioned by another adult and other children who feel exactly the same about *their* point of view. Within the new stepfamily, it can criss-cross affections in all sorts of ways, with disagreements between adults drawing battle lines between the children, or with biological siblings suffering the betrayal of their parent, if they choose to side with their new partner over one issue or another. It can make you feel lost and lonely, a little insecure and very confused. It can also be a dynamic which lasts well into adulthood, lying dormant until some moment (the birth of the first grandchild, perhaps) reveals cracks in the stepfamily – caused by differences in family expectations – all over again.

Katherine Walker is clear in her advice to the adults involved: focus on the potential of the new family to become 'more', rather than seeing it as 'less'. 'We can say "This is something to celebrate, and this union is fresh. It's secure. It's solid, and it may bring, you know, the opportunity for healing and for emotional health and wellbeing that (through nobody's fault) maybe just wasn't available in the previous dynamic."' In our own family, we got there. Days by the pool alternated with days spent looking at cathedrals, with a no judgement clause for those who broke the pattern and opted for more snoozing in the hammock instead.

CEMENT BABIES

When half siblings are born into a stepfamily, creating a blended one, they are sometimes referred to as 'ours' babies (belonging to all of us: she/he is *ours*) or 'cement babies', because 'there is a wish to use the child as a kind of emotional cement', as Brenda Maddox explains, either to 'divorce-proof' the fledgling marriage, or to make all the relationships in the stepfamily closer by creating a child who is genetically linked to everyone in it. (These babies are different to half siblings born, perhaps, as the result of an affair. Their arrival – or discovery later in life – can act like a bomb going off under an intact family, with an often uncontainable emotional fallout. On the other hand, I do also know at least two acquaintances delighted to discover 'bonus' half-sisters and brothers – siblings from their parents' prior relationships – who have been embraced into the fold as a kind of fun mid-life gift.)

For the purposes of the book, I'm talking specifically about babies born into stepfamilies as a result of a new relationship. I like to think these 'ours' babies might have got their name from the 1968 movie *Yours, Mine and Ours* starring Lucille Ball as Helen North and Henry Fonda as Mike Beardsley, a couple who create a blended family by having a new, shared baby together. In it, Mike asks Helen, 'Do you really want this baby?' to which she replies, 'Very much. You see, he won't have to worry whether he's a Beardsley or a North.'

Evidence for 'how effective' these babies actually are at glueing the family together is contradictory, says Dr Blackburn, with about half of studies showing an increase in emotional closeness, and the rest indicating that their birth puts a 'monkey wrench' in the family mechanism. What she has consistently found, however, is that the creation of a half sibling can provide a much clearer playbook for the newly blended family than the stepfamily ever had. The new child can simplify some of the forces which pull at the seams of a stepfamily, by allowing both adults to inhabit the parenting role more unapologetically (with regards to the new baby), with the knock-on effect being that the other siblings feel more unified by their shared sibling status and belonging to a 'brand-new' blended family.

Conversely in a stepfamily, argues Blackburn, there often isn't an established playbook to guide you, which can lead the children to display real confusion about where their loyalties should lie. The stepsibling can be left wondering things like, 'Can I share a secret with my stepsibling? Or is that taboo?' 'Can my stepparent discipline me or not?' 'Should I show affection to my stepsibling, or my stepfather? Or will that upset my dad?' Her research has shown that, in a blended family, thanks to the shared 'genetic markers' in their half sibling (that evolutionary idea again), the relationships between all the siblings can become more straightforward.

It may be more straightforward in some ways, I am sure. New traditions and rules, or rituals and celebrations created for the new baby, can – according to experts like Walker and Sanner – create that more positive experience of the family for everyone, including the step and half siblings. But I can't help thinking about how very different the story each child uses to define their family will be, and how that might affect the identity of the siblings as a group and as adults.

The 'ours' baby, for example, is born into a family with parents who are together and (from their point of view) always have been. Only to find they share the house with a collection of different siblings – who may not live there all the time – and whose parents are not together. To begin with they have no idea that their home contains so many of those 'histories, memories, and scars' that Dr Sanner described. Later on, they might 'struggle to make sense,' says Papernow, of any background tensions in 'their' family (between 'your dad and our mum'), or mismatches in affection between the easier love they have for 'their family' (unencumbered by any of the hard history which took place before they arrived) and the more complicated or ambivalent feelings that their half siblings may hold.

They are also likely to have only hazy ideas about the places the 'outsider' kids vanish to at weekends. 'I felt somewhat bereft that there was this whole other aspect to their lives,' says Professor Alison Pike about her three older half siblings, 'because they saw their father frequently and I wasn't part of it.' Professor Pike was a 'cement' or 'ours' baby, who felt like she was 'missing out'. With the hindsight of age and understanding, however, she can appreciate the benefits to her simpler situation. 'I didn't have to navigate a parental divorce in my childhood or stepparents, which can be wild and wonderful,' she says. 'I now see that I was the lucky one, really.'

As an academic who has spent the majority of her career thinking about the 'nurture' aspects of child (and sibling relationship) development, she also recognises that the different environments experienced by her and her siblings growing up have had a real impact on them all. Unlike full siblings, who tend to travel together between their different homes after a divorce – keeping each other company in the transition from one variety of Bolognese to another – steps and halves are often separated from one another regularly. They might stay put in their nuclear family, while their half siblings scoot off for considerable periods of time, to negotiate life with their other stepfamily (like Pike's). Or they might have a biological parent and more stepsiblings elsewhere, whom they visit while the stepsiblings they live with do the same in another home still. It's an almost endless chain, and in most cases, I would bet, the siblings in these kinds of set-ups won't know much about each other's alternate realities.

This fracturing of the experience is perfectly described in an anonymous blog post I read on Mumsnet. In it, an adult woman remembers going to her stepsister's thirtieth birthday and meeting *her* best friend for the first time. 'I didn't even know her best friend's name,' she writes. 'In fact, I didn't know any of her friends' faces, let alone their names. It struck me that it was always them coming into our lives. We never went into their lives. I don't know what their bedrooms were like, what posters they had on their walls, what their life at their home was like. We went to different schools and were in different years so our friends never overlapped.'

It is a dynamic I can see in some of my own step relationships, and which I hadn't considered before. Having more opportunities to spend time with my stepdad's kids – plus either their mates or ours – would have been a much more natural, and fairer, way to try to build a peer relationship with them, rather than the slightly awkward meals at my mum and stepdad's house. These always felt like they were taking place in a polite bubble, cut off from all the things which usually swirl around teens, and which help to triangulate each other socially: mates, music, people you fancy, clothes, where you hang out, snacks. 'I wonder if we'd been able to spend time with them in their environment, their comfort zone, their turf,' asks the blogger, 'it might've made things less rocky when there were ups and downs. Having my own baby now,' she concludes, 'I can't imagine wanting to encourage her to be besties with a new woman's kids... But I'd like to think I might try.'

Finally, but crucially (as is the case with Professor Pike), the age gap between step and half siblings tends to be bigger than in nuclear families, which makes it more of a challenge for them to gather shared experiences. As adults, Alison Pike and her brothers and sisters have begun a process of getting together to pick over the memories they have each gathered and stored, only to discover just how considerable the variations in their 'supposedly mutual' upbringing actually are. It all goes to show, she reflects, how important the different family dynamics are in creating 'proper individuals', not merely parts of a 'monolithic family unit'.

I have spoken much more about the paradox of siblings, storytelling and perspectives in Chapter 3, and about how one sibling's recollections of childhood can – and do – vary so dramatically to another's. But, having already considered the effect of the size and shape of the family constellation that any baby joins, and how their place in it can influence their identity, I am not surprised when Patricia Papernow underlines that for an 'ours' baby, the narrative can be very complicated indeed. She advises family members to acknowledge and explain everything (when appropriate), to avoid confusion or fresh upset setting in. 'Struggling stepfamilies and successful stepfamilies face the same challenges,' she says briskly. 'Successful stepfamilies just communicate better.'

WHO'S THE FAVOURITE?

The last thing you want, she says, is any child wrongly assuming that they are the root cause of previous mess. The adults in all complex families – step or blended – 'have a lot of power', says Katherine Walker, 'and also the responsibility to do the work needed' to help their children understand and adapt. And as Dr Blackburn found in her research, they can also help siblings in blended families to bond. 'Siblings whose parents emphasise their positive relationship and connection through sharing backstories of their family's origins are more likely to report a positive relationship.' In other words, not glossing over the history like the Bradys, but acknowledging the 'pasts' that each child brings can help build more positive relationships between new siblings, which stand a greater chance of surviving into adulthood.

It's important work and it's difficult, says Walker. 'It's exhausting, and it doesn't happen overnight. And we're increasingly a society that wants a silver bullet. But with any sort of personal development or psychological work, there's just no quick fix.' There is no quick fix, either, for what Brenda Maddox describes as the crux of the whole difficulty for step and blended families: 'So what is to be done about irreconcilables? Children do not like divorce. Adults demand the freedom to live with whom they love.' Like Papernow, Walker and Blackburn, her solution is to face up to the tensions, aiming for honesty and less pretence, in order to make an 'open and tough' new family, which can eventually become 'not a bad place to live'.

5

Siblings as Friends

ROSS: I can't believe you hated me.
MONICA: Now I love you. And not just 'cause I have to.

FRIENDS

Dr Geoffrey Greif, professor at the University of Maryland School of Social Work and an expert in friendship, describes siblings as 'your shadow'. 'Whether you're in contact with them or not,' he explains, 'he, she or they are always part of your life.' When researching his book *Adult Sibling Relationships*, he found that around fifty per cent of people 'consider one of their siblings to be their best friend'. 'And we did not,' he said from his New York office, 'advertise, you know: "come and talk to us about your sibling relationships!" That's more likely to attract people on the extremes – either: "I'm out of touch with my sibling. I want to talk to you about it." Or: "I've got the best relationship in the world. I want to tell you about *that*." So I think we have more of a middle of the road sample.' And yet, of the 703 'middle of the road' people he and his researchers spoke to, half said precisely the same thing: their brother or sister was their closest ally.

WHO'S THE FAVOURITE?

One of the questions I asked every pair of siblings on the podcast was when they became friends. For most (who did) there was a moment or an event which marks the transition from 'someone they shared the back seat of the car with' to 'someone that they choose to hang out with, freely'. For TV historian Dan Snow, the moment came in the pub. He remembers watching his little sister Becca dancing and suddenly saw her through the eyes of the other people who were there – not as his irritating younger sibling, but as someone beautiful, cool and independent. In that moment, he appreciated her in a totally different way, seeing her 'dazzle' on the dance floor. Their relationship changed in a heartbeat. He was very apologetic about the way he treated her before that evening, saying sorry for his 'bullying' and overbearing behaviour. 'I'm ashamed to admit it,' he said, 'I just was mentally quite torturous to her. For some reason I thought by reducing her self-esteem I could build up mine. And to this day I find it extraordinary that I did that… and I feel very guilty… Now she's become one of my best friends and the person I admire most in the world.'

For many of the siblings I spoke to, this morphing from sibling to friend seems to happen around adolescence. Until then, you are usually cloistered away in the family home, with little opportunity for your brother or sister to have much sense of you as a real person 'out in the world'. You are trapped in your 'shared environment', with little autonomy and few choices. It's a scenario ripe for irritation and frustration. Also, because our roles in the family often bear no relation to our behaviour in the wild, it follows that until Dan saw Becca grooving away confidently, he may have had no idea that that was what she was actually like. Perhaps this experience of properly *seeing* others – siblings especially – unfettered from the family is why all teens are more influenced by their peers.

Alison Pike seems to think so. It is not until your teens, she believes, that 'you are seeking a relationship with your sibling of your own volition and crucially can have a relationship which is separate from the parents'. In that moment, your sibling friendship becomes more like a freely chosen one with a peer, and less like being begrudgingly tethered to that annoying 'shadow'.

> 'Siblings that say they never fight are most definitely hiding something.'
>
> LEMONY SNICKET, *HORSERADISH*

With my own sisters, this friendship forging was a bit sputtering. But it did happen, catalysed by several episodes which transformed my two-dimensional idea of them into much fuller pictures. Firstly, I remember finding out that my younger sister was being bullied at school in Holland. The nastiness she described made my throat burn with rage as I imagined what I would say if I ever met one of those girls. In that moment, I saw for the first time what the world was saying about her and making her feel. And that made me suddenly look at her quite differently. Not because I thought the bullies were right – quite the opposite. In the precise instant she confided in me, my perception of her shifted – from a quite vague idea of her as 'just my little sister' to a very clear appreciation of how funny, resilient but also vulnerable she was and of how much more she deserved.

Therapist Erin Runt has a busy practice in Chicago. Her work began as a couples therapist, but the birth of her twin girls four years ago sparked an interest in the importance of brothers and sisters in shaping psychological development. Once she began thinking about how the siblings she treats could build healthy adult relationships with each other, she could immediately see the challenges. 'A regular friendship has this idea of, "I'm opting into this relationship with you, and I can also opt out of it with you later,"' she explains. 'It also has an element of equality – theoretically, there's an exchange here. And you're not very likely to be competing for resources, right? Plus, what is happening in *your* life doesn't necessarily affect what's happening in *my* life… With siblings, what's interesting is – you're navigating this peer thing, but also that person is a direct threat to your resources. They are a direct competition for the support you get, who you are, how you are defined as a person, how your behaviours and accomplishments are measured.' That 'place of competition', she says, can make friendship with a sibling more difficult to achieve, because it's tough to show vulnerability, or feel like an equal with someone you are in that kind of 'competition' with. Her assessment probably rings true for many of the other fifty per cent of people in Dr Greif's book: the fifty per cent who said they are *not* best friends with one of their siblings. Of course, it isn't binary. There are hundreds of ways that brothers and sisters might describe their relationship, with 'friendly' or 'great but not in my top five' being definite possibilities. There will also, of course, be some who don't get along with their siblings at all and this can be very painful.

Dr Greif found his book *Adult Sibling Relationships* had a real impact. He soon had an inbox full of messages – not with people writing a love letter to their brother or sister, but with people asking for help, saying things like, 'Can you do therapy with us? Because I'm struggling with my relationship.' I was really struck by this as it says so much about the giant 'ought' which sits right at the heart of our idea of what it is to be a sibling. We *ought* to be close, we think, to understand one another, to love one another, to have each other's backs, to protect one another, to be friends and to get on.

The idea is fundamental to so many cultures and communities, spoon-fed to us in nurseries, on laps and tucked up in bed. Told to us in songs and stories, in religious texts, in myth and in fairy tale. These stories tell us, 'look what happens when siblings stick together and love one another' – Gretel rescues Hansel from the witch, Lakshmana follows his older brother Lord Rama with unwavering loyalty, Pollux gives up half his immortality to save his mortal twin's life. Aristotle declared that brothers and sisters *should* form an excellent natural friendship. Even the opposite narrative, stories where brothers and sisters did not do what they ought to do – the bitter jealousy between Cain and Abel in Genesis, or the murder of Osiris, the Egyptian god, by his brother Set(h) – read as cautionary tales: no good will come of behaviour like that.

It is this 'ought' which might explain why the majority of books written about siblings are directed at parents: manuals which tend to focus on how to help resolve disputes between squabbling children. Siblings can – according to psychology professor Laurie Kramer – have up to eight fights with each other an hour. An *hour*. That kind of relentless conflict is not what people dream of when they embark on building a family, and it will drive even the most hardened cynic to the self-help section. Many a parent has despaired, thinking, 'Why are they fighting again? They *ought* to get on. They're sisters/brothers. They are supposed to love each other.' Parents of small children will first reach for these books because they need an immediate hack for domestic peace. But I believe there's a long-term aim too: we want these books to show us how to help our children form a lasting, healthy bond; we want them to be lifelong friends.

If anything, the 'oughts' surrounding sibling closeness only grow, becoming a blueprint for platonic relationships more broadly; deployed like an emotional yardstick to measure the depth of other friendships. We find ourselves asking: how close does this come to the sibling ideal? How much do I love them? Like a sister? Like a brother? *That much?* Think how often you hear people say that – in plays, books, films and life – as shorthand for just how much they care. In a seminal scene in *The Sopranos*, moments before Sal 'Big Pussy' Bonpensiero is shot for being a rat, Paulie 'Walnuts'

Gualtieri mutters sadly, 'You were like a brother to me,' to which Tony Soprano dolefully adds, 'To all of us.' Then BANG! A code of loyalty – as strong as one between brothers – has been severed.

Meanwhile, frustrated by the lack of representation of sisters in a lot of foundational sibling research, the feminist scholar Dr Terri Apter addressed the oversight in *The Sister Knot*. She told me, 'I had been previously working on girls' and women's friendships, and this question of where it is that the notion of the idealised "best friend" comes from. And they're talking about "sisterhood" and "soulmates" and there was such an overlap of language between friendship and sistering. The best thing you could say about a friend is "she's like my sister", as if friendships with sisters or relationships with sisters were always good. Added to that, you know, is this broad idea of a "sister", which, of course, I grew up with in the women's movement about sisterhood... that it was all wonderful.'

So there can be an unhappy gap between the 'ought' of the sibling ideal – used to describe what perfect friendship should look like – and the messier reality Apter hints at. There are many who find themselves struggling to connect with their brother or sister, people who may look at that shiny fifty per cent with their 'sibling bff' and wonder, '*How?*' And it's a gap which Dr Greif – fascinated with the dynamics of 'horizontal' relationships (between siblings and friends) – finds frustrating. Along with every single other sibling researcher I have spoken to, he says that (with the exception of intimate partners) the overwhelming focus in academic research and in therapy rooms is on 'vertical' parent–child relationships. He sounded a bit downcast, talking about those unhappy siblings who contacted him asking for help. 'Therapists have been trained,' he says, 'to talk to people about their parents and their kids and their partners, but not about their siblings. And students don't spend a lot of time learning about adult siblings in graduate school, and I think everywhere we go, because your sibling is your shadow, you need to resolve it, hopefully before you die.'

Stephen P. Bank is a former professor of psychology at Wesleyan University in Connecticut. In his groundbreaking book *The Sibling Bond*, co-written with Michael D. Khan, he collected the notes from every patient who presented in their clinic with 'sibling issues' – observing that 'in the emotional, and largely irrational realm of sibling relations we felt as if we were in a foreign country without a map'. The quote resonated with Erin Runt, who is concerned by the neglect of sibling relationships in research. 'There's a lot of peer relationship stuff that we practise in our family of origin,' she explains, 'and there's no attention given to that. And because there's no attention given to that, then other things are underestimated. Sibling abuse, sexual, physical, emotional, is really underestimated. Sibling estrangement is not taken very seriously. Siblings are such a big component, a big percentage of our family experience. They could be such a resource and an emotional support and a community, but they are not seen as being worth the energy, or we're encouraged to prioritise friendships over sibling relationships, even though all of them are incredibly important.'

FRENEMIES

In order to talk meaningfully about the possibility of being *friends* with your grown-up sibling 'shadow', or to resolve whatever grit is preventing the cogs of your sibling relationship from running smoothly, we have to spool back and start somewhere quite different. To rewind from where you are now, to beyond the 'he got more than me' childhood arguments, and right back to the nursery: to Freud and to the origins of the idea of sibling rivalry. This is because the ideas of sibling rivalry and sibling friendship are inseparable, twisted around each other like the very DNA that brothers and sisters share. 'What binds us together,' writes Dr Greif, 'also pulls us apart.' To understand the ways in which siblings might become friends, you have to understand why it might also be hard or downright impossible. 'I think about my very, very close relationship with my sister,' says Dr Apter. 'You know, it was very clear to me, I loved her, I thought I loved her more... or in a way I didn't really love my parents. And I identify with her very, very closely. On the other hand, I also felt something very uncomfortable. You know, she was wiser, she was more confident, she was very successful. It was something that I learned to call envy.'

Although the term 'sibling rivalry' wasn't coined until the 1930s, much of Freud's writing is full of ideas which circle around the concept. 'The jealousy of children towards their brothers and sisters,' he wrote, 'who may represent rivals in love or power, often persists in a disguised form into later life.' Freud knew what he was writing about. When he was just seventeen months old, his younger brother Julius was born, an event Freud greeted with 'rage and wicked death wishes', according to biographer Peter Gay. Could this emotional turmoil be the reason Freud ended up writing so much about siblings (though mostly indirectly)? Not because he was particularly interested in brothers and sisters, but because he was famously obsessed with the mother–child relationship. And, Freud argues, the arrival of a new baby can only ever cause painful disruption to that critical bond. 'It is easy to understand that the loss of the mother's exclusive attention due to the arrival of a new sibling arouses the child's earliest hostile feelings.'

We're familiar with the term 'Oedipus complex', used to describe the (sometimes sexual, sometimes murderous) intensity of the parent–child relationship. Though its tangled legacy would take much too long to unpick here, it remains pertinent to any thinking about siblings. It was Freud who developed the idea that being usurped in your mother's affections by the next child that appears in the nursery can be A Very Big Deal. 'Hostile feelings towards brothers and sisters must be far more frequent in childhood than the unseeing eye of the adult observer can perceive,' Freud declared. It's an idea which still looms large over modern psychotherapy and goes some way towards explaining why there is such an overwhelming focus on vertical relationships, and perhaps why Stephen P. Bank found that 'siblings are rarely described positively. Descriptive language used by most clinicians to depict sibling relationships involves terms like: envy, jealousy, rivalry, and fratricidal wish, which attempt to explain the motives underlying mutual hostility.'

And there it is: envy. Dr Juliet Mitchell, the renowned psychoanalyst who's written extensively about siblinghood throughout her career, stresses the absolute importance of it. The realisation 'that one is not unique, that someone stands exactly in the same place as oneself and that though one has found a friend, this loss of uniqueness is, at least temporarily, equivalent to annihilation… at this later level we have murderous desires, as a response to the danger of annihilation.' Her description of the mixture of joy and grief involved in becoming a sibling hits close to the bone. It's an account Dr Apter finds compelling: 'I was very struck by just her description of envy. The way that someone who is like you and in your world can threaten you by hoovering up all the love and attention that you need to survive… It's somehow "you are all the admirable traits… and somehow you being admirable is a threat to me" and I think that's the brilliance of this depiction.'

'Jem and I fussed a lot, but as we grew older, we found ourselves needing each other more.'
HARPER LEE, *TO KILL A MOCKINGBIRD*

Professor Claire Hughes is a research psychologist and deputy director of the Centre for Child, Adolescent and Family

Research at Cambridge University. Her research provides some much-needed solace for parents in the early-year trenches, as well as a dollop of hope for those of us trying to work on our grown-up sibling relationships. 'Most research on siblings seems to have focused on the negative,' she says, 'and maybe times have changed... or maybe it's always been wrong. But I feel like for most children I know, siblings are a really positive presence in their lives. So, the research doesn't really match reality.' However, as a psychologist steeped in the existing material, she does remember the effect it had on her personally. 'I remember giving a lecture about the birth of a sibling when I was eight months pregnant with my second child,' she laughs, 'and I was almost going [she puts her hands over her ears], I really don't want to hear all this.'

She needn't have worried as her instincts that siblings are a 'positive presence' has been borne out in her family – as well as some of her work. For example, in one study she carried out with children from ages three to six, she found that childish quarrelling at one time or another was 'just not important' – and indeed 'quite normal'. It was only the children who were showing high levels of conflict with their sibling at both time points (so consistently during those three years) who were the ones 'having trouble making friends and maybe engaging in a bit of bullying behaviour and things like that'. Much of the sibling fighting among small children, she concluded, is simply a phase.

And that seemingly simple idea is key when thinking about siblings and friendship – including way beyond childhood. Professor Hughes emphasises just how long sibling relationships can be, how many chapters the story can contain – 'it really does last a lifespan' – and that we should try to keep some sense of perspective. It is ridiculous to try to characterise what a sibling relationship will be like forever by examining it at one fixed point. It would be senseless to say, for example, that the three-year-olds she studied who incessantly squabbled over toys or snacks have a 'bad sibling relationship' with no hope of change.

Kirsten O'Brien is known for having hosted one of the most popular children's TV shows in the UK. She and her little brother Tim came on the podcast to talk about their peripatetic childhood following their dad's engineering career all over the world. They painted vivid stories of growing up together in exciting environments and of bringing back stories from far-flung places to relatives in the North East of England. But the thing I remember most are the descriptions of the fights they had as kids. 'I feel like I wasn't a very kind sister,' Kirsten told me. 'The type of scraps me and my brother had were proper hard core... once the fight started, we would run to the kitchen where my mum had the utensils next to the cooker.' Tim joins in: 'We would arm ourselves... and there were some meat tenderisers which were our weapons of choice. It was very much: whoever got the biggest mallet first would end up battering the other with it.'

When I asked them what their fights were about, they told me they were most likely about 'nothing'. Or maybe the results of some 'button pushing' or silly sibling 'wind-ups'. They couldn't really remember. And what is their relationship like now? Well, they were appearing on a podcast together, squashed in Kirsten's garden office, laughing uncontrollably at their childhood stories and planning what to do with their kids that afternoon. I put it to them that they'd be horrified if their own children behaved as they had. We all recognised it was far from anything you would describe as ideal behaviour – for anyone – and yet, they reminisced with such fondness.

Including their memories is not to make light of anything; especially instances of genuine abuses of power, involving sex or violence between siblings. Those are matters quite apart from what is being described here. Rather, what Kirsten and Tim's long view of their sibling experience provides is an illustration of the ways that ordinary brother–sister relationships can – and most likely will – change dramatically over time, to evolve into something much more functional and mature than you sometimes 'endure' in childhood.

'Siblings are the people we practice on, the people who teach us about fairness and cooperation and kindness and caring – quite often the hard way.'

PAMELA DUGDALE

In *The Sister Knot*, Apter argues for much more nuance in the way we think about sibling rivalry, asking us to take 'a huge step away from the Freud perspective'. There is an ever-evolving tangle of feelings at the heart of what it is to be friends with your siblings – a combination of love, loyalty, irritation and admiration – which feels so distinct from the mixture of emotions that swill around other friendships, and 'rivalry' cannot encompass these subtleties. 'Sister relationships,' she says, 'are built on a foundation of shared experience, but they are also charged with rivalry, envy and conflict.' There is also more open competition in sister relationships, she argues, than in regular friendship between girls and women, because there is more competition between siblings full stop. The legacy of the nursery *can* linger. But, Apter explained, 'if I have this bad feeling towards a friend, let's say. Maybe I'm envious and resentful. It doesn't mean that everything is really bad in that relationship, or that *I'm* really bad because I feel these things – in the moment – towards someone I'm supposed to, or claim to, love.' Like Claire Hughes, she invites people to think of the sibling relationship as always changing and often uncomfortably ambivalent – as well as usually more intimate than any other.

Even as adults, we would do well to remind ourselves of the message in Juliet Mitchell's lecture 'The Sibling Complex', in which she argues that the only way to build a positive sibling relationship is to accept that our siblings are like us, but not identical. 'This,' she explains beautifully, 'leaves room for more than one person to be the mother's child.' As Dr Elizabeth Kilbey, who has spent decades researching sibling rivalry, underlines, 'the goal of the adult sibling relationship has to be: "We are different, but we are *connected*."' There is room for everyone, and we were never really being replaced. The family constellation was merely being added to. There is another star in the sky.

Functional sibling friendship – at any age – is not all down to us as individuals. We don't exist in a vacuum. There are so many other factors at play and many are beyond our control. We have to consider: the family system, the environment we share(d), our parental support and the temperament of older siblings. This can set the tone for the Sibset and affect how likely friendship is to occur, says Professor Alison Pike. 'Different temperamental aspects really can lead to a "lovely" versus "conflictual" sibling relationship. Having a bossy older child is OK because they've got that natural hierarchy, whereas if you have a younger one who's much more forceful in that way, then they can really butt heads. But if you have quite a forceful older one and a relatively kind of compliant younger one, then that combination works super well. And pro-social tendencies in the older one is like the golden ticket.'

THEORY OF MIND

Whatever dispositions siblings have, a psychological milestone – which takes place at around the age of four – may start to help smooth whatever ruffled sibling feathers there are in the nest. It's at that age that children develop what is known as the 'Theory of Mind', explains Professor Hughes. 'When children start lying, they start joking, they start understanding that you don't necessarily mean what you say.' In short, they recognise that different people can think or believe different things. This new-found ability to understand that your brain is kind of private is clearly related to developing the crucial idea that you are an individual: separate from others, including your parents and any new babies they produce. Without your parents doing anything at all to try to mitigate your upset, you might work it out all by yourself. It just takes time.

What's even more amazing about Theory of Mind and siblinghood is that children with a younger brother or sister are twice as likely to show an 'advanced understanding' of it, according to research carried out by Dr Amy Paine, an academic at Cardiff University. Her work has also shown that having two siblings (compared to none) gives an advantage 'comparable to the gains in Theory of Mind children show from age three to age four'. It's quite the boost. It happens, she explains, because siblings act like apprentices. Having them around, as more knowledgeable 'others', may help children understand more about the world, 'by giving them opportunities to engage in the types of play and conversations that they wouldn't otherwise be able to do on their own'. While research has also shown that children can learn from pals at nursery or cousins they see often, I am left wondering about the compounded advantage that the baby of an even larger family might have, when it comes to this psychological development. Their position in the birth order would surely grant them a whole team of more advanced individuals to help them suss things out, and I think this may help explain Alfred Adler's description of younger siblings as 'manipulative'.

'What we do know is that Theory of Mind does tend to be associated with popularity,' Professor Hughes says. 'It can help them develop empathy and compassion – as they can imagine and understand the different ways that their siblings or friends, or siblings *as friends*, might be feeling.' So this precocious achievement could really make the difference in helping children form friendships – either with their siblings or peers outside the home. Theory of Mind is a really exciting thing to research in terms of the proven benefits that being or having a sibling can bring when building friendships – something Hughes is very keen to beat the drum about. 'Because I feel that when I talk to journalists, when I talk to ordinary people, they totally get it. They understand that sibling relationships are super important. When you write a grant for a funding body, it seems a lot harder to make that case.'

A side note about Theory of Mind: because it enables children to be more socially sophisticated, they can use it for manipulative purposes too. 'Let's take Draco Malfoy from *Harry Potter*,' says Hughes, 'who gets Crabbe and Doyle as his henchmen. They're the ones that always get into trouble, and he's the mastermind behind it all. So knowing how other people think doesn't mean you will automatically use that information for *good*.' I think back now to the tricks my sister repeatedly played on me as a small child and of course I fell for them all!

Hughes prefers to think of Theory of Mind like a tool which can be used in any number of ways. 'It's not a given that if your child has developed Theory of Mind early, they're going to go down this love and roses pathway,' she says, although the famous psychotherapist and psychoanalyst John Bowlby's work does show that 'in general, all other things being equal, [children] tend to be quite affiliative in their social goals'. They are motivated to be liked and so will most likely use these skills for making solid friendships. Either way, to have access to it early – thanks to your sibling relationship – could place you at a real early social advantage.

When I interviewed the incredible Irish stage and screen actors (and sisters) Catherine and Eileen Walsh, it was clear how Eileen's position in the family as the adored baby 'Smallie' and youngest of six may have helped her make friends, in just the way Amy Paine's work describes. Eileen recalls how she stomped into nursery, brimming with the confidence of being the 'minded' baby, who was always the centre of attention at home. 'I would be a classic baby, yes,' said Eileen. 'I think I was a funny kid, used to people smiling and enjoying being around you.' She says she was one of those kids 'who know they're loved, they walk in and are like "Hi! We're gonna be friends! I'm great!"' After all, once she was ready to venture out into the wide world, she'd had buckets of practice at playing, talking, sharing, make-believe and caring. She was a hit at the sandpit.

This makes total sense to Professor Hughes, who has also looked into the 'emotional scaffolding' that having a sibling can provide for a child. She also points out that her study 'Toddlers Up' showed that both good sibling relationships and more negative ones had a positive impact on a person's early development. The emotional training from 'mild' rivalry, including teasing and gentle arguing, can pay the same developmental dividends.

WHO'S THE FAVOURITE?

> 'I don't believe an accident of birth makes people sisters or brothers. It makes them siblings, gives them mutuality of parentage. Sisterhood and brotherhood is a condition people have to work at.'
>
> Maya Angelou

There is a statistic about siblings, bandied around the internet a lot, which is helpful for thinking about how a sibling friendship might develop *after* childhood. It is this: by the time you leave home at around eighteen or slightly later, you have probably already spent something like eighty per cent of the total time with your siblings that you will *ever* spend with them. A study in the American journal *Demographic Research* showed that until the age of thirteen, children who have siblings spend about half of all their discretionary time together. As teens they will spend an average of 267 minutes a day together. But by the age of twenty-five, nearly half of American siblings have moved away from home, and by age thirty the number is roughly seventy per cent. 'In less collectivist (Western) cultures, there's a lot of emphasis on growing up and leaving your family,' says Dr Greif. 'You grow up and you move away from your siblings. You're supposed to set up your own life.' A quick rattle through sibling TikTok – #sibtok – throws up reams of emotional reels mainly by teens posting their reactions to versions of the data. For example, 'somebody on here said you have already spent most of ur time with ur sibling and now you're crying while he's sleeping in the room that we're sharing 😢'

But all is not lost. The story is not one of simple divergence, created by a decreasing amount of time spent together. And not all siblings choose distance. In fact, studies show that siblings tend to report increases in closeness and decreases in conflict after leaving home. Probably because whatever relationship they seek to build is now more a matter of choice and less a matter of simply living in the same place. The friction and irritation caused by borrowing each other's things without asking or not doing our fair share of dishwasher emptying is gone and hopefully the process – which can begin in adolescence – of appreciating one another as individuals 'out in the world' continues apace. Actor Tom Holland remembers being a teenager and telling his brother Harry, 'When I am eighteen, I will *never* talk to you ever again.' In the same podcast he concluded, 'and I have been living with him for, like, ten years.'

The 'graph of sibling friendship' doesn't necessarily lead ever upwards, however. After you fly the nest, the trajectory of your relationship is heavily context dependent. Whether you are in the same life stage as your sibling becomes increasingly important and causes the line on the friendship graph to wiggle accordingly. In a paper called '"Can't Live With or Without Them:" Transitions and Young Adults' Perceptions of Sibling Relationships', the authors Alexander Jensen, Shawn Whiteman and Karen Fingerman found that 'When one sibling has undergone a transition that the other has not, it puts the siblings out of sync and makes them dissimilar, as a result, siblings may feel their relationship has declined (less closeness and more conflict).' The line on the graph dips.

When siblings are in sync, there is potential for the opposite to be true. For example, if a young adult gets married before their sibling, this inequality 'may discourage a positive relationship', whereas if they have both tied the knot, 'they may feel that they now have similar experiences and greater equality, and thus, may feel closer'.

The pattern this creates has been best described as an hourglass or egg timer – where the fatter bits at the top and bottom represent the greater amount of contact between siblings in childhood and a closer relationship and perhaps more time spent together again in later life. The skinny middle bit – the life-building early adult years – represents a leaner time for the relationship. In those years, the rapid canter through college or university, towards first homes and jobs, first serious partners then maybe marriage and or possibly babies means there is so much scope for siblings to be out of step, to lose the possibility of understanding each other and our experiences. We are prioritising finding the building blocks of our future. And we are dancing to different beats for a lot of that time.

However, as we get older, there is a greater chance of falling more in line with one another again, as at some point we all arrive at middle age. The life stages are longer and broader, and change is usually less rapid. While there's a huge variation in the idea of 'mid-life', there is usually a kind of wisdom after the age of forty – an empathy for the various paths life takes, the assortment of relationships we can enjoy and the compromises we usually have to make. Even the physical decline binds us – needing reading glasses or being bugged by ligament pain. Not to mention the challenges of raising kids, paying a mortgage or trying to keep our jobs going. The legacy of the rivalry may also have lifted accordingly. 'I'm not competing with my brother, who's older than me, as much as I was, you know, fifty years ago!' laughs Geoffrey Greif when talking about mid-life sibling relationships. His work illustrates that after the more exhausting phases of tussle and comparison in early siblinghood, the calmer 'undercurrents of love and loyalty' tend to remain. A study of siblings in their sixties in the American Midwest backs up his work and his personal experience. It found that sibling relationships become more 'emotionally meaningful and less intense' in later adulthood, with a reluctance expressed by participants to sweat the small sibling stuff: 'older adults often avoid negative interactions and focus on maintaining positive contact with the people they are closest to'. Sister–sister sibling pairs were the best at being in touch, but overall siblings reported being less lonely and depressed if they managed to maintain a good relationship with a sibling. The paper even urges policy makers to think about how to 'attend to the role that sibling relationships play in older adults' health and well-being'.

One of the most touching sibling interviews I have ever done was with Pat and Jean Owtram, sisters who both worked on cracking codes during the Second World War. Born two and a half years apart in the 1920s, they painted vivid pictures of a childhood spent 'visiting ladies' and playing dress-up on the lawn of their home in the North of England. A whole lifetime was then spent largely apart – and sometimes overseas.

WHO'S THE FAVOURITE?

Both women signed the Official Secrets Act and weren't even aware of each other's involvement in the war effort until years after. When I met them, a couple of years before Jean died, they were both over ninety. Husbands had long since died, as had many friends. They were sitting side by side on the sofa, in a sitting room in West London, eating biscuits and drinking coffee. It was such an intimate and comfortable relationship – 'best friends', they told me – but it appeared almost more than that, as if they were a kind of refuge for the other in old age. It made me wonder about the kind of policy that might be designed to house older siblings in the same care community or retirement home. A gentle forage for stories about siblings who have managed this reveals one heart-warming photo after another of elderly siblings beaming from their wing-backed armchairs. 'We never dreamed we'd be reunited in our old age, but none of us can think of a better way to spend our last years,' ninety-three-year-old Georgia Southwick told *People* magazine in 2017. Georgia was housed with her four surviving siblings in sheltered housing near their childhood home in Massachusetts. 'Having each other to talk to every day so many years later has been wonderful,' she said. 'It's a real treat to be together again.' I also found the story of twin sisters Margaret and Winnie who had both been diagnosed with dementia and initially housed in separate care homes. After repeatedly asking for one another, the ninety-year-old sisters were reunited in 2022 at a Cheshire care home – in next-door rooms. 'Oh, it's just the best,' Margaret told the local paper, while Winnie just said, 'We will not be separated again.'

When I try to imagine answering my own question about when my older sister Bex and I became friends, I think it wasn't until we both became mothers. As teens, we were a little bit shell-shocked by everything and struggled to relate during years which were – at times – horribly confused. She was away for long days as a day pupil at a boarding school and then went off to university. I was sent to a different school, and then often left at home alone. So it wasn't until much, much later during a trip to visit her in New Zealand that it really clicked. My eldest child Max was nine months old and she had a toddler and a baby of her own. We shared a three-week holiday; the first time we had spent time together as mums. We organised some childcare and had *fun*. The kind of joyful giddy fun you can only really relish if you've been trapped on a sofa for months on end, with the occasional trip to the GP or a church playgroup for respite. We hired mopeds, ate fish and chips, went to the beach where *The Piano* was filmed and drank delicious wine. We were on exactly the same page: mothering our little boys together. It stands out as one of the best trips of my life, and one of the reasons is that I fell in love with my sister.

Alone at home with a baby, we question everything in an endless, sleep-deprived spiral. How comforting then to be with a sister who is parenting alongside you, because in all your muddle and self-doubt and anxiety about what the holy heck you are doing, there is someone who has the same blueprint for mothering as you. The glorious ease of a shared shorthand for what we found acceptable (rigid bedtimes and enforced broccoli consumption) versus what we did not (children missing naps for no good reason and staying in when we could be at the park, where the shouting was more manageable for all). We may have been making hashes of it, but we were making hashes together. At a stressful time, my sister and I dipped into a mutual pool of inherited knowledge and became friends as a result.

THE COVID EFFECT

I started thinking about siblings seriously in early 2020, when everyone was frightened by the threat of this mysterious disease called Covid-19. Families pulled closer and I watched friends in their forties, fifties and sixties set up Zoom accounts to talk regularly to siblings – some of whom they'd not seen for years. There was something about the stress of it all that made them reach back to the comfort of family and nostalgia. This idea of reconnection in middle age is familiar to anyone with a Facebook account (which instantly ages you for starters) as school friends begin to creep out of the woodwork, sharing old class photos and reminiscing. There is something within us yearning to plot a course backwards, to say 'this is where I came from, and these people know me'. It's a sentiment which has given rise to recent books like Elizabeth Day's *Friendaholic* or *The Virago Book of Friendship* edited by Rachel Cooke, which both consider the significance, beauty and the 'psychic ballast' that an intimate relationship with an old friend can provide in your life.

Perhaps it is part of the second 'contemplative half' of life, where you begin to account for the relationships which have formed you and want to honour them a little, even if that means a rather lame or limp post on social media. It is a strange pull back towards your roots which begins to express itself in your forties and fifties and beyond: a sentimentality for old haunts, old music maybe. There is certainly an urge in me to feel connected to the people I share common history with. I suspect I am one Facebook post away from scurrying down the motorway to the next school reunion.

Dr Nina Howe, research chair of early childhood development at Concordia University, says siblings can serve as good sources of precisely this kind of comfort in later adulthood – as articulated so perfectly by the Owtrams, looking back over the nine decades spent loving and knowing each other so well. 'This is the person that you have known the longest in your life,' she says, 'and you have a shared history.' Erin Runt agrees but says it is often a crisis which pulls (or pushes) us back together as siblings, rather than a sentimental urge (which may see us reconnect with old school friends, or redouble our efforts to catch up with past flatmates). We arrive in mid-life to discover our parents need our help, and we *have* to work together to provide it. 'A lot of times,' explains Runt, 'what happens is siblings might come to therapy and be like "our mom is dying", or "we just have this family thing; we're trying to get along while we go through it". They're not really seeking deeper therapy for their entire relationship. They usually conceptualise it as "help to get through a temporary stressor", or with something they can't agree on… there's usually an external thing driving it.' She helps brothers and sisters who find themselves at this point to carve out new ways to relate, to designate new roles and responsibilities to carry them through the next phase of life as harmoniously as possible.

The risk of reverting to childhood patterns is probably greatest with siblings who have not really kept in touch or encouraged their relationship to evolve and develop beyond adolescence and through all those shifting life stages. When forced together again, they may struggle as old fault lines reappear, says Dr Greif. 'Usually, the problems in relationships between siblings are around favouritism, both as a kid and now. I think twenty-five per cent of people said they were certainly raised in families where favourites were showed. A similar percentage – maybe not the same people – said in adulthood, "I still feel that my mother or father plays favourites." And sometimes favouritism is fine, and other times it's a very lethal kind of knock on a relationship.' That American study into siblings in their sixties also clearly showed that where old sibling arguments like this rear their head, they do real damage, creating increased feelings of loneliness for people and a decrease in wellbeing. 'Professionals working with families in applied settings,' it cautions, 'might design interventions that decrease sibling conflict and perceptions of parental favouritism as well as promote sibling relationships as sources of companionship and support for older adults.'

Getting to grips with historic or fresh grievances like these can be hard, especially when narratives often don't tally.

That's because of that natural tendency to carry major 'main character energy' into sibling interactions. According to Runt, 'We're very self-centred, sometimes, in our experience, so we see all these ways in which our sibling didn't appear to like us, didn't appear to pay attention to us. And we get surprised: "what do you mean *I* hurt *you*?" "HOW?" Because we feel so clear on our own experience, and we're very biased towards being gracious with our own experience. But then we hear about stuff, "You thought that's what I was doing?", "Like, what? I didn't know that upset you. I didn't know you thought this thing about me." And we are surprised to hear how we were perceived.' Dr Greif says it comes down to 'I really don't know what it's like to be *my* brother.'

Talking with your siblings about your parents' health and how to help manage it can be tricky for other reasons. Geography and gender play their part, much as the latter really shouldn't. But even when these negotiations are difficult – old resentments are rekindled or new ones created – they can also present an opportunity: to work on a friendship that can endure, perhaps, or indulge in some nostalgia, as a way of dealing with the present. A little sentimentality can help smooth the painful edges by reminding you where you came from – together. I expect many people reading this have had a version of the experience of clearing a house or care home room, and being sidetracked by an old photo album, sitting cross-legged among the debris and being sucked back into remembering long-gone versions of themselves, before they were the one with power of financial attorney, before he even had big teeth. There are pictures of me squashed into the bathtub with my siblings, all rubbery chubby thighs and bubbles in our hair. Looking at them, all orange toned now, and faded behind plastic which is brittle and crinkled, I think: this is before I had been made an aunty or been labelled as 'bossy' or had introduced a new future brother-in-law. It was way before any of us knew how the story would unfold.

LEAVING SPACE FOR AMBIVALENCE

All that said, I don't think that any chapter on siblings and friendship should create another 'ought'. Not all brothers and sisters can manage to be friends, and that's OK. It's also OK to hold on to the slightly messier idea of a long relationship which can flex and adapt, allowing for feelings of irritation to exist alongside love, or for periods of emotional distance. 'It helps a lot,' says Greif, 'to be realistic, to think about these relationships with three overarching themes: Affection, Ambivalence and Ambiguousness – these tend to be a good way to think about intimate relationships in general. Like "Yes, I have great affection for my wife, but I also occasionally have ambivalent feelings towards her and I don't quite understand what's going on." That's especially true for siblings. "Why did my sister marry that jerk? How can my brother spend time with Dad after everything he did to us? I don't want to spend Christmas with them but it'll create major issues if I don't." In these scenarios, the three "A's" can come in handy.'

It's a viewpoint I believe that Rabbi Levi ben Gershon, a fourteenth-century French Jewish thinker, might have appreciated. He knew his Aristotle (who thought siblings were suited to friendship) but came to a different conclusion, one which chimes with a lot of what Greif expresses. He said that while friends come and go, siblings are in our lives forever. He also said that while friends may be there through thick and thin, siblings are *especially* likely to be there for the tougher moments: 'One who loves [i.e. befriends] another is joined up with his beloved in good times and bad times. This is part and parcel of loving: that one does not abandon one's beloved in time of trouble… He will rejoice when [his friend] does well and assist him when things go badly. While a brother won't be impelled to be joined with his brother in good times, in bad times [for his brother] he will come to his aid, for he is his own flesh and blood.'

Or as Robert Waldinger, a psychiatry professor at Harvard Medical School and the lead author of a study on sibling closeness, more recently concluded: brothers and sisters generally know they can count on one another when needed, even if they're not emotionally close. When the chips are down, said Professor Waldinger, they will often step in to give each other 'instrumental support' – something siblings are shown to offer one another more and more as time marches on. When he asked middle-aged siblings, 'Who could you call in the middle of the night if you were sick or scared?' they could list as many names as they wanted. Some people didn't have a single name to write down. But many, he said, listed a sibling.

6

Sistren and Brethren

Familect

'The language of actual intimacy, the sort we cultivate with kin and close kith.'
    Anne Helen Petersen, *Culture Study* podcast

There are apparently over one million words in the English language, to which we are adding an impressive thousand or so per year. Although strictly speaking not many of them are totally brand new, it is still a dizzying rate of language invention. According to Kerry Maxwell, writing in *Macmillan English Dictionary* magazine, most words which get rolled into the lexicon (and then officially make it into the dictionary) contain a familiar element but they have undergone some kind of linguistic process. These include: being compounded with another word (*furbaby* or *speed dating*), blended (*brunch*), or they have had a recognised affix bolted on to help express a brand-new idea (*to regift*). Other ways of conjuring new words include abbreviation (*taxi* from taximeter cabriolet), repurposing (*to text*, a verb taken from the original noun), or simply borrowing from somewhere else (*pukka* from Hindi, *tsunami* from Japanese, *tattoo* from Tahitian). In fact, in the *Cambridge Encyclopaedia of the English Language*, prolific author and linguist David Crystal explains that 'English, perhaps more than any other language, is an insatiable borrower. Whereas the speakers of some languages take pains to exclude foreign words from their lexicons, English seems always to have welcomed them. Well over 300 languages are on record in the *Oxford English Dictionary* as direct sources of its present-day vocabulary, and the locations of contact are found all over the world.'

English, says Melvyn Bragg, veteran broadcaster and author of many books about English and England, is 'unpretentious', happy to magpie words from anywhere, to fold into a language which is already pretty special because of its diverse roots, found in Romantic, Germanic and Scandinavian languages. He compares English to French, for example, which he says is a totally different kettle of fish. Unlike English, French seems to 'keep the barriers high between print and the spoken word': additions like 'le weekend' are few and far between. Lord Bragg points out that Shakespeare alone used words from over fifty countries and introduced two thousand new words to the English language (such as *alligator*, *elbow room* and *zany*). It was the Bard, for example, who first used the verb 'sistering' in his play *Pericles* in 1609.

When speaking to the etymologist Susie Dent about the origins of other sibling-related and familial words, I found out that 'sistren' (like brethren) was a 'thing' for a time, first spotted in the *Anglo-Saxon Chronicle*, while 'brother' and 'sister' come from the original German *bruder* and *schwester*. To be 'sisterly' pops up as an adverb in the 1800s and is defined as 'to treat someone in a sisterly fashion'; for example, 'she could be mothered and sistered as girls ought to be'. It's a definition which I don't think is as straightforward as it may have seemed at first. Finally, the word 'family' originally meant (in Ancient Rome) 'everyone who lived in your house', including servants or perhaps the retinue of a nobleman'. According to Dent, the word 'sibling' itself has a very strange and surprising root. It is, she explains, 'behind a really unexpected word, "gossip", as a "Godsib" was a relative in the eyes of God – like a godparent. The only way that we can make sense of this connection is that a female godparent would accompany a woman at birth and then stay after and they would chat gossip.' The first recorded use of 'sibling' in English was not until 1908.

Anything more than a cursory poke into the way words arrive in our mouths will take you down a very long and completely fascinating rabbit hole. In Dent's mind, being on the trail of a word's original creation provokes an almost 'sinuous feeling in her head' as she navigates the twists and turns of the language. She comments that even to describe words as having 'roots' is noteworthy, as 'the idea of roots and trees wrap themselves around the English language'. 'Tree' itself probably derives, she says, from 'true'. English *is* fabulously complex, so I appreciate Lord Bragg's description of it as a kind of triple track – or braided language – with one strand being the formal Latin, the second being the vernacular, written English which popped up in the 1500s, and the

WHO'S THE FAVOURITE?

third, the spoken, 'which came from the fields and the streets of the day'. English speakers are part of a long tradition which is happy to hop between all three and to weave in words from everywhere.

nickname, n.
1. A familiar or humorous name given to a person as well as the real name.
Squirtface and Stumblebum: Lillie and Johnny Flynn
Poobles and Preebles: Poorna and Priya Bell
Boogalo and Minefrog: Lucy and Emily Mangan
Mounds and Eggy: Tom and Rob Aitkens

When I started interviewing siblings for the podcast, I was keen to find ways to get under the skin of the family that made them, to understand the culture of 'their people'. I asked them things like: did they tease each other or have in-jokes? Did they have holiday traditions or made-up games? Can they still wind each other up by pressing a button which has worked reliably since they were little? I was trying to get a feel for the texture of their shared childhood, using any strategy I could think of. The answers they provided helped prise the lids off their memory jars, letting them compare and contrast, before – hopefully – alighting upon precious, forgotten details. The specificity of these fragments of memory matter so much when bringing back to mind a fully realised picture of *the way things were*.

One of the most reliable ways, it turned out, was to ask about nicknames. So many brothers and sisters had them for each other, often with a ridiculous origin story to boot. Chef Rob Aitkens was christened 'Mounds' as a boy on account of his slight chubbiness and 'man boobs'. The memory of the nickname led to him and his twin brother Tom sharing all kinds of details about their birth, including Tom's fight for survival as a 'little bag of sugar' who weighed half as much as Rob, and who was given a 50/50 chance of life. It also unlocked some nostalgia about TV, cracking up about the character Roland (or Row-land for anyone who can still hear that pronunciation) from the infamous 1980s programme *Grange Hill*. Roland was a schoolboy who also famously carried a little bit of puppy fat. At a stroke, the sharing of a nickname and its meaning can help unlock the dynamic between the siblings; in this case, slightly protective and very intimate, with a good helping of competition and friendly teasing. I also noticed that something about the act of sharing the name – saying it out loud – generally did something to the tone and attitude of siblings towards each other. They became warmer, sweeter with each other, a bit more reflective, as if they were replaying the home movies of their lives in their minds. It is a privilege to be invited to witness the opening up of that space between people who know each other so well. A single, made-up word can do it.

womb-to-tomb, adj.
1. Expression of twinhood.

Nicknames don't tend to be the only linguistic invention within a family. Often, we develop a whole phrase book, stuffed full of unique sayings, incomprehensible to the outside world. The entries – and the exclusivity they demonstrate – can last a lifetime. These belong to that third strand of the English language – the 'fields and the streets' – although the category needs expanding to include 'the sofa' or 'kitchen table' (more on that later). And, while families are not strictly defined as tribes, which always use language as a signifier of belonging, there is something defining about the way that language created in the domestic setting helps to create 'tribal feelings' in families.

Susie Dent is the daydreamer of her family, with a reputation for clumsiness. She has an older full sister, 'very kind, and more demonstrative than me', a half-sister and a stepsister. They are dotted all over the place, allowing her to feel like she 'has footprints all over the world'. She also had a stepbrother who died some years ago. Her book *Dent's Modern Tribes: The Secret Languages of Britain* is about how language binds groups together. In it she delves into the distinct 'slanguages' of 'tribes', from refuse collectors, who might discover *disco rice* (maggots) on their rounds, to paramedics who might say they are *blueing in* an emergency to hospital. And whether it is birdwatchers or people in the boardroom, she says, all these languages function like codes to make you feel like you belong and, crucially, to keep other people out.

Unlike jargon, which defines particular groups such as athletes or lawyers, 'family slang' is usually more playful, creating both a sense of belonging and 'somewhere to let your hair down'. 'We tend to shuffle on these shared sayings,' Dent explains, 'like a comfy jumper when we go home, the linguistic equivalent of "huffle buffs" – old Scots for the clothes we would traditionally step into on a Friday night and not take off until Monday morning.' Every time you ask someone to pass the *chisog* (cheese) or take something back to *Marks Expensive* (Marks & Spencer) you are flashing the scuffed and much-loved membership card at one another and reaffirming your place in the pack. Every time you ask for the *twidger* to change the TV channel or explain that you need to *bumphle* the sofa cushions to make them plump, it is an affectionate nod to the place and the people that made you.

'To the Doormobile!', idiom.
1. Everyone out of the house.

The kind of language we invent at home with our brothers and sisters (and the rest of the family) is known as 'familyect/ familect', a term coined in 1991 by the Danish linguist Bent Søndergaard in the *Journal of Multilingual and Multicultural Development*. The family Søndergaard studied for his research spoke seven languages and dialects between them, so he was curious to see how they would code-switch in conversations and use wordplay, bearing in mind how many vocabularies they had to choose from. It was reportedly the first time that anyone had really looked at studying these things in the intimate context of a family group. Søndergaard found that while the adults in the home often put in place the invisible 'rules' about how each language was to be used, it was usually the children who were pushing the boundaries, coming up with original wordplay.

Familects – being a relatively young concept – haven't been studied as thoroughly as languages used by other tight-knit groups, which include dialects (languages tethered to geography) or sociolects (languages known among members of the same social group). But Cynthia Gordon, a professor of linguistics at Georgetown University, is one academic who has done extensive research in this field. She is the author of *Making Meanings, Creating Family*, in which she gathered evidence about words used at home, by observing four families in Washington, DC over several days and then by listening to weeks of conversations recorded by the families themselves. She found that repeating words and phrases in a family – which are unique to them – doesn't just result in a bunch of funny, silly or sentimental expressions; it actually has an instrumental role in creating the feeling of family. It is vitally important, she says, for 'binding members of a family together into a distinctive social group'. It is not something to be shared by any Johnny Come Lately. Its very use preserves the intimacy of the only group allowed to use it.

collopsicated, adj.
1. Exhausted or flaked out.

If official words have established routes to creation (compounding and abbreviation, etc.) then how are familects made? The answer, as Søndergaard found in his original study, is often via the children. They are prolific coiners of new words, says Dent, who adds that 'a friend's family still use "foo foos" (her brother's word for shoes) and everyone in my family understands "bontoo" (my brother's word for broken)'. A side note that as children (up until the age of seven or so) are famously obsessed with scatological humour, there will – almost inevitably – be a healthy section of bathroom-related words in any family dictionary. When I asked on the podcast for contributions to our own collection of family slang, we were gifted *bits* (poo) and *bum noise* (farts), to which Susie Dent could add *bubs* (always plural, to clearly distinguish from the term of affection 'bub') and *a packet* (both for 'number 2s').

It's no accident, I think, that one of Roald Dahl's most beloved creations, the BFG, subverts this game and has the adult (the giant) introducing the (more than) slightly prim orphan Sophie to the wonders of 'whizzpopping' after glugging down a lovely glass of 'frobscottle'. 'Us giants is making whizzpoppers all the time!' says the BFG. 'Whizzpopping is a sign of happiness. It is music in our ears!' Dahl had an obvious gift for understanding the way that children's minds work, and that included grasping the sheer delight that they take in a silly-sounding word – or one with an onomatopoeic punch. Children love the feel of those kinds of words in their mouths. In that way, familects are a lot like regional dialects, says Dent, which revel in earthiness, collecting numerous words for the things which make up the very fabric of life, including gas. 'There is so much windy stuff in English,' she continues, 'from "fizzle" which used to mean to break wind quietly, or the fact that a partridge was named after the French word "peter", which means to break wind – because when it took flight apparently it sounded like it was farting.' In familects, as in dialects, there are therefore multiple words for the things we encounter regularly. Dent counted fifty-seven words for the TV remote alone, including *hoofa doofa*, *doojie* or *pogger*.

> Mimsy in the borogoves, idiom.
> *1.* Upset.

Importing words directly from their own dialects (or that of their parents or even grandparents) is one significant way that parents get in on the act of contributing to the family lexicon, according to Christine Mallinson, a professor of linguistics at the University of Maryland. 'They'll introduce words based on where they grew up, bringing their own background to it as well.' In that way, regional words for bread rolls (*bap*, *cob*, *barm cake*, *stotty cake*), alleyways (*ginnel*, *snicket*, *twitten*) or stores (*marts*, *bodegas* and *spas* in the US) can become stirred into the mix of the new family's slang and found popping up in completely different geographical locations. And, says Dent, adopting these words into our family slang is one way to keep some of English's glorious linguistic variation alive. 'It is so important we do pick them up and relish them because like a piece of music they are so much more than the sum of their parts,' she stresses.

It also works similarly for multilingual families – as Søndergaard discovered in his very first study on familects – the members flitting between languages and borrowing words from all their various vocabularies to best express themselves (or have fun). As writer Julie Martinez told *National Geographic*, her husband, whose family emigrated from Mexico, 'delights in mispronouncing Spanish words like *huango* (correctly pronounced WAHN-goh), meaning loose or floppy (and mispronounced WANG-goh), then sticking them into casual conversation: "That chair is wango," or wobbly.' Just like that, a brilliant new word is created for the Martinez family dictionary. (In fact, I might steal it.) And there is an added benefit to this kind of wordplay for families of mixed provenance, says Mallinson. The familect can help maintain a little bit of linguistic heritage. Martinez's kids may not speak Spanish fluently, for example, but they still have access to some of their father's culture and language through their family dialect.

> tanatanatats, n.
> *1.* A checkout till.

In 2008, the Winchester-based charity The English Project (of which Professor David Crystal is a patron) launched something called Kitchen Table Lingo, extending an open invitation to families and individuals to share words from their own familects – words from that third track of English which they use at home, around the kitchen table. The charity was absolutely inundated with contributions, enough to compile into a whole book – which is a delight. And, thumbing through, it is very revealing about how else, aside from dialect cherry-picking and scatological inventions, new family slang words are created.

Because it is a project conceived in England and because words collect around familiar events and things in familects (just as they do in dialects), there are countless words for tea. *Cup of splosh* and a *chupley* (cup of tea… chup of chee… chupley) to name but two. There are also many expressions created simply because they sound just like the thing that they represent – as understood by children who are beginning to talk. In that way ambulances become *nee-naws*, dogs can become *ruff ruffs*, unchewable bits of meat are *giggly bits* and checkout tills (in the 1970s) became *tanatanatats* in Laura Barber's family, because of the sound that the old-fashioned clacky keys and the till roll being printed made to three-year-old ears. (Try it.) These words often remain in use, long after their creators are old enough to know better. 'Kids are naturally delighted by language and all the weird things you can do with it,' says Mallinson, and so playing around with made-up words for things that they recognise and like the sounds of is a perfect introduction to the fun that can be had.

Words which children simply mispronounce often end up being the family slang with the greatest staying power. Susie Dent – who has been obsessed with words ever since she was small, spending long car journeys with her nose stuck in French and German dictionaries – always kept little notebooks to hand ready for her thoughts about language. In them are a few of the things she misheard and/or mispronounced as a child. One entry reads: 'Why is it not pedestranian? [pedestrian] That is so much better.' Likewise for a long time, she thought concrete was called *croncrete*. In our own house, we rarely refer to blueberries as *blueberries*. They are the much more appropriate, berry-shaped-sounding *beebles*, thanks to the fact they were a first favourite of my eldest son, who used to ask for more and more of them, small starfish hands reaching from the highchair and repeatedly chirping *beebles* until I gave in. My best friend's younger twin siblings, meanwhile, christened scaffolding as *scaffbuilding*, which I think is just perfect.

> bouncealine, n.
> *1.* Trampoline.

In a similar, but more collaborative way, there are also words that families conjure up together when the word they need is somehow lacking. Like *bingle* invented by Al Firell and his clan. It describes the alternative event, according to Kitchen Table Lingo, that you plan when rain scuppers your original idea. For example, 'we were going to have a BBQ but it rained, so we had a *bingle* instead.' Or perhaps the *tinkle tonkles*, which Susan Hornby and family hang on their Christmas tree each year. In our own family, we describe a bad hair day as having *ha-ha hair*. It came about – very sweetly – when my little sister CJ came toddling into our bedroom after an afternoon nap. Her downy baby hair, which was chick-blonde and very fine, had been matted by sweaty sleep into a tufty patch on the back of her head. We cracked up, which caused her to stamp crossly away to tell Mum that 'the girls said I have *ha-ha hair*'. In a similar way, her blankie, which deteriorated to the point of being a seven-inch knotted (filthy) rag, became *Deretis* on account of the number of times we would lose it, the panic which would ensue (*Deretis* was essential for sleep) and the sing-song cry of relief when it was found: 'There it is!' When I think of these, I remember the sunny family room we used to play in together, and about how cute my sister's chubby little legs were at that age. It reminds me of what it was like for Bex and me to be the bigger sisters of a baby: how she ate dry brown toast in her pushchair on the school run each morning and how she called to the neighbourhood cats, sitting on the garden bench. About how we cared for her and sometimes left her out. It conjures up a whole dynamic which is sweet, but also a little bit painful given our finite time together in childhood.

schnürf, n. / schnürfy, adj.
1. Cuddly, cosy, loving – you can feel schnürfy or need a schnürf.

That ability to recreate a feeling of family is something that familect can do almost instantly, by transporting you back to the place and time that the word was born. And often, says Cynthia Gordon, that isn't actually one specific moment, but a number of similar repeated moments. That's because families use rituals to create a consistent environment, and a feeling of security and comfort for each other. Sometimes they're daily – especially when children are small, and keeping everyone on an even keel relies on regular food and regular sleep. In her research on the families in Washington, Gordon came across a sweet bedtime routine one family called *rock and rubs*, in which a parent rocked the child before putting her in bed and rubbing her back.

'These smaller rituals are important,' Gordon explains. 'They have symbolic significance for the families in their everyday lives.' Because they are repeated so many times, they (and the words used to name and describe them) work to reinforce memories – in this instance a recollection of comfort and being safe with a parent. Plus, simply because it is repeated so many times, even if it falls out of someone's memory, it would not take much to remind them of it and everything that it meant.

'To the manor born!', idiom.
1. Let's play a game!

But perhaps the loveliest example of familect is in building bridges, helping us to reconcile after a row, offering an easy kind of shortcut to intimacy, reminding each other of the bigger picture and what is at stake. 'Language is a resource that human beings use to tie themselves to other people – and in familect's case, to bind themselves into a family,' says Gordon. It is a way of reaching out to a member of your 'family tribe' and reminding them that you belong to each other. 'For adult siblings who haven't seen each other for a while,' explains Deborah Tannen, another linguistics professor at Georgetown University, 'using familect expressions together can instantly transport them back to their childhood memories.' How often have you tried to make amends with a brother or sister, or to ask a favour, by wheedling their nickname, to appeal to your special claim on their time and energy? Or attempted to comfort them by using a family term of endearment or nickname to try to make them feel as safe and as loved as they did when it was first used? I know I have often done it.

Writing about the resulting *Kitchen Table Lingo* book in the *Guardian*, Harriet Powney pointed out that these words, funny as they often are, are also 'shorthand for moments from a shared past and as such carry an emotional resonance'. She explains that in one friend's house, '"Geoffrey's" means it's time to get ready for dinner... it helps keep alive the memory of an uncle who's no longer with them'. Familects can be playful and inventive, silly and nonsensical (to anyone else) but within the context of the relationship in which they were conceived, they are laden with significance and tenderness. And, in just the same way that the breakdown of a relationship can erase the carefully constructed shared story of your past, the end of a family relationship – by estrangement or death – can completely empty out the words that you used to express things about your shared life, rendering them senseless or impossible to use.

Symonds Yat, n.
1. The little 'lid' you cut off the top of a boiled egg.

When I spoke to Susie Dent, I was able to ask her about our family word *ponky* which was used by all my sisters and was a word (I now know) invented by my mum. It perfectly describes the way a pair of (usually cheap) tight jeans will bag at the knee or how your hair will not be smoothed into a ponytail, but instead is bumpy and... well... ponks horribly on top of your head. I love that I used that word for thirty years without realising it is not to be found in any official record of the English language. I love it even more now that I realise only about five living people know what it means – and I am related to all of them.

7

A Note on Only Children

With much relevance to siblings everywhere

'My parents elected me president of the family when I was four. We actually had an election every year and I always won. I'm an only child, and I could count on my mother's vote.'

CONDOLEEZZA RICE

Toni Falbo, professor of educational psychology at the University of Texas, first had the idea to study only children while attending a psychology class about social stereotypes. The precise catalyst was a piece of research from the 1950s focusing on American couples deciding whether to have a second child. The most common reasoning was that 'they wanted to have another child so the first one would not become an "only"', she remembers. In the eyes of many of these parents, only children spelled trouble; they were lonely, spoiled, inflexible, anxious, precocious, emotionally fragile, pampered – take your pick. 'And that's when I realised,' Falbo tells me, 'I could see a real-world effect of a *stereotype*: another human would *or would not* be born because of it.' That 1950s research had been published when Dr Falbo was a contented little (only) child herself. A self-confessed 'nerd who liked to read', she rarely felt lonely and led a happy childhood not so different to her friends with siblings. 'My mom was very keen for me to get out and do stuff. She would say: "I don't want you to read about life, I want you to live it."'

Falbo's mother was no doubt aware of the cultural attitude towards only children in the 1960s. It was the peak of the baby boom, when the average number of children per US family was 3.62. The recent memory of war and all its losses had sharpened the moral imperative to have a big family, as had the greater influence of the Church. Plus, the birth control pill would not be readily available until 1965. All this contributed to an idea that only children were a bit 'other'. It was a similar story in the UK, where writer Adrian Mourby grew up: 'It was rather like belonging to a racial minority or religious sect… Big families were considered so good that the government gave no child support if you had only one child but did provide it for the second, third and fourth. Just about everyone in my class at school had brothers and sisters – apart from me and Teddy Mercer and we were both regarded as a bit odd.'

I have talked a bit about the 1950s notion of the 'nuclear family' in the chapter on step and half siblings and, suffice to say, it has contributed to a lingering (and overtly misogynistic) judgement on women who only want one baby. In her book *One and Only*, Lauren Sandler points out that men are seldom subjected to the same scrutiny for being fathers of one child. They are rarely labelled 'selfish' or 'unnatural' for pursuing a career first, or for considering the family's finances.

A NOTE ON ONLY CHILDREN

Or simply for wanting to limit how much parenting they have to do (while deeply loving the child they *have* chosen to parent, of course). Only child Sandler replicated her own childhood by having 'just' one child. She writes, 'As only children, we have to get used to lacking something that the majority of people have for better or for worse. As parents who stop at one, we have to get used to the nagging feeling that we are choosing for our own children something they can never undo.'

Dr Falbo gave very little thought to her 'only' status until a memorable visit to see her cousins who lived in a small town in Minnesota. 'They all had large families,' she reminisces, 'and I had so much fun. We had the run of the whole town, to play hide and seek… then I remember them saying, "You don't seem like an only child." And I thought, "Why would you say that? I just like running around, I think, like everybody else?" Then I realised: "Oh, they thought I might be different, and then I disappointed them by being like everybody else."'

Why they thought she would be different was the precise starting point for Falbo's work. She was determined to find out where these negative ideas about only children originated, before starting to test whether there was any actual truth to them. At the time she embarked on the project, the American public's attitude towards only children was overwhelmingly negative. 'The presence of siblings was popularly assumed to have both negative and positive effects,' she explains, 'but the lack of siblings was believed to have only negative consequences.' In the intervening decades, popular culture suggests that not much has changed, from the demon children in horror films (*The Omen*, *The Bad Seed*) to the oddball sidekicks in 1980s sitcoms (*Growing Pains*, *Family Ties*). In *Modern Family*, the tween singleton Manny is a cringingly precocious boy with an overbearing mother. 'In the United States,' says Falbo wearily, 'the only child stereotype in a nutshell is still selfish, lonely, and maladjusted.'

As late as 2023, only three per cent of people believed having one child is 'ideal' – according to a Gallup poll. In fact, on average, Americans' 'ideal' number of children is now 2.7, the highest reported number since 1971. (When you look closely at the data, the story gets a little clearer: more Republicans (fifty per cent of them) want three or more children, compared to forty per cent of Democrats.) There may have been fluctuations in attitudes about what constitutes the ideal family over time, but our general suspicion of one child families has remained steadfast.

Before we go on a spin through history to see where some of the enduring prejudices about only children may have come from, let's consider one of the premises of this book: that a sibling relationship is something that eighty per cent of people experience, and it is likely one of the longest relationships of our lives. For better or worse, our siblings will be there – influencing and protecting us, as well as maybe irritating or upsetting us. They will also hopefully love us, even if our bond is less robust than we might have hoped. So the idea of *not* having a sibling is quite hard to imagine (even if we might sometimes sincerely wish it were the case). Our inability to see beyond the edges of our own experience makes us less dubious than we perhaps should be about only child stereotypes.

It is not a perfect analogy, but I remember as a teen, travelling on a coach to a school sports fixture. Stuck for conversation, I poked the boy sitting on the seat in front of me and lamely asked him, 'What's it like to be a twin?' Maybe I liked this boy, or maybe I just thought I was being cute by showing an interest. I can't remember. What I *do* remember is the retort. 'I don't know,' he shrugged, without bothering to make eye contact. 'I have never *not* been one.' Similarly we might ogle at only children, looking for signs of oddness while they merrily get on with their very normal-to-them lives.

> "'People never like me and I never like people,' she thought. "And I never can talk as the Crawford children could. They were always talking and laughing and making noises.'"
> FRANCES HODGSON BURNETT, *THE SECRET GARDEN*

In August 1911, Frances Hodgson Burnett published *The Secret Garden*. It remains one of the most evocative stories from my childhood: the shadowy house, full of strange nighttime cries, and the overgrown garden, behind a locked gate. The book also featured an only child protagonist. But unlike the saintliness of Hodgson Burnett's other (materially spoiled) singleton heroine – Sara Crewe in *A Little Princess* – Mary Lennox represented almost every single negative stereotype about onlies. Pampered beyond belief, she is also a selfish, 'disagreeable', 'spoiled and pettish' child, whose lonely state is described as 'desolate'.

Despite the acres of difference between Sara and Mary's personalities, both are presented as oddities, to be 'redeemed' and rescued from their isolated states by the friendships they forge: Mary falls in with hardy local lad (and tween heart-throb) Dickon Sowerby, the resident sickly child Colin Craven and a robin. Sara finds connection with Ermengarde, the school 'dunce'; Lottie, a tantrummy four-year-old; and Becky, the scullery maid. In both these stories, there is an almost horror of the unnatural state of the solitary child, which is eased by the author finding them a set of people with whom they can experience 'a proper childhood'.

It's not just Hodgson Burnett. Children's literature is stuffed with solo children. See: Harry Potter, Lyra Belacqua from *His Dark Materials*, Charlie Bucket and Matilda (and so many more Dahl creations), Harriet the Spy, Alex Rider, and the eponymous Margaret, reaching out to God, in Judy Blume's brilliant book about puberty. Having a child on their own is handy for an author as it means fewer complicating relationships to sketch in – including pesky sibling fractiousness. They are also (if they are orphans) freed from the shackles of traditional parental constraints. But more than that, as with Hodgson Burnett's protagonists, there is a concerted attempt to pull at the reader's heartstrings – to make them care. The 'unusualness' of their family set-up is central to their quests; and often we are asked and expected to feel pity for them because of it.

A NOTE ON ONLY CHILDREN

It's probably too much of a stretch to draw any direct link between a gaggle of fictional Victorian-era onlies and orphans (see also Oliver Twist) and the surprisingly influential work carried out by Granville Stanley Hall towards the end of the nineteenth century, which contributed enormously towards the enduring negative reputation of only children. But they do both feel like true products of their time, an era which incubated all kinds of odd ideas, many of which have since been rightly abandoned. No one today uses phrenology (studying the bumps on a person's head) to seriously determine a person's character, but the wrong-headed notions about only children from this period have somehow stubbornly persisted. It is, sighs Falbo, 'a good example of where facts really don't matter'.

But first to the fiction.

Education reformer Hall was a contemporary of Freud's (who first came to America at his invitation). He grew up in rural Massachusetts, free to roam with his siblings and a group of local boys. He somehow concluded that the abundant company of peers along with the chance to amass country craft skills (fishing and hunting for turtle eggs) ranked his childhood as superior to any other kind, and he went on to make silly pronouncements as a result. 'All creatures which have large families, whether beasts or birds, have less trouble in rearing them than those which have only one or two young,' he wrote.

But it was a piece of work published in 1895, *A Study of Peculiar and Exceptional Children*, and written by E. W. Bohannon – one of Hall's protégés – which arguably had the most impact. 'It began innocently enough,' writes environmentalist and author Bill McKibben in the *New York Times*.

'Hall mailed a questionnaire to college instructors in several states, asking them to submit reports on unusual children.' He and Bohannon wanted to find out why some 'kinds of children' might turn out to have certain physical or psychical traits, including being *deft, dainty, nervous, heavy, deformed, strong, loquacious* or *timid*. They studied 1,045 'cases' who each displayed one or more of these 'traits' and found that forty-six were only children – around 4.4 per cent, in his view 'a number entirely out of proportion to that found among children generally'. This prompted a terrific cognitive leap, as he confidently asserted that 'the only child in a family is therefore very likely to be peculiar and exceptional'. It was, says McKibben, whose book *Maybe One* is about the merits of raising one child, an 'ANECDOTAL, LAME-BRAINED, and MEANINGLESS' piece of work. Nevertheless, these conclusions would prove extremely sticky.

It was not until 1920, says McKibben, and the advent of proper scientific methods, that this 'research' began (rightly) to be seriously questioned. But, despite being comprehensively disproved in subsequent decades, the idea that only children were somehow 'peculiar' was ingrained as an 'unchallengeable given', to quote Judith Blake in her paper 'The Only Child in America: Prejudice versus Performance'. It didn't help matters that only a few decades after this work was made public, the Great Depression prompted a spike in only children. Onlies became a sign that a family couldn't afford to have any more, adding to the stigma. Almost a century after Hall's study was published, when asked to identity the specific 'handicap' of being an only child, Blake reported that sixty per cent of people 'cited a personality or character defect – self-centred, domineering, anxious, quarrelsome, spoiled, or overprotected'.

'Being an only child is a disease in itself.'
GRANVILLE STANLEY HALL

Being 'spoiled' along with being narcissistic, selfish and lonely are all 'only' stereotypes which have been proven to be false. And yet, the cultural beliefs are so strong, that in his 2019 paper for the *Social Psychological and Personality Science* journal, Michael Dufner noted that even the only children themselves thought the study would show them to be more narcissistic than children with siblings.

In fact, work done by Dr Falbo in 2015 showed onlies to be more collaborative than their peers with brothers and sisters, who were more used to the sharp elbowing required to gain valuable attention. This contradicts any assumption that singletons somehow fail to learn how to cooperate. In fact, while often content to be alone, they are not only as adept at forming friendships, says Dr Falbo, they are also less selfish within those relationships, perhaps because they value them so highly. Louise Halling, a psychotherapist who has 'just' one child of her own, can see her experience reflected in these findings. 'I've always been good at friendships, they are very important to me: my friends become my family. It is the same with my son, and we have intentionally helped him with that.'

Only children might be as proficient as children with siblings at making friends but it can take them a little longer to get there, because they've calibrated themselves against a different – adult – audience. And that training ground can leave you 'soft', writes novelist Abigail Dean, who cringes at the memory of how off the mark her singleton social skills were as a small child, used to living in a grown-up world, chock-full of attentive people. At school she cut a 'strange and gullible figure in the playground', surprised at being unable to find many (any) fellow five-year-olds willing to 'indulge my eccentricities, my animal facts and stories'. But such harsh awakenings are short-lived, and the long-term scorecard for only children is clear: whatever social deficit they have, says Falbo, is pretty much gone by the age of about twelve. By then, they have 'done what needs to be done to have a relatively successful social life'.

Speaking on American public radio, Lauren Sandler explained her main issue with the lazy labelling of only children as always either lazy or spoiled – or whatever other stereotypes people reach for when describing singletons – is that 'it's a bit of a totalising narrative and tends to be the story that either other people use, or you use yourself to explain various things about yourself. For example, if you feel lonely, it's because you're an only child, even though everyone is lonely in the world.' I think the same kind of 'totalising narrative' can (and is) applied to the sibling experience. So many assumptions are made about the automatic happiness found

A NOTE ON ONLY CHILDREN

in their company, we forget to think critically about all the ways that our humanness can make being a sibling miserable; in just the same way that it could ensure that the experience of being a singleton is wonderful. Sandler understands that we can have a 'very visceral response to seeing a child alone in a sandbox' but encourages us to go beyond that, to be more thoughtful and informed before making false emotional judgements.

'If you have siblings,' says only child Josh, a fourteen-year-old from Dorset, 'you do have a robustness which we may lack. Like, I cannot get shouted at because I will just cry... I can't handle it. I think siblings are less likely to have that, probably because they have been shouted at by their brothers or sisters.' It is a temperament that psychologist Carl Pickhardt sees quite often in his clinical work with onlies, who often struggle to manage conflict, possibly due to that lack of exposure to sibling competitiveness and boisterous play. He has also seen singletons come unstuck with joint decision-making – both issues which are highlighted when they start dating. It's a scenario familiar to Abigail Dean. 'I am not particularly easy to love,' she wrote in the *Guardian*. '"Your definition of compromise," my husband said, "is talking about something – and doing what you intended to do in the first place." It surprised me that anybody would do things differently.'

Conversely, there is a degree of useful sensitivity that Josh believes he's acquired, which siblings can lack, because of that conditioning: 'I am quite tough, but if someone gets hurt I am like, "Oh no!" But with siblings, if their brother or sister is hurt they're like, "They can take it." I talk much more about how fighting can be normalised as part of sibling relationships in Chapter 9, but I wanted to take a moment here to consider whether only children should be thought of (or think of themselves) not as 'too sensitive', but instead as beneficiaries of an altogether kinder emotional education. And perhaps whether we might recognise that our sibling relationships are sometimes too rough and often emotionally careless.

> 'I'm an only child, which means when my parents got divorced, I was the entire drop cloth they threw over the marriage to protect it from shattering.'
> MARIA SEMPLE, *WHERE D'YOU GO, BERNADETTE?*

When thinking about the shape of a single child family, I did wonder about the possibility of the only child trespassing too far into the parents' world. After all, if the family is a system made up of smaller sub-systems (the adults and the kids), what happens when there *isn't* another child? Dr Adrian Mancillas, who has extensively studied only children, says it usually means onlies will have closer bonds with their parent/caregiver, but also acknowledges the potential for them to be 'unduly exposed to parental stress or to endure a more intense relationship that could be mitigated with a sibling'. Family therapist Sarah Epstein also cautions against folding children too much into the adult world, specifically by drawing onlies into parental disputes to 'play referee, to calm each parent down, act out to break the ice, or pass messages between them. It can trap a child in an "unwinnable" situation,' she says, 'between the two most important people in their life'.

The risk is that only children become hypervigilant about their parents' moods and needs, because they are so intertwined. Author and only child Sabine Durrant described it like this: 'the beam of attention worked both ways'. 'I was obsessed with the shift of my mother's moods,' she recalls, 'her irritations, the balance of her opinion. In many photographs from my childhood, I am noticeably leaning into her.' Dr Falbo agrees that the blurring of family systems in the tripod shape of single child families is an interesting issue, because only children obviously spend more time in the company of their parents, so they can become somewhat 'adultised' as a result. 'That one child,' she observes, 'is accustomed to being the "buddy" to their parents, they become kind of the decision maker, and almost an equal.'

The idea of being drawn too far into the parents' 'orbit' is explored more in the chapter on siblings with additional needs, with a focus on children assuming caring duties. That process feels different from this one, which is more about naturally tending to include an only child in the majority of the family's activities, because there isn't another option. 'One of the obvious characteristics of having two or more children,' says Falbo, 'is that the children are expected to spend time alone together. They're told to "go outside and play", just kind of "leave us alone". Parents of siblings end up spending more time privately talking to each other, compared to parents of an only child – who is probably wanting to interact with the parents, and does so much more frequently.' It would be interesting to know what the net result of that dynamic is, whether it creates more mature children, or whether in the absence of a birth order hierarchy, which allows you to be 'more grown up than the next kid', you end up with only children who are more cottoned on to adult conversation, but simultaneously somewhat stuck in a position of 'the family's baby' forever.

ONLY LONELY?

As for any claim that only children are lonely, that is an altogether more nuanced picture, despite the assertion made by influential (conservative) US demographer Judith Blake, in her 1989 book *Family Size and Achievement*, that 'if anything, children from small families are more popular than those from large ones'. I spoke to Patrick, an only child in his fifties, who grew up on a farm outside Cincinnati, with acres of land, a creek and fourteen horses to entertain him – but no siblings. He was lonely then and he can be lonely now – but he doesn't think that's necessarily a bad thing. 'Alone sounds worse,' he says from his New York apartment. 'Alone sounds like you've been abandoned.' Describing visits to his wife's family (she is one of five), he says, 'It's chaos. It's just a house full of people shouting at each other from different rooms.' He enjoys the rough and tumble of those episodes, but is equally content to be by himself, 'making his own fun' as he did during his childhood.

A NOTE ON ONLY CHILDREN

Nevertheless, as an adult he was hugely 'validated' by his wife's reaction to some of his childhood experiences – notably those from during his parents' divorce, which happened when he was eleven. She has been able to reassure him that certain episodes back then were 'not his fault'. And so perhaps, he reflects, having a sibling around during those teenage years might have been something of a comfort. It's hard to say what material difference it might have made – as just like the twin on the bus, it has never been any other way. All he can tell me with certainty is that it was precious that he now had someone able (and willing) to reach back into the past and 'see' him as a child.

There is a danger, when thinking about this issue of loneliness in particular, of comparing the worst possible scenarios for an only child with the best possible for siblings: it is not automatically the desolation of a lonely Victorian manor versus Christmas with the March sisters. It is much more likely that each child's experience, in whatever family they are born into, contains a thread of loneliness, which runs through the opportunities for building friendships and joy. I know I felt it as a child and feel it still; I think we all do. The risk is to assume that having a sibling automatically saves you from that state. It simply can't. It would also be foolish to forget how tremendously valuable it is to learn the skill of being content by yourself, something which reaps lifelong rewards. 'The greatest gift of being an only child is that you learn to be content with your own company and spend a lot of time with yourself. And that's huge,' says Carl Pickhardt, author of *The Future of Your Only Child*. 'After all, our primary relationship in life is with ourselves.'

The resources parents have at their disposal are likely to have a greater bearing on a child's life than the mere fact that they are an only child. If you are less well off, spending all your money on a single baby might well be less materially beneficial to that child than if you had four children but were fabulously wealthy. But then again, cash is not the only valuable resource, as illustrated excellently by anthropologist Dr Vanessa Fong (herself an only child from Beijing), who researched the educational outcomes for only children in China, born under the single child policy. She found – counter-intuitively – that children from blue-collar families often did better at school than the children from more middle-class families. The reason was that more affluent children often had the fallback of a family business to join, so did not need the life raft of qualifications. Furthermore, their parents often worked such long days they simply weren't available to help with homework. Meanwhile, the poorer parents, who had more time to devote to their child's schooling, did so with an intensity which befitted the enormous (and desperately needed) prize at stake.

With just two children, born very close together (the story may be very different with a large age gap, which in some ways mimics the resource allocation experience of having 'two onlies'), I can understand this time and money picture very clearly. Just this week, my second-born got the date for an important exam wrong. A flurry of calls granted him a stay of twenty-four hours, which I devoted entirely to helping him cram. I am sure if I only had one kid, he would never have messed up his timetable so horrifyingly, and if I had more than two children, I could not have spared the same time – or emotional energy perhaps – to dig him out of that hole. It's all about resources.

Broadcaster and feminist campaigner Dame Jenni Murray came into the world at one of the first National Health Service hospitals in Barnsley in the North of England, in 1950. And, because her mother 'nearly died' having her, there was never any question of a sibling. Up until the age of three, she lived with both her parents and her grandparents in a little cottage with an open fire, on which her grandfather made her a full English breakfast every single day. As a toddler she enjoyed the devoted attention of four adults, all funnelling their love directly into just her. 'All the things that a child might want,' she said, 'I got, because I was the only one.'

Adler believed that scarcity of resources lay at the root of all sibling rivalry. The most obvious effect of being an only child is that they are the sole beneficiary of everything their parents have to provide: time, money, effort and emotional support. So it may come as little surprise that, as a result of all those 'undiluted resources', Jenni learned to read at the very early age of two. But the effects of so much quality adult input are complex, explains Carl Pickhardt. 'On balance, that level of parental involvement is a good thing… All that attention is the energy for your self-esteem and achievement.' But, he adds, it can be 'double-edged'. Being the sole target of so much concentrated love can be enriching, but its intensity can suffocate. The phrase 'having all your eggs in one basket' crops up often in the literature – referring to the hopes that parents invest in their solitary offspring. But it works the other way round too, especially during the emotionally turbulent adolescent years. There is a lot on the line as a child attempts to individuate themselves from their little flock, explains Pickhardt. 'You don't want to alienate your parents – they're the most important people in your world.'

For Jenni Murray, her status as an 'only' meant she had elocution lessons, 'which I loved', and was encouraged to attend the 'better' high school. But it was also complicated in the ways that Pickhardt acknowledges. Jenni's 'pushy' mother had actually wanted a boy, referring to Jenni (*in utero*) as 'David Robert'. Consequently, Jenni felt she had to be *everything*. 'My mother was determined that I would go to university,' she explains, 'but because I was a girl I also had to learn to cook and bake, which I HATED. That was the story of my life: I had to be the boy and I had to be the girl.'

> 'There is an unfair responsibility that comes with being an only child – you grow up knowing you aren't allowed to disappoint, you're not even allowed to die. There isn't a replacement toddling around; you're it. It makes you desperate to be flawless, and it also makes you drunk with the power. In such ways are despots made.'
>
> GILLIAN FLYNN, *GONE GIRL*

The only child is the first and last child all rolled into one and represents the only chance at parenting that the parents have.

A NOTE ON ONLY CHILDREN

'I am the favourite and the least favourite, all at the same time,' one teenage only child told me. 'That's pretty cool.' It definitely can have upsides: it might mean opportunities to try all kinds of activities and endless help with algebra homework. That might feel luxurious, especially compared to your peers in larger broods. But, at the same time, you are 'it'. There is no one else to win the swimming badges, pass the exams or become a grade eight flautist. The weight of expectation is the flip side of all that undivided attention. 'Parenting an only child can be "high-pressure parenting"', notes Pickhardt. 'They don't want to make mistakes at the child's expense, and usually, the child feels a comparable obligation to do right by the parents. This is not a laid-back family because everyone is trying extremely hard to do their best by each other.'

Maggie is a middle-aged singleton from the US who travelled the world in her twenties and settled far away from home, which left her feeling very guilty. 'My mum would call crying and begging me to come back,' she remembers. 'In her mind I would marry and move next door and have kids. That is definitely not what happened. I felt a lot of pressure, as once I moved away there was nothing else to take up their time.' If you have brothers or sisters, there is a greater chance that, between you all, you might fulfil the expectations (or at least not be a total disappointment). Without siblings, there is simply 'no one else to buffer you and take the pressure off if you're not quite up to scratch', explains Louise Halling, who felt her parents' dissatisfaction keenly when she took a job they didn't approve of. 'If you have siblings, you might have the oldest child who is a lawyer and other successful kids, whatever. I was just an embarrassment – they didn't want to tell their friends.'

ONE CHILD POLICY

While only children have been seen as slightly unusual in the West, in China they were the enforced norm between 1979 and 2015, which made Xiwen Fu's experience of childhood there remarkable. Fu – who is now a PhD student at the University of Cambridge's Centre for Child, Adolescent and Family Research – was the only person at her school with a sibling, and she hated it. 'When I was at pre-school even the cartoons showed that the ideal family is just three people,' she reminisces, 'so we basically had no idea about what is "a sibling". Even my teacher said, "Oh, why do you have a little brother? Your family is breaking the policy." It was really bad. I had a very hard time. I really love my brother now… But I needed some time to get through that.' Now Fu – together with her research partner Yining Shi – is looking at the transition from the one child policy to the current Chinese government's advice that the ideal number of children is *three*.

It is such a dramatic about-turn for a country which for decades had drummed into its population the message 'one is ideal, two is bad, third is worst.' And it's fascinating to consider the collective psychological journey that families in China have been on as a result, learning about the dynamics introduced into the family system by creating brothers and sisters. A brief rummage on Mandarin-language parenting websites

A NOTE ON ONLY CHILDREN

yielded books such as *Mummy, How Will You Still Love Me?*, *Little Big Sister* and the bluntly titled *Share!* In a nation where siblings were rare for so long, people have had to work hard to absorb the ideas about birth order, age gaps, roles and rivalry, now printed in those playfully illustrated picture books.

What struck me most about Fu and Shi's work, though, is how much it illuminates the central issues of resources and parental expectation in deciding to have more than one child. It strikes right to the heart of why the new three-baby guideline has not been as enthusiastically embraced as the Chinese authorities hoped. In interviews with 155 mothers during their second pregnancy and after they'd given birth, Fu and Shi found that it was those who were only children themselves who worried most about the transition. 'They're very guilty about their firstborn,' explains Fu. 'They feel like, "because I was raised as a single child, I enjoyed all of the resources, but now I'm trying to pull resources away from you."' Mothers who had grown up with a sibling, meanwhile, were a little more sanguine. But so deep were the concerns of the only child mothers that, even after their second was born, they still only had eyes for Number One. 'We asked them, "What do you feel about your second?"' says Fu. 'Most of them will just say, "Oh, I have no idea about them. I only care about my first."'

Under the one child policy, only children were dubbed 'Little Suns' or 'Little Emperors', and lavished with the love, attention and resources of six people – the maternal and paternal grandparents, as well as the parents. But they weren't being merely indulged: they were being *invested in*. They worked hard, attending school six days a week and taking an array of extra-curricular activities on top. The one child policy was about 'quality', says Fu, ensuring that that one child they had became the best they could be: like a 'little king of the family'.

Chinese onlies may well have been fashioned into little monarchs, but they bore very heavy crowns. 'Because the social welfare system in China and a lot of Asian countries is not that good compared to Western countries,' Fu explains, 'they need to look after their parents and their grandparents. They need to pay for their medical services, for example, which is a huge cost. There's just one kid to take care of six people.' That massive attention hopper, which flooded the only child with everything they could possibly need to achieve success, has a calculated economic purpose: it is so that the child can then pivot 180 degrees and become someone that the whole family can depend on.

THE BURDEN OF BEING AN ONLY

Here's the rub – as all children become adults, the flow of resources tends to reverse, no matter where they live. There is an expectation all over the world that as we become middle-aged and our parents grow old, we will help. In some cultures that model is baked in from the start, with multi-generational living as the norm. In the West, there is, instead, an understanding that when the time comes for carers to be employed, retirement homes chosen or hospital stays navigated, the children will step up. If you face this alone, it can be an intense experience.

Adult onlies currently helping their parents told me they certainly feel the burden. 'There is no one to help me share the responsibility,' said one, who relocated her mother, who has Alzheimer's, across the country to a care home close by. 'It can be overwhelming and I wish I had siblings to share some of what is going on.' Another, who cares remotely for three elderly relatives, described the 'loneliness and pressure' as a 'massive' solo responsibility. 'There is no one to phone up and say, "You will never guess what Dad's done,"' she says. 'So, I turn to my friends... but yeah, it's been tough, this phase.' She is so adamant not to replicate the experience for her (only) child, she is already planning for old age – in her forties. 'I am totally open with him and have said, "In the future if you think I need help, tell me and I will get it. I will *not* do this to you."'

But much like preconceptions about only children and loneliness, the picture around care is a little fuzzy. It is not simply the case that 'only children do absolutely all of it while siblings cooperate to divide up the responsibilities nice and equally'. Not at all. Even in big families, one child usually finds themselves the primary carer, through dint of circumstance (more time), geography (lives closest), disposition (most unflappable) or, more likely, gender. In fact, the very notion of 'care' is gendered, found Alice Goisis and Jenny Chanfreau whose research at the UCL Centre for Longitudinal Studies clearly showed that daughters end up doing more of it, even if they have a brother on hand. Their research also highlighted that although only children are one and a half times more likely to care for their parents than those with siblings, the average amount of time that only children spend providing that assistance is pretty much the same as for the *one* sibling who ends up shouldering the lion's share of the care burden in a larger family.

In China, because of poor maternity leave policies and a lack of social care for the elderly, on top of a challenging global economic climate, the generation of only children who are now of childbearing age (and who also anticipate the needs of their ageing relatives) are often resisting having very many babies at all, let alone two or three. 'There are no motivations and no incentives from the government at all right now,' says Fu. 'So it's certainly become unrealistic to raise two children in the way that they were raised back then.' That means there are still a lot of only children in China. And China is not alone. The average fertility rate in America is just 1.8 births per woman; in the UK – based on current data – it's estimated that by 2031, half of all families will be raising one child. Elsewhere in the world, the graphs tell similar stories, of an overall downward trend in birth rates (albeit with some spikes and dips along the way, reflecting wars and recessions as well as periods of calm and prosperity). Elsewhere in Asia, for example, Japan has a fertility rate of 1.2, and South Korea just 0.75. With the exception of China, it is a huge demographic shift. Reasons include: social progress for women, overarchingly, as well as a decline in marriage rates and many having children later;

climate anxiety; suboptimal family leave policies; and the cost of living. At the time of writing, Australia was toying with reintroducing the AU$3,000 'Baby Bonus' to encourage women to have more children – but the sums don't add up: in Australia, as in the UK and the US, raising a child can be prohibitively expensive. The organisation Child Poverty Action Group estimates the current cost of raising a child to age eighteen is £260,000 for a couple and £290,000 for a lone parent – and many only children live in single-parent households.

The wellbeing of parents must also not be discounted as a contributing factor in decisions to 'curtail fertility'. A 2005 study in Denmark showed that while the first child increases the happiness meter of a couple, 'Additional children beyond the first child have a negative effect on subjective well-being for females.' A 2014 paper focusing on parents in Germany and the UK put it very bluntly: 'having the first two children increases happiness, having a third child does not'.

Our populations are ageing and only children are hardly the minority any more. What that means in society on a macro level is an urgent question. But this is a book about families and moreover about the experiences of children within them. I'm left wondering two things. Firstly: if onlies are edging towards becoming the 'new normal', it feels timely to press harder for a wholesale rebrand of their reputation. One that is in line with the facts and which reflects the reality of their experiences. With far more of them, we cannot cling to old assumptions that they will automatically suffer or be spoiled by being alone. Happily, clinical psychologist Susan Newman, who heads up the Only Child Resource Center

– and has previously declared herself 'thoroughly, utterly annoyed' with these myths – has reported the beginnings of a more positive cultural shift. 'People are not apologetic any more about having only one child,' she says.

And secondly: I am really curious about the experiences of only children managing their caring responsibilities. I wonder, for example, whether sibling-less adults might lean more on each other – as friends – to share the burden. With big changes in the shape of the population, I don't think it can continue to be as binary as 'lonely onlies' and 'supported siblings' (not that it ever was that simple). But in the future, with so many single children going through these experiences, there will surely be an opportunity to be somehow 'alone but also together'. I am not sure what that might look like, because imagining any social shift like that relies on innovations and technologies or habits and norms which don't exist yet, but I think they will come. After all, as one contributor to a New York newspaper letters page about onlies so succinctly put it: 'We are only children for eighteen years, but we are only-children adults for the next sixty or seventy.'

8

Glass Siblings

Or Super Siblings

'August is the Sun. Me and Mom and Dad are planets orbiting the Sun. The rest of our family and friends are asteroids and comets floating around the planets orbiting the Sun.'
R. J. Palacio, Wonder

Children who have a brother or sister with additional needs, whether through illness, disability or learning difficulties, can be known as 'glass siblings'. Not because they are fragile, explains entrepreneur Alicia Arenas, who grew up with two brothers with different disabilities. Far from it. 'We are very strong and we have to be, to survive the things we have survived.' They are called glass siblings because 'our parents are so consumed with the needs of our brother or sister that when they look at us, they see straight through us'. Arenas delivers this line in a TEDx talk to a packed auditorium in San Antonio, and even watching on YouTube, I felt the punch of it. She goes on explain what her childhood was like, as the middle child, squashed between the needs of two very loved, but very hard to care for siblings – and it is agonising to hear. Then, when she was eleven, her younger sibling died, and things began to really unravel. Arenas hopes that by sharing her story people will start to recognise siblings like her: so used to putting their own needs last.

She argues that children who have a sibling with a disability or illness can find it hard to carve out a role for themselves that isn't simply being compliant or 'good'. Instead, they squeeze into the spaces left for them. 'We are sensitive to the needs of our mums, dads and siblings, and we know what we face is insignificant. We are very quiet, we become caretakers.' Her powerful talk urges communities to open their eyes to additional needs families generally, but also to make giving attention to the glass siblings a priority. 'Every emotion that the parents of a special needs child feel, whether it's pain, anger, frustration, fear or concern… the healthy child feels all of it too… but with the coping skills of a child.'

Clare Kassa is the CEO of the UK charity Sibs, which represents the siblings of disabled people from childhood right up until older age. (In the sector, these brothers and sisters are called 'Siblings' as shorthand for 'sibling of a child with additional needs'.) She's given a lot of thought to the 'complicated, joyful and difficult' nature of the sibling bond, particularly as it affects the sibling without a diagnosis. 'We try to provide a safe space for them,' she says, 'because you can love and adore your brother or sister and also be annoyed with them, frustrated with them and sad about it at the same time. And I think for some "Siblings", they feel all of those in about five minutes.' Kassa has spent some time thinking about Arenas's talk because the charity has recently been contacted by families needing support for children as young as three. These are very small people with 'very big feelings', she explains, 'of anger, guilt and... guilt at being OK.' The charity is carefully considering how to help them, mindful that a combination of factors – austerity measures, the cost of living and a downturn in volunteering since Covid – has seen the closure of many support groups. 'There are swathes of the country,' Kassa bemoans, 'without any help at all.'

In the UK, at least 1.7 million adults grew up with a disabled sibling. In the US, the charity Sibling and Leadership Network estimates that 'many' of the 6.5 million individuals with developmental disabilities have a brother or sister. What that looks like for each child or adult will vary tremendously, depending on circumstances, the number of siblings and the specific diagnosis. Living with an unpredictable or violent sibling, as Alicia did – she was regularly punched and bitten – is obviously very different to living with a gentler brother or sister. But Sibs recognises the value in connecting all the different islands that 'Siblings live on', as there is always a shared sense of solidarity and empathy between them. 'We run a conference,' explains Kassa, 'and *immediately* friendships are formed. Other people just "get it". Having a place where your shoulders can drop and you can ask the questions that you can't ask anywhere else. It's very powerful.'

At the time of writing this book, my absolute favourite TV show is *Love on The Spectrum*, a reality dating programme which finds matches for adults with autism. There are endless positive things I could say about the programme, which is deft, funny, kind and incredibly moving. But if I had to pick two, I'd say firstly that all the participants clearly belong to the most wonderful families, who must have provided extraordinary support and love to their child. The second is how happy it makes me that the show exists at all. That it was commissioned and has been so successful must say something positive about society's changing attitudes towards neurological difference. I know there are caveats to that, but it is still hard to imagine a programme like this being made when I was small: it was only during the 1980s that children with Down's syndrome were allowed to attend mainstream school in England. When Arenas's older brother Mario, who has severe autism, was born in the 1970s, her parents were accused (by medical staff) of abusing him and the support for her struggling family was virtually nil.

My own cousin David was born in the summer of 1968. We didn't see a lot of him and his sister Hazel as our family moved around, spending a few years in Portugal before we moved to Holland in 1984. But I have always known that, as a tiny boy, David was treated in hospital after pulling the flex on a boiling kettle and burning himself badly. Once admitted, some of his developmental issues were registered for the first time, and doctors were keen to investigate. Hazel said it was all these tests that gave David a pathological fear of people in white coats. Despite being only fifteen months older, she vividly remembers being upset watching through glass as a doctor checked 'Davey's' reflexes by striking his knee with a hammer. 'He screamed,' she said. 'And I just thought that the doctor was battering him.' In the end, explains Hazel, 'Our

GP said, "Do yourselves a favour. Get him away from anybody medical. Go and chill out."' They took him home without a diagnosis, and within weeks David started to talk, smile, walk and laugh. It was only later that a chance sighting of a newspaper article about 'Pixie Children' finally provided the answer. David had a rare genetic disorder called Williams syndrome.

Regardless of the label, he needed a lot more attention when he was small. And thinking back, Hazel remembers how independent that made her at a very young age. 'I was quite capable,' she says, 'and obviously David wasn't as capable. So I was sort of forced into a position of having to get on with it, to stand on my own two feet.' She also grew increasingly protective towards David, finding any unkindness unbearable. When kids used to follow him around the amusement arcade, mocking him and trying to steal his money, she didn't hesitate. 'I'm sure it's a bit of dramatic licence,' she says, 'but Mum reckons I could take on about three of them. I knew I had to look out for him.' In a family system, where resources are finite, it is easy to see how having a disabled child can lead to the picture that Alicia and Hazel paint, of capable and supportive siblings, valued for requiring *less* than their sibling, at the same time as being asked for more.

SIBLING CARE

Clare Kassa says that although not all 'Siblings' they support are carers, many fall in and out of that definition over the course of their relationship. (And the lockdown pushed more young people into that role than ever before.) But talking to her, and to 'Siblings' themselves, it's clear how many hesitate or struggle to identify as carers, saying 'he's just my brother' and that's that. As with all families, the river we swim in is all we have ever known. Many bizarre, difficult, entitled or ridiculous things in a family are accepted at face value, barely examined or understood until much later (and only then if you gain enough distance to have perspective). Loving your sibling as children – even if it is challenging – can easily bleed into acts of support and care which you may struggle to label that way. Clare Kassa herself has a brother with a learning disability. 'I didn't meet another Sibling [of a disabled person] until I was in my twenties. Quite often, we meet adult Siblings who have no idea that it's even a *thing*,' she says. 'I went to a presentation at a conference where there was an Australian academic talking about research into Siblings like *me*, and I just suddenly saw, well, my life on a PowerPoint. And it was... shocking.'

This sense of isolation is why she is so keen to encourage schools to look into whether a student has a sibling with additional needs. Surprisingly, this is not done automatically. In 2024, Sibs published a report called 'If Only You Knew', which showed forty-three per cent of the two hundred children they asked said the hardest thing about school was 'School not understanding what it is like for me.' Children who took part reported being told off for being late, being bullied, or punished for failing to complete homework, and finding it hard to manage emotionally. One child said they would just like some 'compassion'. 'It's just not easy to plan when he has so many seizures every day. Sometimes I am about to leave for school and he has one, so I help my mum. Sometimes this makes me late, and I get a detention.' Although some UK schools have accepted specialist training from Sibs, a concerning seventy-four per cent of children still admitted, 'No one at school ever offers to help.' As children can fail to realise that their home life is in any way exceptional, it's easy to imagine that they may not feel worthy of special attention or grace from the system. It's why the report recommends that staff should approach the child to ask about their sibling and home life, rather than the other way round.

Priyanka is a seventeen-year-old girl who lives in Nottingham. She is in the middle of four brothers, and both younger boys have multiple additional needs. Nevertheless, she sees her role as 'simply' a sister. When I ask her whether her brothers *need* her, she hesitates. 'They won't need me for the medical things,' she says, 'because I know nothing about that, but like, if they need some sister time and caring and loving and just playing around. That's me. I'll be there.' Both little boys are tube fed and have complex diagnoses. When we talk more, she admits, 'I don't have specialty in medicine, but, if I have to guess what to give a child or what to do at that moment, I could do that.' She also uses expressions like 'having a day off' when she doesn't look after her brothers at all and is just free to 'chill'. 'Everybody needs a break. So that day, one of my other siblings looks after them, or moms look after them, and I don't look after anyone.' When I speak to her mother, who is a paediatrician, she is clear: 'All my three teens are young carers. They can tube feed, give emergency meds if they had to and know the emergency airway position as well.' Later, she sends me some baby monitor footage of Priyanka reading a bedtime story to her smallest brother, who is blind. Unaware she's being filmed, she holds the book down near his little face, taking great care to describe the pictures he cannot see, with gorgeous sensitivity. As for how she feels about having the brothers she does, she is both wise and unequivocal. 'We are lucky to have them in our family. There is joy and sorrow and anger and all those things; they just bring it all together and they literally fill up our family.'

'Everybody is valuable. Everybody is unique.'
DAVID JAY, *PEOPLE LIKE US*

I have already explored the idea that siblinghood starts as a vertical bond, with us 'bigger' or 'smaller' than the other, ahead or behind. The older ones demonstrate as the younger ones watch. Later in life, as we 'catch up', those vertical relationships become more horizontal, making us peers (and hopefully friends). There are moments, of course, when the hierarchy can reassert itself, to plan a special party, make a financial decision or coordinate care. But when you have a sibling with a disability, it is a different story.

Some children grow up quickly as a result of having a brother or sister with additional needs, feeling a sense of responsibility for their siblings. This is known as 'parentification'. Coined by the Hungarian-American psychiatrist Ivan Boszormenyi-Nagy, it describes when the roles of parents and children are reversed, and parents look to their children for emotional and/or practical support, rather than providing it themselves. It is a simple enough idea, but manifests in lots of ways. Firstly, there is a scale from moderate to extreme. And secondly it can switch on and off, with children sometimes 'filling in' temporarily to cover a crisis, like illness, before reverting to their normal role. These instances of parentification are (mainly) parent focused, but the term is also used for children who act like another parent, to help take care of a sibling.

Research shows that there are generally more negative outcomes associated with parenting a parent, starkly described in the book *Lost Childhoods: The Plight of the Parentified Child* by Gregory Jurkovic as a 'violation of intergenerational boundaries'. This is different from caring for a sibling 'like a parent', which is found to be a much less troubling proposition. (Although it is easy to see how one may bleed into the other: for instance, a parent with a sick child may end up inappropriately sharing too many of their worries with their other children.) But, in general, it makes sense, as there are already some expectations around 'looking out' for each other baked into siblinghood. In families with an additional need, instead of the older sibling automatically caring for the younger sibling, the chain runs from the sibling who *can* help, to the one who needs it. Even if the help they provide comes nowhere near to the official definition of parentification, it is almost inevitable that they will be asked to give of their time, patience and understanding (rather than helping administer meds or doing the vacuuming).

A sibling might have a broad spectrum of needs, depending on their specific disability. Siblings with addictions, eating disorders and other chronic or acute mental health issues may also require extra time and attention. In her TEDx talk, Alicia Arenas includes them all in her definition of 'additional needs'. It makes sense. If our roles as siblings are (partly) shaped by what demands are placed on the family resources, it is easy to imagine that the ongoing extra needs of one child, for whatever reason, may deprive another of attention – or lead a parent to borrow some of their physical or emotional energy to cope.

How that affects siblings varies hugely. In a 2023 Italian study in *Frontiers in Psychiatry*, researchers talked to older siblings (aged 19–26) who had been parentified – to various degrees – meeting the needs of their disabled sibling. Annalisa Levante and her team found that if family relationships were poor and the social support surrounding the family weak, the experience eventually led to 'a deterioration of the sibling bond' itself. But if the family had decent social support and the 'parentified sibling' saw their role as beneficial to *them*, the narrative flipped completely. Put simply, their relationship with their brother or sister became stronger.

Research by academics in Alabama found that while too much sibling parentification can lead to children feeling anxious, worried and isolated, a moderate amount can have lots of benefits including increased resilience, empathy, joy, maturity and self-esteem. These advantages are also cited by Levante and her team and feel completely familiar to sisters Carlotta and Sara. They are aged eighteen and twenty-six and have a middle sister, Federica, who is twenty-three and has Down's syndrome. The girls say they remember feeling almost sorry for families they visited as children who didn't have (specifically) *their* sister living there. The families seemed much less fun and more 'independent' of each other, they said, lacking in the 'second nature, this kind of caring-ness' that the girls feel they have in spades. They also describe the 'privilege of unity' that Federica has gifted the family. And, even though they recognise that Carlotta is definitely a 'kind of parental figure', they say it only serves to bring the unit together, rather than pulling them apart. Having a sister with a disability has also been enormously helpful in sorting out the wheat from the chaff when it comes to friendships or (potential) boyfriends. 'It's so good,' they laugh. 'It shows you so much about a person, it makes life very simple.' Anyone who reacts badly – and is old enough to know better – is swiftly rejected from a universe which has been shaped by a sister they describe as 'so pure in the way that she is, that the only way to act is to reciprocate that. You can't show anything but pure love back.'

But a child can't muster all the positivity they need to protect themselves (and their sibling bonds) alone. These girls did not. They had their parents right behind them. As Emily Holl, director of the Sibling Support Project in the US, explains, 'the single strongest factor affecting a sibling's interpretation of the disability is the parent's interpretation of the disability'. Parents who are able to be more positive can help to shore up the sibling relationship. But it's also important that space is left for 'everyone's narrative', even if that is sometimes uncomfortable. On a podcast about glass siblings, Holl remembers being thirteen years old, very upset and crying to her mum about her brother. 'I said, "It's so unfair!"' She meant it was not only unfair for her brother Pete – who has a developmental delay – and for the family as a whole, but also for *her*. Her mum's response still helps her cope today. 'She said, "You're right, sweetie. It is unfair. Life can be unfair." And I felt so seen.'

When I speak to Carlotta, Federica and Sara's mother, she is clear that she and her husband have championed an attitude to difference and disability which focuses on the person, not the label. 'From day one, we have treated Federica as an individual, not as someone "with Down's syndrome"', she explains. 'So that is all the girls have ever seen. It all came so naturally. And of course, they did realise that Federica was special, but they don't treat her in a *special* way. They get angry at her, too.'

BEYOND THE LITTLE UNIVERSE

When Sara tries to remember when it dawned on her that her older sister was 'different', she describes starting school, aged four or five, and saw that Federica – who had almost finished primary school by then – was sometimes slightly isolated or treated just a little bit differently during the school day. The experience was confusing and 'kind of shocking' to her, as up until then she had existed in a little universe where her sister was simply her playmate. 'It was uncomfortable to start encountering other children and their families, and realising "Oh, there's different dynamics." And "Oh, these children aren't like her." I really remember witnessing that.' It was very moving to hear her describe those playground memories, especially considering how young she was, and how much they upset her worldview. It wasn't until much later that she realised these scenes were so difficult because they mark the moment where her 'pure' love for Federica first bumped into a painful realisation of her vulnerability in the world. She sees that clearly now and says that over time that growing awareness of her sister needing protection is one reason that their relationship, which at that stage was 'like twins', began to change.

Now, she says she has 'kind of overtaken' Federica. 'But her sister didn't really notice,' according to their mother. 'She never said, "Why isn't Sara playing with me any more?" So maybe it was natural for her, too.' It is a funny idea, to be 'ahead' of your older sister – and all the words I can think of to describe the shift that can happen in additional needs families sound a little unkind, which is why Sara put big air quotes around 'overtaken' when she used it. I think she was being respectful of her big sister and her status. The shape the family settles into now – as the three girls become adults – is something the whole family is wrestling with, because Sara will leave home this autumn, and Federica is not quite ready to fledge. Their mother wonders how she will ever be able to 'let go' of her child, who will always be the baby of the group, and yet not the youngest. They all want to respect Federica's adult wishes and preferences, to encourage independence and push her to reach all of her potential, but remain mindful of her need for their joint protection.

Their desire to 'get it right' was as clear as the fact that they revel in still having her at home. 'She's the one who, if we're angry or sad or whatever, will give us a smile and brings us back together,' her mother says. Speaking to this family, I was reminded of a specific episode of *Love on the Spectrum* (the Australian version... I told you I was a fan), in which Mr A Plus (aka Michael Theo) makes his family laugh at the dinner table. I can't remember what he said (although I think it was something about sex) but I can remember how his mum reacted. 'Everyone,' she said, 'needs a Michael.'

A family at the end of their rope should not be made to feel bad for being unable to put a Panglossian spin on the reality of living with a child with more challenging behaviours. In her TEDx talk, Alicia Arenas is unflinching in her descriptions of what life was like with her profoundly autistic brother Mario, who she describes as 'a whirlwind of destruction', who made 'holes in the wall from his fist, his head or us... My mom bears the marks of my brother, perfect indentations of teeth marks up and down her arms.' These families need to be given lots of extra resources. With that support, it is more likely that parents will find the extra bandwidth to devote time and attention to *all* their children, something Clare

Kassa from Sibs finds hugely valuable. 'To put your child(ren) without additional needs first, just occasionally, will make a dramatic difference to a caring sibling, who is used to hearing the message "just wait". It may help parents muster the energy to find joy in their situation, before reflecting that back to a child who may be struggling to see it.

This is exactly the kind of work that Emily Holl's organisation does in the States, with the full-on 'Sibshops' – activity sessions which bring together brothers and sisters with shared experiences to hang out with each other, away from their family. 'It's still surprising to me,' she says, 'that so often the definition of family support services just means the parents. We are always reminding people that siblings are very important members of their families and must also be considered.' In the UK, Kassa underlines the fact that this is exactly the kind of community support which needs funding. 'We have Siblings who have brilliant relationships with their brothers and sisters [with disabilities],' she says, 'and those who don't. For some it's very traumatic. We work with adult Siblings who have PTSD because of the complex and challenging experiences that shaped their childhoods.'

A photography research project supported by an organisation called Family Fund – providing small grants to families raising a disabled or seriously ill child in the UK – gave me perhaps the clearest insight into some of the challenges that some very young siblings face, especially if they also come from lower income families. For those children, the charity finds, the blurring of caring and parentified roles is commonplace, with siblings wearing many hats. They can be a support for parents struggling with mental health issues, as well as possibly providing interpreting skills, on top of being a brother or sister to a child with a disability. The project aimed to show what their life looks like by asking them to take a single photo which best sums it up. Children took pictures of butterflies 'because I want to fly away', of bolts on their bedroom door, installed for their own safety, of wide blue skies 'which show how alone I feel'. They sent in images of huge chests of drawers full of labelled medicines and of a steep lane, because 'it's a never-ending uphill struggle'.

They sent much cheerier photos too. Of peas in a pod, puzzle pieces fitting snugly together and of hobbies they share with their brother or sister. But the overwhelming impression from those siblings – for whom so many challenges can intersect – is of a difficult and quite lonely childhood.

'She may be different, but she's not less.'
THE OTHER SISTER (1999)

For ten years, management consultant Roger Fielding was a trustee of Sibs. He has two grown-up daughters from a previous marriage and had three sons with his current wife: two of whom were born with disabilities. The needs of his family have been – and still are – profound. His oldest boy Oliver died just before his thirteenth birthday, fourteen years ago. 'I can't tell you how painful that was,' he says simply. That left 'normal, neurotypical' Louis, and Max, who is now twenty-one and who has recently learned to move his foot, when someone needs to put a sock on it. 'Brilliant,' says Roger. 'Can't tell you how helpful that is really, it was bloody hard to put his socks on when he's just a dead weight. So: small gains.'

Roger spotted an advert for the role in a newspaper, having never really considered the idea of sibling support. 'I thought, that's really interesting. It's a charity focusing not on the child with a disability, but on their brother or sister.' But when he broached it with Louis, the feedback was a little bit unexpected. 'He said the charity was not for him as at no time did he think being a Sibling was disadvantageous. He told me, "I love being his brother. I *love* Max." He spends all the time he can with him. He does not see it as a compromise.' When we speak, Louis is on his gap year in India but has planned to fly home early to join Max on a speedboat trip for adults with disabilities. 'Louis, who's now twenty-two, has seen his elder brother die,' says Roger, 'and he's seen his younger brother survive, but with severe learning difficulties. His brothers have made Louis the man he is. He's got immense maturity and emotional intelligence. I know he's my son, but you can't speak too highly of him.' From his decade at Sibs – and from being part of the additional needs community – Roger says he realises every situation is unique, and others will need to rely more heavily on the support Sibs provides, to help them cope.

Roger's conviction that having a sibling with a disability can shape children in positive ways is something sibling expert and therapist Dr Avidan Milevsky wishes was understood better. Writing in the journal *Research in Developmental*

Disabilities, he says most of the academic focus has been elsewhere, concentrating on the 'deficiency model', focusing on 'poor academic performance, behaviour problems, adjustment difficulties, and stress experienced by well siblings of children with disabilities'. He argues that there has been insufficient research done into the 'strengths' gained by growing up with a sibling with a disability, to provide a full picture. The evidence is skewed.

In her truly superb BBC documentary *A World Without Down's Syndrome*, comedian Sally Phillips illustrates this point perfectly. Sally has three sons, the oldest of whom, Olly, has the condition. In the programme, Sally reads out the NHS leaflet on Down's syndrome routinely handed out to pregnant women. 'Complications, heart problems, gut problems, hearing problems, vision problems, thyroid problems, dementia...' she reads. 'I think that just makes you frightened,' she exclaims, before adding, 'What about all the possible things that can go wrong with a typical person?' By the same measure as the pamphlet, Sally is 'a neurotypical person with forty-six chromosomes, childhood asthma and a family history of glaucoma'. 'Does that describe me?' she challenges. Her point is that we need to have much more qualitative evidence gathered from those who have a child (or sibling) with an additional need to understand what the experience is like – in all the detail it deserves. 'To me,' she concludes, 'Down's syndrome is much more than a list of health problems, but that's because I know Olly.'

In his report, Dr Milevsky notes that many adults who grew up in a family alongside a sibling with an additional need go on to pursue careers in 'helping professions', putting into practice many of the enhanced psychological skills they gained in childhood. This definitely applies to Carlotta, who is training to be a doctor, and credits her sister with the decision. 'It all comes down to her.' She vividly remembers when Federica, aged four, was a patient at Great Ormond Street Hospital, having open heart surgery. 'Just seeing all these scenes wired my brain a certain way, and it's definitely given me an empathy that I would not have had if she didn't exist.' Carlotta was just seven years old. She believes this empathy sets her apart from some medical colleagues, who were not 'thrown into' the same situations as children. Her youngest sister describes the perspective they have been given as 'grounding', 'real' and 'something that some people can't even really grasp'. And as something they are both very grateful for.

Clare Kassa believes that people with a brother or sister who is disabled, neurodiverse or has a long-term medical illness experience 'amplified' feelings about their siblinghood. That the 'joy, mess and anger' of their lifelong relationships are more pronounced. But it is when these Siblings grow up that their experiences really diverge from their peers.

For some, she says, it means that the choices they make are influenced by feelings of obligation and guilt. 'We have Siblings who don't take that job, don't go to uni,' she says, 'who don't make lots of life decisions because they are part of a care team at home.' But even for Siblings able and encouraged to spread their wings, she adds, there can be a struggle to adjust to a life where they have permission to put themselves first. It is a pattern which family therapist and psychologist Patricia Papernow recognises. 'One summer I had three young women who'd all gone away to their freshman year of college and fallen apart, and every single one of them was the sibling of a child in trouble,' she said. 'One had a bipolar brother, one a kid on the spectrum, and the third one had a medical issue. And they had held it together for the entire time that they lived in their family. They were the "good kid". Then they went away to college, and when they didn't have to hold it together... Boom.' She mimes an explosion with her hands.

In any family, our position is *relative* to those of our siblings. We are made and shaped in that system. Now imagine how it might work in a family where the centre of gravity is often focused elsewhere, and part of your identity is partly created as a result of someone else's need. Regardless of whether that experience is positive, negative or mixed, it is not difficult to see how it might – in those circumstances – feel destabilising to spin off into the wide world, away from all the very particular forces that have made your family and your very valuable role within it.

'It's not going to happen, OK? It's not going to happen ever. You're not going to leave me.'
What's Eating Gilbert Grape (1993)

But it is only later still in life that the most profound and consistent point of difference emerges for siblings in this position. 'I call it the ticking time bomb effect,' says Kassa. 'You know, at some point you are going to have to step in, step up, take the place, perhaps, of your parents. You know it's coming.' Decisions about care might happen as an adult, but they're anticipated much earlier. Siblings are usually very aware of their brother or sister's vulnerability in the world and have a desire (maybe mixed with a feeling of obligation) to protect them. Kassa says she recently worked with an eight-year-old girl who said she wasn't 'ever' going to get married, because she was going to look after her brother. 'So that was the trajectory of the future,' she says, 'of knowing that this is for her lifespan.'

For Siblings in this position, facing up to what their relationship will look like once their parents have gone is a huge source of concern. It is referenced in every study I read about these kinds of adult sibling relationships, including Dr Milevsky's. He writes about siblings being 'preoccupied' with the question of the future and that decision is often a source of 'significant stress'. My own cousin Hazel remembers responding to her mother's death with a very clear sense that she now had 'massive' responsibilities. 'Firstly, I didn't know how David was going to take it,' she tells me. 'I do remember feeling very sensible, but sort of going, "Oh, God. This is it now, this is a real-life responsibility." And it weighed heavily.' In the end David only lived for another year, before dying very suddenly of cancer, able to spend his last days at home in the community he had been a happy part of since he was eighteen. Hazel had regular sleepovers and would climb on to his bed for cuddles. There is some guilt in her retelling of that year, about how she felt overwhelmed by the responsibility, only to lose her beloved brother so quickly. But she wasn't to know.

In an interview about her documentary on the Down's syndrome community, which includes her son Olly, Sally Phillips says his long-term care has been a priority since the very beginning. She explains that her decision to try to have two more children was completely intentional, because she 'didn't want to leave one sibling alone as a carer'. Having spoken to my cousin about the reality of being alone, feeling responsible for her brother, I can really understand her determination. But having learned about the way that the care burden is typically carved up between siblings, I am not surprised when Clare Kassa tells me that in families where one child has a disability, there is still – usually – one (often female) sibling who shoulders most of the responsibility. She also points out that the caring role can be hard to quantify, especially if it takes place at a distance: answering multiple calls a day from an anxious sibling, for example, or filling in government paperwork and managing finances. 'I'm a distance carer,' she says, 'and just because I don't live next door to my brother doesn't mean I'm not involved. Every day this week I've dealt with something. And then there's the question of being on constant high alert. At Sibs we've run a couple of sessions for adult Siblings about distance care, and some have acknowledged for the first time, "Oh gosh, I am a carer. I hadn't really thought about it."'

I am reminded of Laura Linney's character in the film *Love Actually*, whose mobile phone is constantly ringing

– at her desk, during meetings, and also in the precise moment she finally gets the colleague she is head over heels in love with up to her bedroom. It is always, *always* her brother calling, from what we later learn is some kind of secure medical facility. She invariably picks up, with the identical bright greeting each time: 'Hello, my darling!' The film shows her managing quite an extreme situation alone with an immense amount of patience and grace. But, even if you are not facing it alone, it strikes me that convening care successfully as a sibling team might also be a challenge. Arranging help for parents is a process famously fraught with emotional potholes for brothers and sisters to navigate, stressed by the new responsibility. Perhaps the same is true for siblings trying to organise and negotiate care for their brother or sister. Except the needs might be more complex and the arrangements may last for decades. Everything is amplified.

For Emily Holl from the Sibling Support Project, her own 'future planning process' was initiated by her brother Pete. Their mother was in the hospital, 'and he called me,' recounts Holl, 'and said, "When Mom and Dad die, I can't live in this house by myself."' She was thoroughly taken aback. 'I said, "Oh. We're having that conversation now?"' But in the end, she was grateful, especially because her brother was 'driving the bus' on the issue. She now thinks including the disabled sibling in that conversation 'to the greatest extent possible' is vital because 'they will have lots of feelings and opinions about what their life should look like too'.

In the UK, there is no legal obligation to care for siblings in adulthood, once parents are older or gone, and for some families it just isn't possible, for several reasons. But for those who do 'step up' – like Juliet, who built an annexe on her house for her younger sister Eleanor – negotiating their sibling relationship now, in among all the myriad of practical and financial arrangements, can be far from straightforward. Although the large age gap between them meant that she was once mistaken for her sister's mum 'when I was like, eleven?' she laughs, until her sister moved into the flat, their relationship was definitely a more traditional sibling one. Now she treads a line between sister, carer and companion, while also managing some aspects of Eleanor's life with their mother, who is still alive. She is also married, with four secondary school-aged children and has her own career, so the juggle is intense.

Because of what she has learned in the last seven years, she's very relieved their original plan to all live in a big house together (her family, her sister and their parents) was never executed. 'It would have been an *absolute* nightmare,' she says, 'because grown-up siblings and parents can't actually care together. Your agenda is similar, but the depth of your preoccupation with that person is so different.' Her mother's anxiety that Eleanor was reaching her potential 'every day' is in tension with Juliet's stretched resources. 'I have to say to myself, "Maybe Eleanor's not completely happy all of the time. Maybe she hasn't got someone to talk to every single moment. And, actually, that's OK." Whereas for my mum that can be really difficult.'

It can also be tough for the parent, says Emily Holl, to respect the unique perspective siblinghood brings. Siblings have the benefit of a 'slightly more unsentimental' view of their brother or sister, as well as a (maybe) more accurate idea of their abilities. 'We keep it real… we know what our siblings are capable of.' Holl advises that, whether a child or an adult, the siblings' expertise should be welcomed and included, whether in school meetings or with social services. But they should equally understand that they are not obliged to play any particular role. 'They should be given the right to refuse,' she states. And for all Siblings, 'Their value should never be tied to their role as helper.'

'I often compare myself to my brother a lot. Which is a big mistake. I would often label him as a fresh cutted meat from God.'

MICHAEL THEO, ACTOR AND STAR OF
LOVE ON THE SPECTRUM

Juliet is quick to highlight the benefits of her arrangement, which are 'the amazing joy' at being able to have such a positive role in her sister's life, and the fact that her children are being taught some of the same valuable life lessons that she was as a child. 'They have never had a chance to assume that life is all about money and achievement, because they've got this complete, palpable, constant presence that is clearly a life as valuable as every other, but who can't be measured according to the normal success: intellectual success, financial. That's a really positive thing.'

Yet she has to continue to accept that her sister, because of her disability, will always be her mother's priority, just as she was in childhood. As a parent she understands, because sometimes she makes the tough choice to put *her* children first, when Eleanor is also clamouring for attention. But it remains hurtful for siblings like her to be as transparent as glass in the eyes of their parents, no matter how understandable. 'I'm on a Facebook group for siblings,' Juliet says, 'and it's the issue that comes up *most* – after understanding the benefits system. The dynamics between the parents, the disabled sibling and the caring sibling is massive.' It is something that she finds hard. 'When my mum comes over, the first nine out of ten things she says are something to do with Eleanor, rather than "how are you?" And that's fine. I'm not a very "how are you" person. You know, I'm happy, I'll get on with things. But it's really noticeable.' I think about Emily Holl's advice for people greeting younger siblings who help care for their brother and sister. She says, instead of commending them on being so 'good' all the time, we should instead train ourselves to say, 'Wow, you really help a lot; what's that like for you?'

Looking ahead, there will be a natural simplification of the situation when their parents pass away, but Juliet still worries about the future. 'I was only ever a big sister to my other siblings in the kind of annoying way. That I knew how to niggle, you know. Whereas with Eleanor, I am that big sister who needs to take her hand, teach her about life *and* help her across the road and make sure she's OK. And it's sort of never-ending.' This enduringly 'vertical' nature of the relationship is what she finds hardest to talk honestly about. 'I don't know how to say this without sounding horrid, but you can't have a totally normal friendship with someone whose intellectual capacities are severely limited, because friendship between siblings or anyone is based on some kind of wavelength. You don't have to be equals in any particular way, but you have to sort of "get" each other. So if actually, in every single conversation, you're the person who gets everything that's going on and the other person doesn't… you're just constantly aware of it.'

It is a feeling that Clare Kassa thinks is commonplace. And for many, she says, 'the awareness of an "uneven, imbalanced relationship" starts young'. On its website, Sibs has a page for Siblings – up to the age of 17 – to ask an advisor any question they like: about their brother or sister's condition, school life, or how to talk to friends about disability. 'A couple of weeks ago,' she says, 'a little girl messaged that her brother liked to play a certain game, and she liked to play another game. And she typed… "is it alright to play the game that I like?"' The key, she has found, is to help them come to an acceptance that 'this is how it is, you know, and it can be hard and that's OK'. Emily Holl agrees. Research carried out by her Sibling Support Network shows that brothers and sisters who have had permission to be honest (including about the really hard things) are more likely to step into a caring role later. 'The Siblings who want to come back as advocates,' she writes, 'are also those who were supported in having their own journey along the way… one which has nothing to do with disability. Who were allowed to really figure out "who am *I*? What makes *me* tick?"'

Carlotta and Sara have already started thinking about the future of their relationship with Federica. 'I know I want kids,' says Carlotta. 'And I have had it sort of in my mind that Federica will be very much close to me, whether that's living with me, or living nearby. We will always have active care for her.' The girls have ongoing conversations with their parents, who have planned financially to ensure that the burden on them is as light as possible. Both girls are clear that they don't feel obligation, in any negative sense. Their mother chimes in, 'I tell them, "You don't need to worry about her." And they go, "We want to worry about her. Leave us alone please. She will be OK."' They protest that they love Federica and will always want to keep her safe. Their minds are made up. They want to try to balance career ambition, independence and families of their own, with an idea of lives which will always involve caring for their sister.

When it comes to Louis and Max, who will have been on that speedboat by now, Roger is balancing the grief he and his wife feel at looking for a 'forever home' for Max, with the joy that Louis's first response to any suggested location they find is to work out how quickly he can get there by train.

9

Estrangement

With a side serving of favouritism

'Their childhood had bound them, their blood, their shared past. And yet they had spent years barely speaking, as though those very things had forced them apart.'
ELIZABETH STROUT, *OLIVE AGAIN*

Fern Schumer Chapman is the author of *Brothers, Sisters, Strangers*, a book about sibling estrangement. After experiencing a rupture in her relationship with her brother, she now coaches other families in the same situation. 'Sibling estrangement is *horribly* stigmatised,' she says. Her passion for trying to bring the issue into the light comes from hearing about the impact sibling estrangement can have. 'It ripples through your identity and life, affecting your self-esteem, your friendships, your wellbeing, your ability to trust. Not to mention wider family relationships, because people align themselves with one side or the other... It's a really complicated experience.' It's complicated, misunderstood and, apparently, very common.

WHO'S THE FAVOURITE?

Karsten Hank and Anja Steinbach collected data from ten thousand sibling pairs in Germany for a paper published in 2023. Twenty-eight per cent of respondents reported at least one period of estrangement from a sibling, and fourteen per cent reported more than one. In the US, Cornell University's Family Estrangement and Reconciliation Project led by sociologist Dr Karl Pillemer carried out its own survey. It asked: 'Do you have a relative with whom you have no contact at all?' Twenty-seven per cent of people answered 'yes', and eight per cent said the relative they were cut off from was a brother or a sister.

Despite these statistics – and there are others which indicate similar patterns – there has been such scant research into sibling estrangement that Fern Schumer Chapman and the handful of others working in the field feel frustrated and alone. When Chapman was writing her book, she wanted to put the word 'estrangement' in the subtitle. Her publisher said, 'No. Nobody knows what that word means.' This was in 2021. Likewise, when Dr Pillemer began his research, despite the advice columns chock-full of letters asking for guidance with estrangement, he found nothing about it at all in the weightiest tome about family relationships, *The Handbook of Family Therapy*. It was a refrain I heard over and over from the small community of therapists and academics writing about the issue: research into the sibling relationship was limited. Work focused on why the bond between brothers and sisters frays or snaps was rarer still.

One of the reasons might be that the term is a little slippery. Estrangement is defined in the dictionary as 'A feeling that you do not understand someone or do not have any connection with him or her', a meaning which is broad enough to include sibling relationships where there is absolutely no contact (as in the Cornell study); relationships which are emotionally distant but functional enough to allow for the occasional family gathering; and those where one person feels estranged from the other because their emotional needs – what they desperately want from their sibling bond – are not met. Estrangement is also not binary – siblings can cycle in and out of estrangement, closer at some points but often with a certain tension aggregating in the background.

In her sibling love story *Marrow* about the loss of her sister Maggie to cancer, and the years immediately preceding her death, Elizabeth Lesser is unusually clear-eyed about their fluctuating sibling relationship. 'We were similar in some ways,' she writes, 'yet different enough to misunderstand each other, to judge each other, to reject each other. Sometimes we were close and sometimes we were strangers.' The book is reflective about the forces which swill around siblings as they grow. How the choices that brothers and sisters make as they fledge into adulthood can pull them into spaces and places beyond the reach and understanding of the other. In their case, Maggie chose to stay close to home – marrying locally and living nearby. Elizabeth moved to the city, to pursue a life far away from smallholdings and log cabins. The acres of experience between them coupled with that inevitable busyness of building a grown-up identity and an independent life meant that they didn't pause to talk honestly about their realities. Instead, they imagined what lay behind the other's decisions – and got it quite wrong. Maggie felt left behind, as if her choices were being derided, Elizabeth as though her decision to leave was a pointed rejection of a life they had previously shared. It is not until serious illness arrived and painfully stripped out everything except what really mattered, that the sisters admitted the whole, nuanced, messy truth to each other. In the end they learned that neither of them had been perfectly content with their choices (who is?) and both had felt wistful about the life their sister was living. The terrible diagnosis spun the sisters back into each other's orbits again, casting out misunderstandings and allowing for reconciliation.

THE CATALYSTS

The conditions surrounding an estrangement vary dramatically. It may come about for exactly the reasons that Lesser describes: the widening distance between siblings in their twenties which, if left unmonitored for long enough, can create a vacuum between two lives. Communication slides into formal fact-sharing about job promotions or new flats, rather than little hooks into the fabric of each other's day-to-day lives. The longer you leave it, the more surface and sweeping the scope of the catch-ups, until the connection is emptied of emotional intimacy and becomes all about practical headlines. These bulletins are dull to deliver, boring to receive and can feel duty-laden. Not a fun basis for really getting to know what makes your adult brother or sister tick.

Other – very practical – reasons like geography can also conspire against sibling closeness. My own older sister Bex moved to New Zealand in her twenties, and maintaining regular contact was tough: time zones are a pain and flights are long and expensive. I would often fancy a chat at around five o'clock in the evening, while poking in the fridge and looking for something to cook or drinking tea on the sofa after a tiring day at work. I'd look at the clock and realise it was 4 a.m. in New Zealand, and therefore hopeless. Often, we would be forced to wait far longer than we both wanted before scheduling a convenient time, so the calls rarely felt spontaneous. It wasn't until I had a baby that it became much easier. Then I could call at 2 a.m. and almost guarantee she would pick up. Moreover, she had small boys of her own and so could reach across the world and into the weary dark of our wakeful nursery, reassuring me – from big sister to little sister – that I was doing brilliantly. I was so grateful.

As children, siblings may be pulled apart as a result of a wider family crisis, like separation or divorce, the children pressured to take sides, causing family rifts. When I spoke to the poet Benjamin Zephaniah for the podcast, he told me how the violence he had witnessed at home dramatically divided him and his siblings. When he saw his father beat his mother, he 'would fight him. But my other brothers and sisters would run away. So they would run in one direction. And I'd be running in the other: towards her.' Eventually the abuse became too much for his mum, and she left. Benjamin was the only child to go with her. The siblings picked their sides, and stuck to them, pretty rigidly. 'My brothers and sisters think Mom wasn't a good mom because she abandoned us. And Dad was a hero because he raised seven kids on his own. That's a great man. And I think the opposite, I think Mom was a hero, because she had the guts to get out of a violent marriage. And that he was horrible because he beat women. There's always a kind of tension underneath.' It was an estrangement that lasted decades. When I interviewed him in 2023, not long before he died, Benjamin said the relationships had only very recently showed some small signs of recovering as the siblings rallied to care for their mum, who was very sick.

But in other – less explosively – unhappy families, parental conflict can also have long-term effects on the relationship between siblings. Research conducted in the Netherlands by Anne-Rigt Poortman in 2008 showed that brothers and sisters who have grown up in a family with a lot of arguing – and where the marriage eventually fails – had less contact as adults, and significantly more conflict in their relationship. It stands to reason that sibling relationships developed in a miserable family will have a fainter pattern of happiness to trace as they grow, and that their loyalties to one another may be weaker as a result.

Estrangement can also occur after one single event. An explosive argument in which both parties retreat, wounded, to their corners; the relationship is suddenly and violently damaged. Or it can come about as the result of a simple misunderstanding which grows and festers in the darkness of a communication blackout, and on to which the worst imagined versions of the other are imagined and embedded. More customary, though, are the quiet, slow withdrawals: regular but rare texts or phone calls from your brother or sister petering into eventual silence. There is often no definable moment or active decision which severs the emotional bind. Rather it can thin imperceptibly over time, stretching into barely there threads, like wisps of old cobweb on the breeze, no longer able to keep your hearts tethered together.

'Happy families are all alike; every unhappy family is unhappy in its own way.'
LEO TOLSTOY, *ANNA KARENINA*

So far, I have relied on the idea of the family as a system – a constellation of individuals bound together, usually, by blood. It is both a robust and reliable arrangement and a worryingly fragile one, where the actions and choices of each member create unavoidable vibrations for everyone else, with the potential to knock the whole thing off kilter. The hope is that a mixture of love, acceptance, forgiveness, shared history and DNA is enough to withstand the grievances. It is a beautiful ideal. But human pride and vulnerability – our susceptibility to feeling hurt and angry – make it prone to failure.

Our shared history is, as we know, impossible to verify. Memories clash and the stories we carry about ourselves and each other can be a source of upset as often as they are a source of joy. The length of sibling relationships – likely the vast majority of our lives – changes the stakes. The sense of permanence of their existence means that on the one hand we should invest in our siblings and try to find harmony, but on the other, perhaps, that we feel there's no real rush to do so. Death is not something we automatically think about with our siblings in the way we do with our ageing parents, where we may more easily accept and forgive them 'before it's too late'.

The challenge is made harder by the fact that, during those (possible) decades of loving each other, our sibling relationships will evolve. So in order to stay close, we must find ways to navigate the changes together: from the nursery to playmates, to grown-up peers, to becoming brothers- and sisters-in-law, perhaps, before maybe making each other aunties and uncles. Later in life, we will most likely be pulled back together again, to gather around our parents, to try to figure out ways to cooperate and organise, to provide care. And then, eventually, we will grieve together for them, before hopefully growing old together ourselves. It's a huge ask.

I have written about how we are given – or assume – our roles in this arrangement, sometimes complementing our siblings, sometimes in uncomfortable tension, or chafing against each other in ways which are uniquely irritating. I've described the ways in which the parts we play can start to cause malfunction in this fragile arrangement, when siblings feel forced into a role by the weight of parental expectation (or the behaviour of other family members) which is damaging and unhealthy. About the creation of scapegoats who don't or won't fit the mould – or even worse, are forced to carry the burden of the family's unhappiness. There are also, of course, more extreme instances when siblings hurt each other badly, abuse acting like a wrecking ball to the family structure, smashing ties between siblings and wreaking chaos. The evidence seems clear that, despite a deep need to belong in our sibling relationships, to find comfort *inside* the family constellation, for many that just isn't possible.

'For the better part of forty years, my only sibling – a brother and I – had almost no relationship,' writes Fern Schumer Chapman in the opening of her book. 'Eventually I hardly knew who my brother was anymore.' Her tone flip-flops between a slightly brisk retelling of the facts – 'we simply didn't have much to say to each other' – and a disarmingly honest description of the emotional toll that the rift with her brother wrought, the 'suffering' and 'shame' that came with the relationship breakdown, which she found almost too painful to admit to the world.

And it's odd, because the pain she describes about her own estrangement is in spite of the fact that she acknowledges the bond between brothers and sisters can be really complicated, weathering periods of emotional distance and patches of scanty communication. But Chapman still found a vast difference between how people react to the more socially acceptable admission that you 'don't really get on with your sibling', and to letting slip that you don't have any contact *at all*. The latter, she says, can make you feel horribly exposed to judgement by people who may wonder whether you are capable of maintaining *any* relationships, if you 'can't even have one with your own brother'. A 2024 survey by *Time* magazine on the 'estrangement epidemic' in the USA corroborates her experience. It found 'most Americans would condemn the behavior of those who are cutting off family, whether they were triggered or not'. When her sibling relationship broke down, Fern summed it up simply as 'an utter contradiction of the very nature of family'.

Failing to maintain the 'very nature of family' is something that psychotherapist Ali-John Chaudhary is very familiar with. He runs an online community to support estranged siblings and describes the issue as 'a silent epidemic'. One in three people find their sibling relationship difficult, 'yet you can't really talk with people about it'. Chaudhary speaks from experience. He has one sister, with whom he has 'a tumultuous, low-contact, superficial relationship', and has done for decades. Brought up by parents who encouraged their children to live 'individual lives', he describes ending up existing on totally 'parallel tracks' to her, struggling to find any connection at all. He also feels his parents exacerbated the problem, casting his sister as the Golden Child and him as the Black Sheep.

It was only when he began his work as a therapist that he realised how common his experience was, and that many people are quietly estranged from their sibling, their relationship so harmed by the dysfunction in the family around them. 'And it's so sad,' Chaudhary says, 'because families should be a safe place where you can be yourself,' not a place which tugs at and distorts the relationships between the children in it, causing them to buckle and snap.

Determined to normalise the issue of estrangement through his work, he has found solace in the company of other siblings he meets online, and has made progress towards understanding how his relationship with his sister ended up so damaged. Nevertheless, he still describes walking through life feeling like 'one shoelace is untied'. The undone lace of a failed relationship generates a lingering feeling of precariousness and incompleteness, which he's constantly having to negotiate with care. I think it also captures a certain vulnerability that is occasionally visible to others: something about you is 'off'.

> Cutoff: 'the process of separation, isolation, withdrawal, running away, or denying the importance of the parental family.'
> MURRAY BOWEN, *FAMILY THERAPY IN CLINICAL PRACTICE*

Murray Bowen was a pioneer of family therapy in the 1960s and 1970s. He believed that a person's relationships with their family members are by far the most important: trumping friendships or romantic relationships. His work casts a long shadow and may explain why – until very recently – sibling estrangement has been a shrouded issue. In fact, Bowen's belief in the 'primacy of family attachment' led him to be explicitly negative about the idea of using 'emotional cutoff' to deal with conflict at all. He also argued that what looks like a neat solution to a messy problem can actually store up troubles for the future.

Bowen thought that people who estrange simply defer the problem, leaving the underlying issues lying dormant and ready to rear their head once given the chance. He also believed that without addressing the root causes of family upset, individuals are vulnerable to repeating the same patterns of behaviour in the families they go on to create, leading to cycles of dysfunction rippling down the generations. 'People who cut off from their families often seek intense emotional closeness in other relationships, only to struggle with the same unresolved emotional issues,' he explained. He also warned that by 'cutting off' a relative you forfeit a huge source of emotional support, and tend to become more anxious as a result. It's a pretty miserable list.

Bowen's legacy has lingered, says Chaudhary, producing a generation of therapists who are not 'estrangement informed'. He has found many professionals lack the tools to deal with sibling rifts in a nuanced way, by helping to ease the pain of separation or guiding those affected towards a life with 'more peace' – even if that means living out of relationship with their sibling(s).

Clinical psychologist Dr Lucy Blake, an expert in estrangement, agrees that Bowen's theories have contributed to the way that 'The Family' has been culturally venerated and idealised. She argues that 'for people affected by family estrangement, this idea of what things could be or should be, or ideal family relationships, seems really key to the experience' and adds to their sense of loss and failure. I will talk about social media later, and the role it has played in starting more open conversations about estrangement, but first let me apportion some blame to Instagram with its turbo-charged idealisation of #familylife. One which is full of picture-perfect 'candid' moments in matchy-matchy Christmas pyjamas or frolicking on a beach at sunset.

A doomscroll through this kind of faux reality, with all the compromises filtered out, can create a nagging feeling of inadequacy in anyone. And, says Blake – who wrote a book called *Home Truths* – 'can prevent us from acknowledging and engaging with the normality of complicated lives' in which we feel 'anger and distress and confusion and love and guilt, all the things that make our relationships rich and difficult and valuable'. A large part of her work looks at the ways siblings can learn to build and foster meaningful (and indeed *imperfect*) relationships, so that they don't slide into being 'strangers under the same roof'.

I started my podcast about siblings five years ago and began working in earnest on this book three years later, amidst the media frenzy created by the publication of Prince Harry's memoir *Spare*. That book spotlighted the complexity of sibling dynamics generally, giving it due prominence on a global stage, and brought into sharp focus the idea of sibling estrangement in particular. Since then, the Murdoch siblings seemingly have had their own (very public) estrangement picked over on social media, as have (allegedly) the Beckham brothers, spawning all kinds of think pieces about these kinds of breakdowns. Writing this chapter on estrangement in 2025, I feel as if it is sitting on a kind of cusp, looking back at the old ways that cutoff was thought about, and then looking forward a little, at what research has revealed to date, together with a growing awareness of the issue. 'Now it's all over the place,' says Fern Schumer Chapman. 'The minute you mention it, people rush forward to say, "Yeah, it happened to me as well." So things are changing quickly.' She cites the pandemic years as the point that the idea of sibling estrangement started to seep into the public consciousness. Covid saw family relationships rekindle, with individuals holding out a hand to distant siblings, liberated from the awkwardness by the far more powerful force of existential dread.

In his book *Fault Lines,* sociologist Dr Pillemer described sibling reconciliations as the 'silver lining' of the pandemic. The realistic possibility of death or serious illness allowed some to realise they may not be granted the luxury of 'one day' deciding to send the email or voice note hinting at a desire to reconnect. Disaster sharpens the mind and clears out some of the clutter in our hearts: Covid reminded us all that life is short.

The years we lived under the shadow of the virus amplified some specific things, says Dr Pillemer, who surveyed 1,700 people for his book. One was the feeling that time suddenly isn't stretching infinitely out in front of them – which is called 'socioemotional selectivity'. 'When people perceive the time horizon as short,' he explains, 'they place a higher value on relationships, including those with family members.' The second was our sense of 'anticipatory regret' – the sorrow we think we may feel in the future if we do not act now. The awful threat of a global pandemic made us all suddenly vulnerable, by dismantling the 'normal order of things' in a frightening way. The luxury of thinking we could wait until 'life was less busy', perhaps, to invest in our sibling relationships – or rebuild them from scratch – was snatched away.

Ironically, Covid then gave many of us a sudden, huge and horrible amount of free time: more than enough to try to absorb the jolting reprioritisation of what we discovered really mattered to us, but painfully little freedom to act on it. Trapped at home and unable to travel, meet and hug, we were faced with the real and shocking possibility that we might die, and that – therefore – so might our siblings. Writer Kimberly Witt's brother (with whom she had a 'peripheral' sibling relationship before 2020) was working in an ICU department in Iowa when the virus began. She describes being 'overwhelmed with worry for him', because of the serious risk of exposure to infection. Stuck in their respective homes, she and her sister invited him to a new WhatsApp group, sharing 'real talk', photos of their grey roots and silly memes as the pandemic spread around them. 'Confused, scared, and tired,' she reflects, 'we turned to one another for support.'

TIKTOKIFICATION

Other changes were taking place alongside Covid and the lockdowns. With people forced by the pandemic to live life more online than ever before, TikTok took off. It remains *the* place for video content about *everything*, including siblings. From rose-tinted videos full of #sister adoration, from Anna and Elsa (sisters from Disney's *Frozen*) memes to declarations: 'forever best friends who will be there no matter what' (usually featuring a sunset), to posts mining the well of family upset, including arguments *and* estrangement.

A quick search yields podcast clips discussing the Murdoch siblings and their 2024 fall-out over the future of their father's media empire; videos of estranged people tearfully 'accepting that I'll never, never be able to cry to her about a stupid boy, I'll never be able to "borrow" clothes from her closet and I will always be a stranger to her'. There are also plenty of videos exhorting the benefits of 'cutting off' a sibling who is 'toxic' and others confidently explaining 'the (4) ways you can tell if your sibling is "a narcissist"'. To be clear, there are a lot of videos about adult children saying similar things about their parents too. In this kind of online arena, cutting ties with your sibling (or parent) is commonly described as 'going no contact' and it has generated a lot of attention and considerable controversy.

As a parent of two digital natives, I've clocked the general bleed of 'therapy speak' (relationships becoming 'toxic', people being 'narcissists') into everyday language. I would suggest with confidence that it is something that TikTok has accelerated, and it can be tremendously useful, giving people language to help them describe difficult experiences. Online videos about all kinds of personal issues can give people struggling to cope some sense of community and source of comfort. I'd also argue that TikTok has helped destigmatise a host of common human experiences, from acne to the menopause, ADHD to, of course, sibling estrangement.

But if you are the one deploying that kind of language to publicly diagnose your sibling as 'toxic' or 'narcissistic' before 'going no contact', it does give you an unfair protection from any comeback. It is a phenomenon which psychologist Dr Terri Apter has noticed: 'It is more prevalent among millennials, many of whom believe that levelling accusations and airing grievances against their family may achieve a better version of themselves than they believe is possible if they remain in the orbit of those they blame [and may have been encouraged to blame by armies of therapists] for being obstacles to a desired self.' In other words, awareness might be raised but the communication is very one-sided, creating self-righteousness on the one hand and powerlessness on the other.

But it isn't just 'normal people' making estrangement videos about their brothers and sisters. Speaking to the *New York Times*, Dr Katy Murphy – who trains early-career therapists at the University of South Dakota – is scathing about professionals, those 'armies of therapists', who are also busy making online content about sibling relationship breakdown. Her worry is that videos exhorting the benefits of 'going no contact' will find users susceptible to suggestion and vulnerable to manipulation. 'My personal opinion,' says Dr Murphy, 'is that TikTok therapists are destroying the trust and professionalism that took forever to build up in this field.' The article explains that Dr Murphy has started reporting individual therapists to licensing boards explaining her cynicism about their motivations. 'What they want is to generate revenue,' she said. 'They all have podcasts. They all have books.'

Dr Ali-John Chaudhary and Dr Lucy Blake were keen to reiterate that estrangement is a really complicated issue, as hard to define as it can be to achieve. The simplistic way it is presented online, says Dr Chaudhary, might well be gaining prominence for the issue generally, but it does not represent anything like the full spectrum of 'experiences of estrangement' which exist. Combined with the lack of research to date and only nascent cultural awareness, the result is that all the different kinds of estrangement are being 'lumped together' in one unhelpful homogeneous pile.

'I'm not, personally, a fan,' Dr Blake tells me, 'of the narrative that "people are just cutting each other off for no reason"... It is usually something that's extremely painful which people spend decades grappling with, rather than a quick and dry, thoughtless action.' Estrangement can be a sad, confusing and exhausting process, 'a difficult kind of achievement', as well as a decision which might grant you 'space and time and freedom' from a bad sibling relationship. It is not easy to extricate yourself from a dysfunctional or even an abusive relationship, and it will take maintenance.

Estrangement does not equate to liberation. Choosing to distance yourself from a sibling may result in you losing and mourning several other identities and roles. It might mean you are no longer a sister-in-law or an aunty. If you have a partner or children, they will also lose the mirror image of that: *their* aunty, *their* uncle and *their* cousins. How you negotiate your estrangement in the face of everyone else's response to your decision may also prove to be very stressful. Reverberations will be felt on many branches of the family tree. It will also raise all kinds of questions: from more trivial ones about table plans at weddings, to really fraught emotional dilemmas. If your brother gets really sick, will you visit? If your sister has a baby, will you acknowledge their arrival? If your estranged sibling dies, how and with whom will you mourn?

It is perhaps not surprising, given the collateral damage caused by estrangement, that parents often intervene, distressed that their kids have fallen out and desperate to restore harmony (or the appearance of harmony) to the family. Some will even exert pressure on their children, says Dr Pillemer, who says that 'unresolved rifts often create chronic stress for all family members involved. The evidence clearly demonstrates that this type of stress can lead to depression and anxiety, and even manifest itself in physical health problems.'

'There is no absence so terrible as the absence of one who has never left you.'
CHLOE BENJAMIN, *THE IMMORTALISTS*

Jane is estranged from her brother in Australia. When we speak, she tells me ruefully, 'The ocean is a good boundary.' She says her mother is in 'weapons grade denial' about the state of their brother–sister relationship, and 'views the estrangement as all my fault... that it is all my choice, rather than the ways my brother has behaved'. Phone calls and visits are peppered with (not-so) subtle 'brother PR': 'he really does care for you, you know'. The result is that they are not '100 per cent no contact', and Jane sends her nephew gifts and cards for his birthday and Christmas, but that is all. 'Simply, I didn't receive a text from him last birthday, so I didn't send one back, and so that was the end of that. The door is not entirely closed, but it's just barely cracked open.'

Any meaningful relationship has evaporated and what is left exists only to protect her mum and to hold on to a last glimmer of hope. 'There's this almost, but not really, charade, for the sake of appearances,' Jane explains. She is not sure whether the performance will continue once her parents die. 'Honestly, I don't know. I don't want to say "no" because I'd like to believe people are capable of changing for the better.' For now, she is reluctant to cause more pain to her mother – who comes from a Jewish family with a history of flight, loss and displacement, and for whom family comes first. 'Family above everything and peace at any price,' she says quietly. Her mother talks to her own sister every single day.

Published in 2023, *Spare* – from the title onwards – pulls no punches about the rift between Princes Harry and William. The drama plays out against a rarefied backdrop of monarchy, immense wealth and the international media. But it does little to conceal the fact that it is – at its heart – a tale of sibling strife. Consider this description of the bedroom given to the young princes. Take away the view of the fountain (and the question of the throne) and you're left with something familiar, the pouting tone of baby brothers everywhere.

> Adults called it the nursery. Willy had the larger half, with a double bed, a good-sized basin, a cupboard with mirrored doors, a beautiful window looking down on the courtyard, the fountain, the bronze statue of a roe deer buck. My half of the room was far smaller, less luxurious. I never asked why. I didn't care. But I also didn't need to ask. Two years older than me, Willy was the Heir, whereas I was the Spare.

When Fern Schumer Chapman read the book, she was quick to spot many of the ingredients which recur frequently in her work with siblings, and which she has compiled into a checklist of 'risk factors for estrangement'. Things which can wreak havoc between siblings in any family, regardless of background, include: childhood trauma (like the death of a parent at a young age); parental favouritism (the line of succession presents the ultimate in favouritism); and poor communication skills. 'The monarchy is notoriously bad at resolving personal problems,' she says, 'and the brothers probably were never taught, never learned, how to negotiate differences, family values, judgements and choices.' It is hard to comment on what was – or was not – modelled to the princes, in terms of conflict resolution, but it is clear that Harry feels his choice of spouse was contentious (another one of Chapman's risk factors) and went against the grain. 'He'd actually been pretty discouraging about my even dating Meg,' writes Harry. 'One day, sitting together in his garden, he'd predicted a host of difficulties I could expect if I hooked up with an "American actress", a phrase he always managed to make sound like "convicted felon". Who your sibling chooses as a partner is a 'perilous' moment for your rapport with them, says Chapman, prompting basic questions like 'will I like them?' and 'how will they fit into our family?' The new relationship might also test the sibling bond, by creating feelings of jealousy about the new romance (which can run both ways) or worry about the suitability of their brother or sister's choice – whether, simply, they are *good enough* for your sibling.

Following the 2024 US election, there was a flurry of articles and videos on social media collecting the experiences of siblings whose relationships had suddenly ended over 'which side' they had voted for – differences in political affiliations also rank highly on Chapman's list. 'I'm a gay man, so I've cut off my parents, sister, and extended family since they support a man who doesn't believe in equality for LGBTQ people,' wrote one man in a Buzzfeed article that year. 'Both of our parents are dead so she is the only family I have left,' explained one woman on Reddit, after being cut off for voting for Trump. 'I am devastated because she is my sister who I love more than anything.'

For Jane, from Australia, who is estranged from her brother, it was his devotion to right-wing politics that did the most damage to their relationship. But in their case (and I suspect many others) that simple clash isn't the whole story.

'It became,' she explains, 'not about what my brother was doing, but about the fact that I was mad at him about it.' Her inability to swallow something was the problem, not his politics. She was labelled unreasonable because kicking up a fuss contradicted her role in the family as the pliable and agreeable girl. 'In the end I called my mother and said, "It sounds like you have the choice between getting him to stop doing the political things he's doing and getting me not to care. You're putting the pressure on me not to care." And she basically said, "yes... because that's easier."'

It is important to think a bit about how the simple idea of 'not behaving in the way that this family expects' can actually be more complex than that. It can often be a case of 'you are not performing your *role* in the way that allows this family to repeatedly paper over the cracks and carry on in the way it always has'. In instances like that, making any kind of stand can be confronting and very uncomfortable.

> 'In some ways he was my mirror, in some ways he was my opposite. My beloved brother, my arch-nemesis, how had that happened?'
>
> PRINCE HARRY, *SPARE*

Spare, says Lucy Blake, was a something of a gift to the estrangement community, who had previously felt unheard. 'I used to think my family was very different from other people's families and "less" than other people's families,' she says. 'I now have this understanding that actually the estrangement in my family tree makes my family much more like other people's families, and I found that to be a big comfort.' The public telling of estrangement stories will definitely provide solace to the siblings who contact Fern Schumer Chapman, who are struggling with the false idea that they are alone in their misery. 'I will tell you the first line of all the emails that come to me,' she says, 'it is almost always the same. They say: "I thought I was the only one."'

Hearing Prince Harry say on primetime TV, 'I would like to have my brother back,' but also describing the kinds of fights he had with him was very powerful because it showed the truth of a troubled sibling relationship: with both the conflict and the yearning for connection – the kind of agonising 'both-and' which makes the idea of sibling estrangement so tangled. The lure of the familiar can be strong, and fighting against the belief that only your family can give you a true sense of belonging is tough. 'They constantly come back to this idea that "Oh, maybe one day" or "they're not really that bad"', says Chapman, 'and "we had so many good times as children". To accept that perhaps they simply cannot depend on a sibling is very difficult.'

The struggle she describes in the individuals who seek her help is partly due to the way we can sometimes see sibling relationships as set apart from others in our lives. 'It is a relationship which we tend to sentimentalise,' says Jane, who tells me she is often 'a prophet of doom' to friends keen to have a second child 'so their first won't be lonely'. She urges them to pause and think of her and her brother. 'Don't have another child for the sake of your only child,' she says, 'who's probably quite happy, just rubbing along being their own selves.'

While there is potential for a lifelong bond with our brothers and sisters, it will likely take more work than we tend to acknowledge, without a cast-iron guarantee of friendship in the end. We should discard any belief that being 'somebody's brother or sister' demands that we overcome or heal whatever hurts we have experienced as a result of our relationship with them. That is not true at all – any more than it is true in other relationships, like friendships or marriages. We should face up honestly to the ways our siblings have influenced and shaped us, and that honesty should encompass the possibility that sometimes they might have hurt us too much to maintain the relationship. 'Some relationships are too violent,' says Chapman, 'too insulting, too injurious to continue.'

Dr Lucy Blake reckons the tendency to think sibling relationships operate according to different rules can lead to accepting some pretty ugly behaviour. 'I had a conversation with someone who breezily said, "Well, you know, my sister chased me round and kicked me till she broke her toe!"' Blake believes we need a much more critical approach to sibling aggression and abuse, which, she says, is common. 'It feels really important to acknowledge that while we have this image of siblings kind of being "best friends for life"… they can actually be the most violent relationships people ever experience.'

How physical fighting between siblings is viewed is something of a bellwether for the way we regard a sibling relationship generally, I think. The fact that physical arguments between younger siblings are often dismissed by adults, who turn a blind eye to events which in any other context would be considered shocking, reveals a disregard for the important relationship building that siblings should be doing. It's a complaint Dr Chaudhary hears often in his sibling estrangement support groups, from people furious that they face the consequences of their parents' failure to teach 'what is right and what is wrong'.

Abuse between siblings is a problem which is made more complicated to talk about as there is no standardised definition for it in either academic research or law. Instead, it's lumped under general terms like 'domestic violence', 'child maltreatment' or 'family violence'. Yet, a 2018 study by the University of Austin, Texas found that sibling abuse is more prevalent than both child abuse and domestic abuse combined – with nearly fifty per cent of siblings who were asked reporting having engaged in severe violence in the previous year.

Professionals can also be dismissive, says Vernon Wiehe in his book on sibling violence, labelling physical fighting as 'normal sibling rivalry' or 'rough play', even when the behaviour is clearly harmful, and would be viewed very differently if it was between friends or lovers. I should point out that he – along with all the experts I consulted – stressed the difference between abuse and the kind of childish 'roughhousing' which is quite normal, consensual and mutual, and often includes a parent. It was a regular Sunday night event in our house when my two boys were smaller. For quite a few years, their favourite pre-bathtime game was 'Wrestling', with Dad as a 'partner'. All the sofa cushions were deployed as a crash mat and they could select levels from one, 'amateur', to five, 'Olympic'. But alongside accepting this kind of physical play when they were small, we also instituted a strict 'you hit you lose' mantra, to underline the idea that violence must never be used to solve disputes or express emotions.

FAVOURITISM

One of the hardest and most exposing things to talk about among your grown-up siblings may prove to be one of the most common factors in estrangement: favouritism. A 2005 study in the *Journal of Family Psychology* found that up to seventy-four per cent of mothers and seventy per cent of fathers in the UK said they had a favourite child, but only ten per cent of them would admit it publicly.

Until now it is also a topic which I have purposefully (mostly) skirted around – despite the title of the book. That is because, although it has strong links to ideas around birth order (eldest daughters are more likely to receive preferential treatment from their parents) and what roles we adopt in the family (the favourite is more likely to be cast as the Golden Child), it is brought into sharpest focus at the point of sibling relationship breakdown. See William and Harry.

Favouritism is the issue which most clearly demonstrates how difficult it can be to transition into functioning and honest adult siblings if issues created in childhood are not properly resolved. Favouritism can be expressed by different means, including money, time and tolerance. And it most clearly shows the damage that can be done to the bonds between children in a family by the interference of their parents.

Unlike the issue of estrangement, there *is* a body of research into sibling favouritism, or Parental Differential Treatment (PDT) as it is known. Although vanishingly little of this research focuses specifically on looking for a causal link to estrangement, some studies do describe the effects that favouritism has on siblings and their relationships later in life. An article in the *Journals of Gerontology*, for example, indicated higher depression rates among respondents who identified themselves as 'being the children in whom the mothers were most disappointed'. It's one of the most moving lines of academic research I read while writing this book: the idea that someone has carried a sense of maternal disappointment with them for so long, and that its effects are so profound.

A much larger piece of work published in 2025 was more illuminating still. It showed that siblings who receive favoured parental treatment tend to experience better mental health, exhibit fewer 'problem behaviours', achieve greater academic success, enjoy better self-regulation and report healthier relationships. And the inverse – for the non-favourite – was also shown to be broadly true. The study, in the *Journal of Family Theory and Review*, drew its conclusions using data collated from every available piece of research on favouritism. When it comes to sibling relationships, the research found that 'in childhood, adolescence, and adulthood, siblings feel and express less warmth and more hostility toward one another when a parent favors one child over others'.

It is not hard to imagine how this lack of warmth is created between the 'chosen', favoured child and the other, who only feels the chill of their parents' disappointment. Instead of allowing the sibling sub-system to develop unimpeded, the parents' interference has conspired to create a chasm of experience between them. An adult sibling I spoke to about how favouritism had affected her life explained how her sisters had both received extravagant presents, driving lessons and treats during their childhood, and she had not. 'They also got so much more attention, right from the word go,' she said. Elsewhere, an anonymous person wrote to the *Observer*'s agony aunt describing her experience as a sidelined sibling, saying, 'My childhood was marred by favouritism. I was the middle child of three: the black sheep, the difficult one, the sickly one. These aren't labels I've given myself – they were said to, or about, me regularly. My elder sibling was always the most treasured by my parents. This dynamic has continued into adulthood.'

While peer-reviewed research may be playing catch-up on the link between favouritism and estrangement, a dive into the websites of therapists who routinely deal with the fallout from PDT helps to paint a fuller picture. I learn that, sometimes, parents lavish more attention and praise on the child who is struggling, keen to make up for a kind of perceived 'shortfall'. Behaviour which the other siblings – who are succeeding and quietly 'getting on with it' – find deeply unjust. But much more often parents favour the Golden Child – for their flawless performance as bearer of the family standard, or by living their ambitions vicariously. Both can drive a wedge between the children.

The favoured child becomes confused by the leniency shown to them compared to their brothers or sisters, who in turn become resentful. 'The favourite might feel gleeful,' explains Professor Helen Dent, who has worked with families where one child is made the Scapegoat, 'and relieved that they're getting the approval, but they will also, consciously or subconsciously, feel guilt and a lack of safety because, if their parents' love isn't unconditional, who knows what may happen to them next?'

For favoured Golden Children it can be an especially fraught experience, torn between the natural alliance they should be fostering with their siblings, and being seduced by that privileged (but vulnerable) position with their parents. They are trapped in a lonely kind of double bind, where they are disliked by their siblings for being treated as special, for playing a part they did not ask for and may not enjoy. The family system is bent out of shape.

Remember, too, that siblings raised by the same parents will not all have comparable relationships with them. Differences in temperament, gender and interests between the children will all influence the ways that they're raised – not all favouritism is intentional. Parents may just naturally get on a lot better with one of their children. A paper published in the American Psychological Association's journal says – perhaps unsurprisingly – that 'parents may be inclined to provide relatively favored treatment to daughters, conscientious children, and agreeable children'. As a daughter, it bothers me to think of the crossover between gender and 'good' behaviour, but as a parent, I can understand the allure of the more manageable child.

Thinking about the myriad ways that birth order, family roles and the different environments and relationships experienced by siblings growing up might create upset and resentments, it feels like the idea of favouritism (real or perceived, intentional or not) runs like a thread throughout the whole course of a sibling relationship. How it relates to the quality of those bonds in adulthood is an area ripe for further investigation, says Lucy Blake. 'What can be really damaging is a family dynamic where parents play siblings off against one another, where they feel like they've been pitted against each other for "who will be a winner and win the parents love?", or "who can do the most?" That can lead them to feel as if their long-term sibling relationship is really strained. It's hard to say much about without more data, but we know it's important and we really need to dive into it.'

In a piece in the *Guardian*, one sibling highlighted a surprising way that favouritism can prevent adult siblings becoming close. 'Margaret' revealed her resolve to end her relationship with her mother if the grandchildren are treated as unequally as she and her sister were. And she then explains the reason why the unfairness in their childhood has made it harder for her sister – the favourite – to cope with being her friend: resilience. 'We have tried to be close,' writes 'Margaret', 'but it doesn't work. I suspect she feels guilty about how I was treated, but also – because she grew up walking this rose-strewn path that my parents laid before her – she wasn't prepared for the fact that real life is tough. I've ended up doing better than her professionally, and she finds that very hard.'

WHO'S THE FAVOURITE?

By failing to resolve issues lingering from childhood, adult siblings can really struggle when forced back into close contact, typically to deal with the care or the death of their parents. But successfully navigating those twin challenges still leaves one more potential emotional landmine: inheritance. Questions around who gets what and why can press squarely on any psychological bruising caused by the experience of favouritism in childhood. It is to do with fairness *and* money, which both cause all kinds of sibling upset, as the author and screenwriter Daisy Goodwin explained in her viral Substack newsletter about being disinherited. 'When a parent makes a will,' she writes, 'they should be aware that although their children may be reasonable adults in every other respect, when it comes to inheritance, maturity dissolves into a puddle of childish resentments. Because when a beloved parent dies, what is being parcelled out may look like goods and chattels but it feels a lot like love. A parent's will is not just a legal document, it is the last expression of their thoughts and feelings towards their children.'

Goodwin coped with the situation by making the 'most grown-up decision of her life' and summoning the grace to 'let it go', choosing peace with her siblings over indulging any churning sense of resentment that the will could easily have caused. It also made her determined to do the precise opposite when her time comes. 'In my will I am leaving all that I possess to be divided equally between my two daughters,' she resolves, 'even if one of them invents the next Facebook and the other is living in a tent. I want my legacy to them to be unconditional love.'

In families where siblings lack the supreme grace of Goodwin – or whose relationships are flimsy – arguments and upsets caused by any 'unfair' dividing up of estates can create an environment ripe for estrangement, according to Fern Schumer Chapman. 'Siblings, at the end of the last parent's life, make a last-ditch effort for power and love and family loyalty,' she says, 'and those conflicts often result in a divide. I have talked to many people who – at this moment – discover who their sibling really is, whether it's through the sibling stealing from them or scooping up precious family treasures.' It's a very vulnerable moment for relationships already teetering on shallow foundations.

Psychologist Laurie Kramer strongly recommends not waiting for arguments to blow up in mid-life before addressing the issue of favouritism with your siblings, but to confront it honestly as soon as you can. While it might be (probably will be) difficult to admit you feel guilt at being the favourite, or painful to acknowledge the hurt you experienced because you weren't, it will be worth it. The foundational dynamic created by our parents is probably not the healthiest way to progress through adult siblinghood. Unless we are mindful enough to consistently spend time talking to our siblings, about our experiences, our relationships with each other, about how it all felt and looked from our specific point of view, while being gracious enough to realise that might be very different to anyone else's, it will be hard to progress beyond our childhood roles. Without that kind of communication, the loss of your parents can feel like the anchor of the family ship being hauled up, leaving everyone unsure how to relate to each other, without them at the centre to emotionally (and practically) tether everyone together. In the absence of holiday gatherings to see the grandparents, or regular correspondence to manage their old-age care, siblings may find they drift quietly away from each other, sometimes unaware of the emotional distance opening up between them.

MISMATCHED EXPECTATIONS

Clear water between brothers and sisters can be a feature of their adult relationship from the very start, if they simply don't expect – or need – intimacy from it. 'For some people, the fact they might see their sibling once a year is kind of business as usual,' says Dr Blake. 'Whereas some researchers might say, well, that's estrangement, they might not identify with that word. They might just think, "Oh, we see each other and we send cards: it's fine."' That may be 'fine' if the feelings are mutual. But where there is a mismatch – a sibling who yearns for closeness and whose affections are unrequited – failure to build a solid bond with their brother or sister as an adult has been described as 'more painful than divorce', according to Blake. Wanting more than your brother or sister is prepared to give can really hurt. In those cases, all the talking in the world may come to little. That is because estrangement caused by this kind of 'emotional misalignment' is so complicated to talk about. There's so little shared basis for understanding. Both parties feel the other is being unreasonable: one too distant and the other too needy.

It is also common, according to the findings of Ali-John Chaudhary and Lucy Blake, to have one sibling keen to 'go deeper' in their relationships with their brothers and sisters, to explore the family's psychology and chew over their histories. They assume a kind of emotional processor role; sometimes, but not always, because they have done some 'work', perhaps had therapy, and are keen to share. For their brother or sister, meanwhile – contentedly trundling along in a more superficial way – it can be uncomfortable to have complicated or buried feelings stirred up and can lead to real friction between them.

In our own family, it was my older sister who first assumed the processor mantle. She had met people who encouraged her to think more deeply about our childhood and its effects on us, and she was enthusiastic to talk to me about it. I'll admit I found it hard and became very irritated whenever she strayed into the territory of *feelings*. I was unused to facing emotional issues head on, and mistakenly believed she was 'dredging up stuff' unnecessarily, 'making a fuss'. I was – says Chaudhary – behaving in a very Anglo-Saxon way. 'There's this whole saying from a Pink Floyd song,' he says, 'something about quiet desperation being uniquely English.' Over time, I have (obviously) changed my mind, and credit my sister (as well as good therapy) with helping me do that.

For siblings who prefer to keep things lighter by talking about 'the weather or the state of the roads', it can be doubly irritating that their sibling even *has* this new role, explains Chaudhary. Their 'emotional intervention' can feel like a very unwelcome reconfiguration of the family's status quo, which may have limped along, but survived nonetheless. In his experience, it can end up causing so much frustration and upset that the relationship breaks down completely. Change is hard.

'Blood is thicker than water.'
English Proverb

What then of the siblings who do seek to reconcile, who are matched in their desire to connect and can meet the other 'where they are'? Karl Pillemer, clear in his mission, wrote *Fault Lines* to help families navigating estrangement. It contains stories from dozens of people who have repaired relationship rifts, allowing Pillemer to lay out 'a road map to reconciliation'. Siblings leave their testimonies on his website, including one pair of sisters who became estranged following a row on a family holiday: 'Almost twenty-five years later, my sister called me but did not leave a message. I checked the phone number and the area code was hers. I thought about it for a couple of days and called the number, and it was my sister. I think it was a year later when we began visiting each other, and she is now the only family I have left.'

Navigating sibling reconciliation is 'one of the thinnest pieces of ice you'll ever walk on', according to clinical psychologist Linda Blair, author of *Siblings*, who recommends not excavating too much of the past, but focusing on positives in the present instead. 'Leaving recriminations by the wayside and recognising the futility of seeking retribution or contrition' is often the only solution, agrees Fern Schumer Chapman, who has helped many siblings gently plot the beginnings of renewed relationships.

But the process is exposing, warns Dr Pillemer. 'It requires taking risks and imagining an alternative future that is very different from the present.' A quarter of a century of silence is significant. But Chapman says she finds nearly all estranged siblings carry hope for a different future into her coaching sessions. 'They feel lonely, they feel bereft, they feel abandoned, and most of them are stuck on hope.' Where possible, she builds on that to help her clients find a route back to closeness, even if that might mean drawing up 'codes of conduct', no-go conversational areas and even a 'safe word' to prevent reopening old wounds and starting fresh arguments.

Reconciliation might not be neatly linear; periods of more closeness may be followed by times when distance creeps back in and old patterns re-emerge. And, sometimes, I believe, it's right to acknowledge that it is just impossible. Sibling relationships do not have to be necessarily – or always – lifelong, significant or supportive. Sibling relationships are not exempt from normal rules and sometimes, cautions Dr Chaudhary, that means it is OK to recognise that there is simply not enough 'goodwill' in your family – or between you and your brother or sister – to keep you happy, or even safe.

Genetically we share somewhere between thirty-seven and sixty-one per cent of our DNA with a sibling – and even identical twins don't necessarily share 100 per cent with each other. That means that the amount of DNA you share with each sibling varies, a fact which may help to explain why you gel so well with one sibling (who shares your sense of humour, for example), and grate so horribly with another.

Biologically speaking, each parent passes down one of two copies of each gene to each child. Overall, a child has a fifty per cent chance of inheriting either copy. The same is true for the other parent's version of that same gene. 'Each gene is a coin toss,' says Carl Zimmer, whose book *She Has Her Mother's Laugh* is all about heredity. 'And that's why some sibling pairs end up sharing more genes and some end up sharing less.' That genetic pick and mix, he explains, is why 'some of our siblings are more like our identical twins, others more like cousins'. (And in fact, in Hawaii, the same word can be used for both female cousin and sister.)

Maybe, then, just maybe, it could be considered a bit arbitrary to draw a line around your little nuclear family, making up rules about how close you ought to feel and how well those relationships should sustain you. Reading about children estranged from parents who refuse to accept their sexuality, I learned about the expression 'compulsory kinship'. It describes how people can feel bound by societal expectations to conform to the idea that the family-of-origin relationships are 'central, natural, and inevitable'. I would argue that a provable variation in genetic make-up *on top* of all the other ways that you experience life differently as brothers and sisters means it's simply OK to accept some distance between you, for however long it lasts. It is also OK to mourn it and not to feel any shame.

And if it helps, the medieval saying 'blood is thicker than water' was reinterpreted over 100 years ago by American clergyman Henry Turnbull to read 'the blood of the covenant is thicker than the water of the womb', so its meaning was brought more into line with the biblical proverb 'There is a friend that sticks closer than a brother.' I like the thought that all those years ago, Turnbull described what feels like a very modern idea: that blood ties do not necessarily guarantee intimacy, but shared *life*, with whatever family nurtures you – birth or chosen – might be what really matters.

10

Bereavement

'My sister will die over and over again for the rest of my life. Grief is forever. It doesn't go away; it becomes a part of you, step for step, breath for breath.'

JANDY NELSON, *THE SKY IS EVERYWHERE*

When Elizabeth DeVita-Raeburn's older brother Ted died, he was seventeen and a half. 'I always include the half,' she writes, 'because six months is a very long time in a short life.' Ted was Elizabeth's only sibling. She's since written about the experience of losing him in *The Empty Room*, a process she found positive and necessary – a way of claiming her personal story of loss. But finding a way through the devastation that her brother's death caused her family, in order to confront her own grief, was incredibly fraught. Right from the beginning, her grief was sidelined. 'I was standing by his open grave,' she recalls, 'and I was dying inside just wanting to jump into the hole myself. And this – I'm sure very well-intentioned – woman walked up to me and grabbed me by the arm and sort of leaned down and whispered, "You're going to have to be very good because your parents are going through a lot."' At just fourteen years old, she was left (by this encounter and countless others which followed) feeling ashamed for longing for space and time to talk about what losing her older brother felt like. He was the one who had taught her how 'to navigate life' and now he wasn't there.

It is why she argues so fiercely in her book against any notion of grief hierarchy, in which you are expected to advocate for your sadness, and prove your experience is somehow valid before you are allowed to fall apart. 'The truth is,' she writes, 'the worst loss is the one that is happening to you, the one that has picked you up and thrown you down and left you struggling to put your life back together.'

Bereaved siblings are often 'The Forgotten Mourners' – sitting outside the nucleus of anguish occupied by the parents for whom the loss is considered titanic. For mothers and fathers, the loss of a child is recognised as such an affront to the natural order of things that it can eclipse all else. The loss of a child can be so unbearable, isolating and consuming that it can leave marriages torn apart. Amid this turmoil, people's capacity to view the devastation from another perspective is limited. For parents especially, being able to get up in the morning might be the most you can hope for. This can – sometimes – leave bereaved brothers and sisters neglected, both in the lead-up (particularly when a child has been ill for a while), in the moment of death and in the months and years after. Despite the many tropes around sibling competition and rivalry, similarity and difference, their experiences of loss have not been considered. Sibling bereavement is the most under-researched familial loss of all, and as such their grief is greatly underestimated.

BEREAVEMENT

In 1989, Professor Kenneth Doka coined the phrase 'disenfranchised grief' – 'the grief that persons experience when they incur a loss that is not or cannot be openly acknowledged, publicly mourned, or socially supported'. A bereaved sibling is left with precisely this feeling. A grief overshadowed by the upset of others: the parents of the deceased, or the deceased's partner or children, if they had them. Yet in the United States alone, nearly 62,000 children and adolescents lose a sibling each year, and between five and eight per cent of people will experience the death of a sibling prior to adulthood. After all we have explored about the sibling relationship, in all of its beauty, complexity and ambivalence, it feels like sibling grief should only ever be considered as acute and primary. If our identities are partly shaped by our relationships to our brothers and sisters, then to wake up in a world without them is a tectonic shift in our emotional landscapes. As one woman, who lost her sister as a teenager, shared on a blog for other bereaved siblings: 'for brothers and sisters, our siblings have almost always existed. They are the world, and for us, always or almost always have been. Take part of that away, and it is like someone removing a continent. It's like Africa goes missing in the middle of the night. You wake up, and the planet has fundamentally changed.'

'The world has shifted, and nothing can be put back exactly as it was before. There is a hole in the shape of him, and I have to learn to live around it.'

JOANNE LIMBURG, *SMALL PIECES*

WHO'S THE FAVOURITE?

In her beautiful book about the death of her brother Julian, Joanne Limburg quotes a letter she sent to a rabbi about him, explaining that his death had 'sent out cracks in all directions – all the way through the family story, past and future'. When I read that, I picture Joanne standing on a piece of Arctic ice, a web of fissures spreading out around her. She is rooted to the spot she used to occupy with Julian, afraid to move lest the ground gives way. Peering back over their shoulders, they would have been able to see the 'Climbing Tree' they scaled as kids, or the bus stop where teenage Julian was once picked on by pupils from another school. Looking together towards the expected horizon, they may have imagined Joanne's son (aged five at the time of Julian's death) growing up and getting to know his uncle better. Instead, the letter resumes: 'I'm the one that's left.'

The poignancy of this grief comes from the sense that your sibling is your contemporary. You had a mutual vantage point from which you bore witness to each other's histories, and from where you expected to strike out as travelling companions on a journey into a shared future. I have seen people on chat rooms and forums dedicated to sibling loss explain it like this: when your parents die, you lose your past; when your spouse dies, you lose your present; and when your child dies, you lose your future. But when a sibling dies, you lose the past, present *and the future*. You have to step off that fragile ice float alone and make your way into the next day, week and year, without them by your side. It feels, as Joanne Limburg explains, 'like an affront'. Since most siblings are roughly similar ages – members of the same generation

BEREAVEMENT

– there is also the added shock of your own mortality to contend with, one which has a very different texture to the feeling of being made adult orphans, for example.

> 'To lose your younger sister is a terrible thing, there's no one alive to check the truth.'
> BLAKE MORRISON, *Two Sisters*

Comedy writer Jason Hazeley lost his sister Millie when she was forty-seven, and the kind of grief which followed the absolute shock of her death was something he hadn't anticipated. 'Let's call it horizontal grief,' he wrote in the *Guardian*. 'I'd done vertical grief. My father died years ago, and I have lost grandparents and aunts and uncles – but losing the only other member of the family who went to the same primary school as me and with whom I shared the back seat of the Austin Maxi and argued over the Kellogg's variety pack on day one of every holiday was something new and dreadful.' He reflects that the loss of a sibling is something quite apart as they were someone who knew you in a way that others could never do. Someone who knew where you came from and held pieces of your story, sometimes so you didn't have to: Jason's sister is the only person who knew the name of the boy at the French holiday camp who told him, aged ten, how babies were made. I have written about the paradox of 'sharing memories' in families, a process which can be as complicated and contested as it can be comforting. Despite the fact that we are all bound to be unreliable narrators, your siblings and their (version of) stories are still integral to a communal past, and their death severs one of the threads tethering you to it.

'When she died, she took the memory of not one but two childhoods with her,' explained Jason, 'in all their vivid, silly, scattered, doesn't-matter-but-it-does detail… Memories are the stories we tell ourselves, and they are the building blocks of the self. But if you can't remember the stories, who are you?' His grief was compounded by not being able to ask Millie any more questions, to check things – both small and large – against the versions of the memories he held. 'I feel as though I have lost a witness, someone who can attest to what happened to us both.' It is a loss which feels fundamental.

As I embarked upon this book, a friend had just lost her sister, Jess. The time from diagnosis to death was a scant few weeks and she was left reeling. She is also now her parents' only living child. She is the sole memory to be relied upon, if she ever wants to bring to mind the childhood they shared. When we first talked about her sister, she told me that when they were little, the family had a cat, and the girls used to say to each other that if you blinked at her and she blinked back, it meant that she loved you. Before she died, Jess was on life support. The only thing she could do was blink. Nobody else in the world could feel the significance of this. And with her death, these stories come to an end, never to be replicated or replayed.

When I interviewed the bestselling authors and twin TV doctors Xand and Chris van Tulleken, Chris eloquently described what it is like to inhabit a world with the knowledge that there is another person walking around who looks identical to you, who somehow represents you even when you're not there. Their intimate relationship was formed in the womb, and after they were born, their closely matched DNA continues to bind them together for life – even when they are physically apart. Chris even said that if someone has met him and likes him, he knows they will probably go on to like Xand too. It can be a very efficient way of making friends or working a room. And yet, their relationship is fractious and they squabble, sometimes badly. They have had therapy to help deal with disharmony and they describe themselves as having different personalities and correspondingly different approaches to life and work. Chris loves to plan while Xand is allergic to diaries.

Twins provide the clearest way of illustrating this idea of shared perspective and the wrenching grief of sibling loss. The intimacy of their lives from the very beginning is a bit like a hand in a glove and each is reliant on the other for the way that they function individually as well as together. As the Hon. Timothy Knatchbull, who lost his twin Nicholas in an IRA bombing in 1979, explained, 'Nick's heart started beating next to mine, three weeks after our conception, and we'd hardly been separated in the fourteen years and nine months since our birth… I was utterly devastated. Nick was my soulmate. I didn't think I'd know how to lead my life without him.' This theme of utter togetherness is also explored by Emma Spearing in her visceral one-woman play *Whole* about the loss of her twin sister Charlie to cancer. The production is

Emma's primal scream, which forces the audience to confront the physical devastation she felt in losing 'a part of herself' when her sister died.

If we accept the theory of sibling deidentification, that siblings create a distinct identity to one another to attract parental attention, then even though twins have so much of their identity bound up in their intimately shared experience, they must also claim a niche which is unique to them: they are not the *same* person. In their twinness they seem more alive than other siblings to this doling out of labels, including strengths and weaknesses. They must see so clearly – in relief – what the other has that they do not and vice versa. So when one twin dies, it very easily follows that the other will feel as though a part of their intertwined identity has vanished at the same time. In Emma's case, when Charlie died, she was explicit that she had lost 'the Batman to her Robin'. In life, they were a duo who depended on each other being there to make sense of their individual identities.

These examples might feel a little over the top to you, perhaps as a non-twin or someone with an average, not-super-close relationship to your brother or sister, but I will wager that there are things about your sibling which you do admire, which you do not possess in your own personality and which in some way you may have come to rely on as existing in your world. 'In my family there are many roles to be filled: some play Provider, Peacemaker, Problem Solver, Helper and Healer,' wrote Richard A. Dew in *Rachel's Cry: A Journey Through Grief* about the loss of his son and its devastating effects on his daughter, and the shape of the family.

'Others are: Encourager, Comforter, Nurturer, and still others Fixer, Learner and Teacher. But given the cast that we depend on, who stands in when the Fun-maker's gone?'

My own little sister CJ, for example, is the 'Fun-maker' in our family; she is entertaining at a party in a way that I am not. Going out with her puts me at ease as I don't have to try to be fun (though I make a very good wing-woman). She is the same way at family gatherings, holding court at the dinner table, with story after story, one funny accent after another. I can only imagine the awful absence if she were gone. The imbalance in our sibling unit would expose both Bex and me. It is because as brothers and sisters, we are born into a family system, in which we form key parts of our identity by being in relation to our siblings. Losing one suddenly rearranges everything that you have ever known.

To help tell the story of her brother Ted's death, DeVita-Raeburn interviewed seventy-seven other bereaved siblings and found that the impact of the loss of their brother or sister on their own identity was a recurring theme. They would say things like: 'he was my confidence', 'she was the one who understood me', 'he was the social one'. When you lose a sibling you lose more than a person who performed a particular role in the family. Like a piece of a jigsaw going missing, you can no longer stand with your brothers and sisters as a team, certain that whatever you lack, they may be able to compensate.

Journalist Georgia Coan lost her little brother Elliot, following a routine operation to mend a broken collarbone. It was unexpected, very traumatic and the effects on her were existential. 'The sibling relationship is so complicated and so special and so important,' she said, 'that when you lose it, you're no longer the person that you used to be or that you were growing up.' Exactly how this occurs is described in a 2024 paper in the *Sociology* journal, which says, 'Issues of identity and relationality reside at the core of sibling relationships, regardless of the quality or closeness of connection.' The paper goes on to explain the idea that, as fundamentally social creatures, when a sibling dies, whatever part of our identity we constructed in relation – even in *opposition* – to them will also be lost forever.

Our siblings do not just help us figure out our identities in childhood and adolescence. It is obviously where a lot of the heavy lifting is done, but they remain influential forever; whether we talk to them daily, or have a trickier, more ambivalent relationship. All feelings about our siblings are helpful for us in thinking about who we are becoming – because of how we inevitably position ourselves in relation to them. Whether that means: 'I now know that I am kind and caring. Look at me, organising all those appointments for Mum, while she selfishly pursues her career.' Or: 'He's so great with my kids, and really thoughtful. I feel bad that I'm so much more disorganised with birthdays and things.' When you lose a sibling, you can no longer compare yourself with them as you both grow and change. 'It's almost as though your DNA changes,' explains Georgia Coan. 'And you kind of have to come to terms with that, even if you don't want it, even if you reject it. It's like: I don't want this for myself. But you have no option but to continue.'

BEREAVEMENT

Time does not stop when someone dies, though you might desperately want it to. You can't refuse to ever move forward again, hollowed out and lost about 'who you are'. As Georgia says, life carries on, and, somehow, we have to as well. But, without your brother or sister around any more to help shape who you become, you must plot a new course, leaning on different guides. Other people who travel along with us – our friends or partners – will become more important, helping with that making and remaking of us: smoothing out our hard edges, or encouraging us to be braver or more confident. But it is a big ask.

In her characteristically uninhibited and beautiful account of how she coped with the death of her sister, circus owner Nell Gifford, journalist Clover Stroud describes how she 'fantasized about vanishing into the place I'd come from, before I was born, and finding my sister there'. Furious that she couldn't time travel back to that place where they could find each other – either as floating stardust before being formed in the womb, or physically in their shared childhood, riding 'scruffy ponies' and dressing up family kittens – she finally realised something which offered a kind of peace. She would never *really* lose Nell. 'I couldn't lose something that was inside me,' she wrote, 'and actually was me, and I knew she was there, as bright as the red of my blood.' You may not be able to see them, to laugh over childhood memories, cry over others, but you still know them intimately and carry them with you. The characters of the dead remain inscribed in the hearts of survivors they leave behind. So you can also hold yourself up to *that* version of them, even if it is slightly shadowy; even if they will never change, as you must.

How we do that, how we learn to see ourselves in relation to the brother or sister we have lost is a little bit dizzying, like looking at ourselves in a wavy mirror at the fair. As at each new stage of our lives, we can only compare ourselves now, solidly in the present, to the memory of our sibling. We can also ask others who knew them to colour in the parts we cannot, providing more and different details about the person *they* knew. But still, the dynamic of our bond will be different to one between living siblings.

That said, there can be a strange comfort found in making comparisons with the sibling you have lost. Even physical resemblance – which may have been anathema to you as children, perpetually annoyed at people pointing out that you were 'peas in a pod' – may become one of the most reassuring reminders of the 'red of the blood' you share. A facial expression, particular gesture, aversion to sport or love of Marmite will link you forever to the person you lost. It can act like an outward sign of belonging to someone else, reminding people that you are the sibling and your relationship is unique and inimitable. It announces to the world that you, your claim on your sibling bond – *and* the pain of the grief which you have suffered as a result of losing them – should not be forgotten.

Similarly, I would wager that as children or teens, you were often unable (or maybe unwilling) to acknowledge some of the ways that your personalities were actually alike. But, that as an adult, having learned to live without your sibling, you may be more open to noticing traits in yourself which you had thought belonged solely to them. What you begrudged in life, you may warmly welcome after their death. Research undertaken in 2018 by sociologist Laura Towers shows that embracing similarities in this way 'enables bereaved siblings to continue bonds and maintain a connection with their deceased sibling following their death... by emphasising a sense of sameness and belonging'. Enabling some kind of continuing 'bond' with the sibling who died is enormously valuable, helping us to deal better with their loss. It helps us realise that part of our mourning is the pain of transforming their physical presence into something else, a different kind of tie, sustained by memories and stories as well as how we make sense of any resemblance to them now.

MAKING SENSE OF LOSS

As siblings, one of the most obvious ways that we construct our identities in relation to our brothers and sisters is through birth order. Even if you reject the idea that your place in the family has much to do with shaping your character, if you are 'the baby', for example, you can't escape the fact that you are the youngest and will never 'catch up' with the others. Ditto the eldest, who will always reach the milestone birthdays first. When a sibling dies, that changes and you might feel utterly unprepared for what that means.

How bereaved siblings answer questions like 'how many brothers and sisters do you have?' or 'are you the youngest?' was part of Laura Towers's focus. She found that many really struggled with the scrambling up of the order, saying things like 'I was never meant to be older than him'. Bereaved younger siblings lose the person they hoped might guide them through certain life stages, whereas older siblings are denied the opportunity to provide a 'route map' for them. 'When I turned nineteen,' said Britney, 'and became the same age as he was, and then when I turned twenty, I was like, "weird". I still feel younger, even though I've lived longer. I got a college education that he never got and I did things he never did. But I definitely do feel younger in my mind.' Others wrestled between 'head and heart', knowing that their sibling had died and so was always frozen in time, but finding it hard to imagine or express. 'She died a few days before her thirteenth birthday, and so she's always a little girl right and yet she's always the eldest too right? And so she's not a little girl. I never see her as a little girl cause she was my older sister... I don't think that will ever change,' Samantha remembered.

Most of the siblings that Towers surveyed preferred to continue to self-identify in relation to their deceased sibling – keeping their old place in line. Towers says this highlights how important the 'ongoing lateral kinship tie' is to the way people see themselves in the world. A recent Facebook post which I spotted, by close family friends Sam and Layla who lost their older sister Hannah years ago in an almost unbelievable helicopter crash, read: 'Happy Birthday to our "forever young older sis"'. There is value, says Towers, in recognising that 'the dead can continue to maintain an important and influential, albeit liminal, position in the webs of relationships in which people are embedded'.

These tricks of time are made harder and more painful, says Georgia Coan, when the gap between your age *now* and the final age your sibling reached stretches further apart, and you reach more and more milestones without them. Her brother was a teenager when he died, but would have turned twenty-eight in April 2025, just as I type this. 'I feel that in moments of career success specifically, that there is a bit of guilt,' she says. 'I know that he would be happy for me, and he would obviously want all of this for me, but you still feel guilt that you're the one that's been able to do all of this and that your sibling hasn't.'

The feeling is familiar to Callum Fairhurst, founder of the bereavement charity Sibling Support. After his big brother Liam died at the age of fourteen, he found arriving at important life events, such as starting sixth form college, agonisingly difficult. 'I was like: this is meant to be Liam doing this. I found it really overwhelmingly emotional… and then moving to uni, that was also really emotional, and then leaving uni: bloody hell. Like, what? My parents didn't ever go to a graduation of Liam's, but that's what we always, always expected.' If you were planning to follow in someone's footsteps (and had been for years), it can feel unnatural to strike out alone and exposed. To embark on a whole new life stage without them, with no one to tell you what to expect and no one to reflect on it with afterwards, is unsettling. I suspect that for siblings who lose their brother or sister when they are very young, that process of becoming an adult and leaving them behind in childhood, as Callum describes, can sometimes feel cold-hearted. Like you've betrayed them by growing up when they can't.

WHO'S THE FAVOURITE?

In both sibling bereavement and estrangement, we find the pain of a relationship being truncated before it 'ought' to have been. I am not talking about the anticipated death of an eighty-year-old sibling here (although, of course that will be very sad, all those years of knowing and loving someone and then having to say goodbye), but of premature deaths, when there was still the expectation of many chapters to come in your mind.

We often take siblings for granted – they are always just… *there* – and consequently might not invest in them in the same way we do our chosen friends or partners. Their loss may make us feel bad for not spending more time together, or for prioritising careers or other relationships. We might simply feel rotten for saying awful things to them during heated arguments. So it is especially interesting to learn how sibling ambivalence directly affects the experience of grieving their loss. Helen Rosen, author of *Unspoken Grief: Coping with Childhood Sibling Loss*, has researched the experience of sibling bereavement in detail. To do it, she came up with two dimensions to characterise the kinds of sibling relationships she was looking at first, before seeing which are most affected by death. The dimensions are two axes on a graph, and the first is called 'closeness–distance'. At one end are siblings who are in constant contact with each other; at the other, those who seldom speak. The other dimension Helen calls 'warmth–hostility'. At one end of that axis are the siblings who have warm, supportive relationships, and at the other those who constantly argue or consciously choose to limit contact. Rosen discovered that the more a relationship veered towards the end of either continuum, the more intense the grief.

That means it's not only the close and warm relationships we grieve, or grieve most. We will also intensely mourn the sister who angrily broke off contact with us years before, or the brother with whom we have always struggled to connect or whose life choices we can't quite respect. But in those cases, we will also experience those other emotions like guilt or regret, alongside our sadness – making the grief more complicated and the feelings harder to unpick. The same is true of relationships which are right at the extreme end of warmth and closeness. Those kinds of highly interwoven, co-dependent relationships tend to be predictive of a grief which is more difficult for the remaining sibling to navigate. Barbara Lazear Ascher says in her book *Landscape Without Gravity*, written after the death of her younger brother from Aids, 'Siblings may be ambivalent about their relationships in life, but in death the power of their bond strangles the surviving heart. Were you close? Yes, but we didn't know it then.'

MOVING FORWARD

Survivor guilt is common. 'There's a huge amount of feeling that "it should have been me, not them"', says Callum Fairhurst. 'They were more academic than me, were more successful than me, were nicer than me. Why was it not me? I don't understand it.' This kind of guilt is hard to let go of. Helen Rosen identifies another dimension that adds to the complexity. It is called 'Family Legacy', and describes the feeling among children that they 'owe' their parent for their existence. For her research, Rosen spoke to 159 people who had lost a brother or sister and found that this feeling of debt was increased 'dramatically' by their death. It is as if the remaining sibling has their life plus their sibling's life to live.

Both the idea of legacy and survivor's guilt can be exacerbated if the sibling who has died is actively idealised – either by the family or by the bereaved sibling themselves. It can happen as a result of good intentions, trying to keep a connection through more flattering stories and memories. But if it tips into hagiography, it can create an impossible standard for the surviving sibling to live up to. My older sister Bex, who is a trained celebrant, would love it if instead we adopted the funeral traditions from Pacific Micronesia. At a funeral on the island of Mogmog, travel writer Judith Fein describes hearing mourners speaking honestly and openly in front of the whole community 'about the shadow side of the departed'. Her translator explained, 'it was psychologically healthy for the people who had been hurt or harmed to speak their truth… It was even more important for the man who had died to have the truth spoken about him, and how he behaved in life.' It's sort of similar to how Bex has asked me to approach speaking at her funeral, if I ever have to. I have her full permission to steer away from general platitudes and to include 'the specifics – both positive and negative'. I will tell people gathered that she was incredibly competitive, for example, but only when she thought she might win; therefore fearsome at Bananagrams, but outright refused to play Trivial Pursuit. And I think it is a good idea: to be honest about our sibling's *full* humanity. It might lessen the guilt about any ambivalence we felt towards them in life, and prevent us trying to chase approval, or left feeling that we need to be more special, gifted or clever than they were, to somehow prove that we are worthy of living after their death.

The emptiness felt in a family following the loss of a sibling can feel so awful that some surviving brothers and sisters report actively trying to expand themselves to fill it, by assuming some of their sibling's character or role into theirs. Siblings left suddenly 'as if Africa vanished overnight' feel it might help the family recover faster, by reconfiguring the system so that the absence appears a little less apparent. If the sibling who died was a repository of parental ambition, for instance – destined to achieve academic greatness – there can be a sense of duty in the surviving brother or sister to 'make up' for what has been lost. A 2008 article on bereavement published in the *Family Journal* notes that grieving siblings sometimes actively do this to 'comfort the parents or relieve their grief'. It is a horrible reminder of the sibling's place in the mourners' hierarchy, their grief put aside in service of others. 'Children,' it says, 'are often the barometer of family tensions and may try to comfort, cheer up, or distract parents having difficulty with loss issues.' It is another indication of the multitude of losses that a sibling suffers when their brother or sister dies.

Not only does the death of a sibling steal a shared past and future from their surviving brother or sister, but it also takes away the parents they once knew. The bereaved sibling instantly loses the parents unaffected by loss, not broken by the death of their child. The parents who – perhaps – they did not have to look after before, now becoming hypervigilant to their emotions. It is another relationship which they must mourn. The parents will be forever altered – as all members of the family will be – and a new relationship with them will have to be carefully constructed to accommodate the absence of the missing family member. Children who are relatively young when they lose a sibling also have to face up to the more existential shock of their parents' powerlessness: they were not able to save their sibling and keep the family safe. It is a hard truth to bear. The cracks really do go out in all directions at once.

For some, there are the brothers and sisters 'on the mantelpiece', who died before they were even born. Children born after an older sibling has died are called rainbow babies now (the same name is given to those children born after miscarried and stillborn babies) and their grief is very particular. It shares so many of the same ingredients as other bereaved siblings, but is even less discussed, because – says the Rev. Giles Fraser, whose older brother Johnathan died before he had a chance to know him – it feels almost impossible to 'own'. 'It feels illegitimate to have grief for someone you have never met, never been alive at the same time as... but I do feel that way. The pain extends through the generations.' Just as with other bereaved siblings, that pain changed his parents into people whose loss was always palpable to Giles, even as a little boy, who never knew the old carefree versions of them. Their grief had a profound impact on how they raised him: he and his younger brother were 'clung on to', he says, and 'loved to the point of overprotection' by a mother whose tears were always close to the surface.

How the grief of a parent for a sibling they never knew feels to the child who lives is the subject of a moving essay by Joyce Hayden for Al Jazeera. It's written like a letter to her brother Gerry, who drowned before she was born. 'In family pictures,' she writes, 'I have never seen Mom as happy as she was in the photographs before you died. She never looked that happy or thrilled to be alive again.' The piece describes little Joyce, at home from school on a snow day, sifting secretly through dusty shoeboxes, stuffed to the back of wardrobes. She finds faded cards, crayoned by her brother for her father's birthday and a pair of small brown corduroys, which she presses to her face, desperate to find out what her brother smelt like. 'Even now,' she writes, 'I feel closer to you on snowy days. Even now, snow on my tongue tastes of grief.'

The day before we spoke, Giles's mother had marked his brother's birthday by placing flowers in the place she had scattered his ashes – the stone birdbath on the lawn at the family home. 'His birthday comes first, and mine follows,' explains Giles, a fact he says he was 'always made aware of' while growing up. Despite that, at the age of fifty-seven, he got tied up in a bit of a knot when describing where he 'comes' in the family order. 'I am the oldest, but I haven't always been the oldest… but even that isn't right. Goodness, where do we start?' He told me that Johnathan was seven months old when he died in the night, a victim of Sudden Infant Death Syndrome (SIDS), known as 'cot death' when it happened in the 1960s. His parents thought he was sleeping in and had been grateful – enjoying a cup of tea in the kitchen together, before making the horrifying discovery. 'My dad ran into the street,' Giles says, welling up, 'and wouldn't come back.' Family friends came to tend to the body, and are still close, part of the 'web of survivors' who help to describe the 'gentle' child who was lost: to both his parents and also to Giles.

Children born after loss are sometimes still referred to as 'replacement children' or 'subsequent children', 'conceived consciously or unconsciously, to fill the void left by their deceased sibling', says Sarah Vollman, a social worker and bereavement expert, in an article for *Psychology Today*. In past centuries, it was common even to give these babies the same name as their older sibling, a practice which has now, thankfully, fallen by the wayside. Nevertheless, says Vollman, 'being born as that child can have a significant impact upon their identity, attachments, and life story'. That resonates for Giles, who still finds his grief confusing, but who now realises – as an adult – that he lived in a house full of trauma, some of which he now carries, second hand. For example, he was extremely vigilant and anxious about the temperature in his own children's bedrooms, because of a potential link between that and SIDS. 'Let's say technology has been "well deployed" in the Fraser household,' he says. He can also see that his mother was broken open by the loss (and the losses of several miscarried babies before) and fully understands why she held her surviving children tighter as a result. As a priest, he can't think of a better response, even if he found it almost claustrophobic as a teenager. As a parent, he admits doing the same.

BEREAVEMENT

There is a Portuguese word, *saudade*, which means to be in a state of longing or a nostalgia for something or someone that is absent or lost. There is no equivalent in English, so I think this beautiful word should be adopted to describe precisely this kind of grief, the sadness of mourning someone you may never have known. Giles says he talks about Johnathan regularly – but not often – with his parents, in conversations he describes as very intimate. 'I want to say I love him,' says Giles, '... and he is certainly my brother and... I rather like his gentle presence amongst his other brothers who are more robust than him. He definitely has his place in the family.'

'We live in a culture that only wants to talk about what is going well. Anything that is not going well is positioned as a detour from the main road. The truth is that pain is not a detour from the main road. Pain is part of the road we walk as human beings.'

SUSAN CAIN, *BITTERSWEET*

Callum Fairhurst was still at primary school when his older brother Liam was diagnosed with cancer in his leg. On the day the doctor phoned to give his parents the news, he remembers being at home watching *The Simpsons* together on the sofa – 'that was the day his, and rather selfishly, my, childhood ended'. Four years later, after an illness which went 'on and on', Callum went into his brother's bedroom to kiss him goodbye. Liam was fourteen and Callum was just twelve. 'I kissed him, and I said to him that I will live a great life,' he recalls, 'and I said I will try and help other people… I wanted to live his life for him with those two promises. They're the two most important promises I have ever made to anyone, and I will ever make in my life.' Living Liam's life for him initially meant carrying on raising money and awareness for the disease, something which his older brother had done with huge enthusiasm, despite his tender age and diagnosis.

It wasn't until Callum was at university and decided to tackle his grief head on – but struggled to find help which was sibling-specific – that he realised how else he could honour his promises. That was when he decided to set up Sibling Support, which provides help for overlooked bereaved brothers and sisters. At the time Callum was searching for support, he found excellent charities designed to help children who have lost parents or grandparents and organisations to help mums and dads navigate the loss of their child. But he found nothing that was specifically for him. It made little sense, says Callum, because 'Every family with more than one child will at some point experience sibling bereavement, yet there was a real lack of specific support for a grief which can be really confusing, fractious and profound.'

Meeting others who have been through similar loss and sharing stories about their siblings provided some comfort, especially in the early stages of Georgia Coan's raw and traumatic grief. She went on organised weekends away and sat in circles with other bereaved brothers and sisters who talked about their experiences of loss. It helped her to feel less alone, suffering with strange and distressing symptoms caused by the absolute shock of Elliot's death. 'There were actually moments,' she said, 'where it was almost physically painful to be inside my body, if that makes sense. And like some kind of alien, I wanted to just zip this... this human skin off.' It made sense to me, having heard about the 'series of unfortunate events' which led to her brother's death: horseplay at school, in which his collarbone broke (but inwards, rather than the usual outwards). An operation to mend it was delayed and then became complicated after a vein became adhered to the bone. Two days after being finally discharged, Elliot suddenly collapsed and died, having suffered a massive internal bleed. At just nineteen, why would Georgia *not* want to be rid of a fragile body which might also let her down?

Thankfully, years later – and after lots of psychological help – she feels like she has made enormous progress and doesn't feel like she needs to go on the residential weekends any more: she has a network of people to lean on, and her mental health is 'way better'. But, Georgia says, not everyone she met since losing Elliot is able to keep moving forward without their brother or sister. 'Very sadly,' she said, 'I know of at least two siblings who unfortunately took their own lives... I think if you already have mental health issues and you go through such a traumatic loss... and you don't have the support system, you can easily understand why people end up going down that path.'

A 2013 study undertaken by Stockholm University and led by Mikael Rostila looked into the risk of suicide following sibling bereavement. It found that for women, the suicide risk was 1.55 times that of non-bereaved persons, and in men it was 1.28 times higher. The risk of a sibling taking their life, if their brother or sister did the same, is even higher. 'Facts are the harshest and the hardest part of life,' wrote Yiyun Lee in her book *Things in Nature Merely Grow*, 'and yet facts, unalterable, bring with them some order and logic.' Her sons Vincent and James both died by suicide: first Vincent and then James. The cold, troubling facts about the effects of sibling death are these: that it has been shown to lead to negative lifelong physical and psychological outcomes such as substance abuse, impaired relationships, poor academic performance, suicide and early mortality. And that because siblings are often hypervigilant about the grief of their parents (and others), they end up 'adaptively coping' with their own loss, squeezed, as it often is, out of plain sight.

It's not uncommon for bereaved siblings to struggle with their grief for years, even decades later, burdened by a secondary set of feelings caused by their 'maladaptive coping' mechanisms to their sibling's death. And, says a 2022 paper in the *Journal of Paediatric Nursing*, it is often the case that siblings manage all of that alongside destructive thoughts and behaviours. These rather bleak findings led to a call for a much more 'robust understanding of the risk' facing siblings who are trying to cope with the loss of their brother or sister. It also explains why Callum Fairhurst 'ended up finding groups of friends that have had sibling bereavement, just kind of accidentally, and then you feel there's this weird connection. Those that I know who have grieved at a young age are more likely to find escapism through harmful choices, most commonly excessive alcohol or drug taking.'

'I needed actions that matched the enormity of my feelings, because there was a cathedral collapsing inside my soul every day, and I wanted to know how to express it.'
CLOVER STROUD, *THE RED OF MY BLOOD*

In the midst of a grief which is so unexpected and makes you feel 'so out of control', Georgia feels empathy towards people looking for 'crutches' to help them cope. There is such a turmoil of feelings, she says, in among which 'you suddenly realise you're not immortal'. So 'ridiculous as it might seem', drinks or drugs can look like the answer to an impossible problem. By contrast, Georgia found herself struggling with obsessive compulsive disorder, something she has had since she was twelve. 'After Elliot died, it became a lot worse, it was almost as if I had to have control over something.' Although she is a lot better now, she still tries to keep herself 'safe'. She does not drink, and says the anxiety she still has prevents her from taking too many risks. It is a hangover from those early 'dark days', when she was extremely cautious about letting anything bad happen to her, because of the potential of upsetting her already shattered parents: 'Because I knew that obviously they will naturally worry more about me now that's happened… It's become less so as I've got older. But I'm still not the sort of person that's doing anything wildly crazy, if I'm honest.'

> 'Shall we finish this episode with a hug?'
> 'I will put that in a jar on a shelf, marked "Brother Joth".'
> NICHOLAS AND JONATHAN DIMBLEBY,
> *THE BRIGHT SIDE OF LIFE*, BBC RADIO 4

Five years after it was founded, Callum's organisation provides exactly the kind of compassionate support for siblings that he wished had been available to him – and which made the difference for Georgia. But with the passing of time, something else has also happened: Callum's grief has changed from something simply 'awful' into something he calls his 'superpower', something which helps him fully embrace everything in life. Despite missing his brother every day, and finding milestones particularly painful, he says that now he sees that his death 'showed me all the beauty of life. I walk out the door and generally, most days, I feel just so lucky to be alive. I love the trees and all of that. And that's because of the grief.'

Georgia experienced something similar, but is honest about the painful irony of the process. Because Elliot's sudden death made her realise how fragile life is, and because she 'lost' so much time immediately after he died, frozen in the period of early grief, she is now sometimes in a state of uncomfortable 'panic', desperate to make the most of the opportunities she has. 'Because, actually, we do only get one life. I know it's a cliché, but we need to do more and experience more. I do feel a definite pressure to not waste time.' To live with a tug of guilt about a sibling who is left in the past, together with a drive to propel yourself forward, sucking the marrow out of the life you have been granted, is a tough mental place to exist. Especially for Georgia, who found it impossible to 'seize the day' for quite a long time, mired instead in horrible mental health struggles.

Now, she is beginning to take up more of life's opportunities; planning to travel more as her confidence increases and trying not to let the feeling of time passing become something frightening. It is fair to say both she and Callum now live with gratitude, because their siblings did not get the chance to. What they are experiencing – becoming adults, getting jobs, winning awards, throwing parties in their flats – Liam and Elliot will never experience. The horizontal grief of sibling loss, which can put an unhealthy pressure on us to fill a void left by our brother or sister, can also be a beautiful invitation – given the right support – not to waste what you have been given, and Georgia and Callum have not.

I wondered about this in 2023, when I made a pair of programmes for BBC Radio 4 with Nicholas and Jonathan Dimbleby called *The Bright Side of Life*, all about the experience of horizontal grief and the idea of savouring the life you have. The brothers were facing up to Nicholas's diagnosis with motor neurone disease, which progressed rapidly in the course of production. The brothers – both in their seventies, one increasingly frail – sat at Nicholas's kitchen table with the ticking clock marking precious time in the background. They talked about their lives together and how they felt, knowing Nicholas was dying. Their gratitude at having the time to say their goodbyes was palpable, as was Nicholas's joy at a life enriched by family, friends and art. 'I'm living in a memorial service,' he explains in a slurred and laboured voice. 'Because I wasn't hit by a bus, people had the nerve to write and say "we loved you and you made the house so nice… we always loved coming there."' At the end of the final programme, Jonathan asks, 'Shall we just finish this [episode] with a hug?' And Nicholas replies, 'I will put that in a jar on a shelf, marked "Brother Joth".' The chairs scrape on the stone floor and you feel the heartbreak of them both. 'Oh God,' Nicholas quietly concludes.

Susan Cain explores all these ideas in her book *Bittersweet*, about 'how sorrow and longing make us whole'. When we grieve, we long for connection, 'to reunite with those we are separated from and our sorrow at not being able to'. It is not a new idea, that the contrast between pain and joy gives meaning to both, but the book is a lovely retelling of truths found in different philosophies from all over the world, including Taoism, with its light with the dark, and the philosophy of Nietzsche: 'Have you ever said Yes to a single joy? O my friends, then you have said Yes too to all woe.'

Experiencing joy once you have the knowledge of pain is a strange kind of gift from grief. It is similar to the feeling that creeps upon us as we age, that our time is limited and that happiness has to be seized, because we have – almost inevitably – learned how hard life can be. It is also like the knowledge that those who are given a second chance at life receive:

that death is a real possibility. The loss of a sibling is a mixture of all of these at once: we are well, we know what it is to mourn, life is a gift and it doesn't last forever. The effect on how the bereaved sibling approaches life can be as magnificent as the burden of the grief is terrible.

> 'Sea—Ship—drown'd—Shipwreck—so it came
> The meek, the brave, the good, was gone;
> He who had been our living John
> Was nothing but a name.'
>
> WILLIAM WORDSWORTH,
> 'IN MEMORY OF MY BROTHER, JOHN WORDSWORTH'

In 1805, the Romantic poet William Wordsworth lost his younger brother John in a shipwreck, off the rocky coast of Dorset. Known on board as the 'Philosopher', this reputedly quiet and thoughtful man had just embarked on a trading voyage to China when he died. His plan had been to share the profits from the trip with his older brother, to enable him to carry on writing poetry. When news of his death reached William at Grasmere in the Lake District, it left him utterly devastated. He wrote that he would 'never forget him' and eulogised that John's 'eye for the beauties of nature was as fine and delicate as ever poet or painter was gifted with'. But it was a devastation which ultimately left William feeling a lot like Callum: heartbroken but not bleak and hopeless. Instead, as he wrote in 'Elegiac Stanzas Suggested by a Picture of Peele

WHO'S THE FAVOURITE?

Castle in a Storm, Painted by Sir George Beaumont', John's death was an experience which 'humanised' his soul giving him access to the entire palette of human emotions, including a new and awed appreciation of what it means to be fully alive.

> So once it would have been,—'tis so no more;
> I have submitted to a new control:
> A power is gone, which nothing can restore;
> A deep distress hath humanised my Soul.
>
> Not for a moment could I now behold
> A smiling sea and be what I have been:
> The feeling of my loss will ne'er be old;
> This, which I know, I speak with mind serene.

After John's death, Wordsworth was forever changed, knowing what it is to suffer and mourn, as well as how it feels to have the world fully revealed to him as a result, in all its beauty and capacity for pain. It reminded him of the shock he felt seeing a painting of a familiar scene – the view of the calm seas from Peele Castle – rendered instead as a riot of dark and violent storms. The knowledge that benign blue skies can be transformed by 'That Hulk which labours in the deadly swell' is precisely what John's death has granted him, and which – he laments – is hidden from those who ignorantly take millpond waters or moments of innocent joy for granted. 'Such happiness, wherever it be known/Is to be pitied; for 'tis surely blind.' He sees grief as part of a life – to be treasured just the same.

Callum shares in this mission with Sibling Support. 'Often when we talk about death and grief, we're actually not talking about death and grief,' he explains. 'We should be talking about life and joy. There's nothing we can do to bring back that dead person, but there's everything we can do to stop you from kind of having a dead soul.' I was especially touched, I want to add, that when reading about how Wordsworth coped after John's death, I learned he started collecting artefacts from shipwrecks, 'psychological crutches' discovered by Dr Sean Kingsley, the British maritime archaeologist, who said Wordsworth 'leaned on them desperately to keep John's memory alive'. The yearning to live fully exists alongside a desperate longing to feel the sibling bond, and is just as strong as the enduring pain of the physical separation. Callum channels all of that into the positive work of his charity, which has the added benefit of honouring the vows that he made to his brother Liam. Wordsworth treasured his collection of polished wooden boxes and shared his beautiful poems with the world. They both use their longing and their sorrow to help bereaved siblings everywhere.

Afterword

As I put the finishing touches to this book, my sister Bex is about to turn fifty. Therefore, I can safely assume we have loved each other for almost forty-eight years. Meanwhile, the baby – 'Squidge/t' – is firmly in her forties, joining us in the Badlands of middle age, at last! The bonds between us have gradually tilted over the decades from vertical to horizontal. And now we stand shoulder to shoulder, on the same ground, looking ahead.

I can appreciate that underpinning the simple story of maturing beyond our foundational roles of eldest, middle and baby are a multitude of other influences that have shaped us. And we will never truly reconcile our different versions of events. Sometimes our narratives more or less match. Mostly we find our perspectives challenged, diminished, appropriated and remade. The thing is, we may grow up together with our siblings, but we experience so much of life alone with our thoughts. And these are much more convincing – particularly in childhood – than what may or may not have actually happened.

Along with every therapist and academic I have spoken to for this book, I am desperate for there to be more research in the field. From what has already been published – and from what I have witnessed during my many interviews – our character development is, in no small part, influenced by our siblings. It's why I called my podcast *Relatively*. Whatever form our relationships with our brothers and sisters may take, they help us to figure out our place within the family, which in turn provides a blueprint for how we relate to people in the real world.

For five years, I have been repeatedly struck by people's appetite for conversation about their brothers and sisters – and crucially by how they *feel* about these. A mere mention of the subject tends to be met with a kind of outpouring: a jumble of memories, caveats, laughter, eyerolls, verbal cul-de-sacs and convoluted side-bars, attempts to provide context and backstory. People want to make their timelines clear – to justify how and why things unfolded as they did: early evidence of favouritism, labelling, arguments still unresolved, the impact of new schools, house moves, divorces, bereavements, births, and so on. Sometimes seemingly minor details from childhood get interwoven into more significant adult experiences, exacerbating or alleviating these: the pain of disappointing relationships or the hand-to-heart 'can't live without them' joy of describing the bonds which sustain them. Invited to share these, 'people stammer and hesitate, tripped up by memory and sudden bursts of unexpected emotion', wrote journalist Erica E. Goode, when she described researching a piece about brothers and sisters for the *New York Times*. I found exactly the same.

AFTERWORD

Experiences of being a sibling are rarely given the requisite time or space, often subsumed by the role our parents played in constructing our sense of self. My strong suspicion is that this will change, and that the same emotional intelligence and language which we have adopted for that primary parent–child relationship will soon be applied to our sibling attachments too. Therapy – which sees the individual as part of a larger family constellation, in which we can feel both a sense of belonging and the possibility of individuality – will (should) become the process by which we are encouraged to see and understand ourselves as adults. Thanks to the willingness of today's youth to share openly about all kinds of emotional issues, it won't be long, I'm sure.

I recently spotted a post on Instagram titled 'Ten questions to ask your sibling now'. Along with a healthy sprinkle of sentimental prompts (favourite games as children, etc.) were these three very thoughtful ones which I plan to use:

> Is there anything about our relationship you would like to change?
> What do you hope our future looks like?
> Is there something you'd like to say to me but haven't known how to?

This kind of emotional introspection, endemic to social media, gives me hope that we can evolve out of the bad habits that keep us closed off.

Just this week, the writer Esther Freud was on the radio talking about her relationship with her older sister, the fashion designer Bella Freud. Asked if it had 'changed over time', she answered with a laugh: 'It changes almost week by week.' In a subsequent piece for *Vogue*, Esther wrote, 'I'm aware myself how carefully the younger sister needs to tread, how mindful she must be not to threaten the equilibrium, not to blossom too early or too obviously, if she wants to keep her sibling as a friend.' I was stunned by the sensitivity of this. She was aware of her relative role and chose to preserve the closeness with her sister over a sense of individual entitlement.

While writing the latter chapters of this book, I found myself unexpectedly recalling my maternal grandmother Edith. Born in 1917, she was of a generation which articulated things very differently to those of us alive today. Of course, she may not have *felt* all that different. Edith's brother Eric had served in the Royal Air Force in the Second World War, but his plane was shot down 'somewhere over Europe', and he was presumed dead at the age of twenty-one. Not long afterwards, my grandma ('code' name Blossom) signed up to serve with Council of Voluntary War Work. She later told me she volunteered because she wanted to 'replace him' in the fight. I like to think that perhaps she wanted to feel closer to him by setting sail for North Africa, rather than staying put near Wolverhampton.

On the wall in her house in Devon, she hung a letter from an unnamed pilot to his family, intended to be sent in the event of his death during the same war. I think it was published in a newspaper, but to her it was intensely personal, and she often touched it with her fingertips or dusted it with the cuff of her dressing gown. When I stayed with her as a child, she would occasionally take it down, angle it to the light and read it to me. I tried to make the right sympathetic noises but found it awkward. I didn't have the perspective to see her as anyone's sister – someone who had squabbled over toys, or who – as a teen – may have looked up to her handsome big brother in uniform, preparing for war: she was just my grandma. Later, I learned that she had helped support her other brother, John, through school by going out to work when she was still very young – a sacrifice I don't think I have fully appreciated, even now. John died of motor neurone disease aged seventy-nine.

I can only assume she would have loved dearly to have grown old with both Eric and John in her life. She didn't have the chance to know Eric as an adult; their relationship was forever vertical. I know she often imagined what kind of man he might have become. But it is not until getting on a bit myself, and then thinking deeply about what it means to have a sibling, about the tragedy of losing them too soon, that I can start to appreciate how acutely and how long she must have grieved them – their shared histories and their lost futures – before she finally died aged ninety-nine.

This book was not intended to stray into the realms of parenting. As such, I have tried to steer a course which only occasionally brushes up against explicit ideas about how to think about the children you may be raising. What I have tried to do instead is write about brothers and sisters in a way which feels inviting to grown-up siblings, keen to reflect on the ways their own relationships may have been formed and then gone on to shape them as individuals. But of course, that has involved travelling back to childhood, and so I realise that a lot of what I have included may also be useful in thinking about your own children, or grandchildren.

Because my sons are growing up and getting ready to fledge, I have found myself reminiscing about these life stages – both as I experienced them and from the point of view of my parents. I'm so much more able to understand their passionate desire that we 'all get on'. Despite everything I have learned about the ways in which children from the same family can differ and diverge, I am clinging to the same hope of harmony and intimacy for Max and Theo that my mum and dad have for Bex, CJ and me. I don't think you can help it as a parent, and it's why the hurt brought about by sibling estrangement weighs so heavily.

Building and trying to maintain intimacy with my sisters had to be an intentional act, harder than for many siblings, who can draw so effortlessly on a range of shared experiences. But, it must be said, it was a lot easier than for others, for whom a rupture (for whatever reason) may be beyond repair. Writing this book has only made me more determined to put in the effort, to not let them slip through the cross-currents of daily life and the responsibilities that present themselves more urgently.

At a recent lunch with my sisters and our dad, he rummaged in his rucksack and pulled out three lovely, matching leather notebooks. He handed one to each of us, encouraging us to record anything that we felt was important: memories, funny or poignant anecdotes, perhaps. I haven't

AFTERWORD

yet decided how I will use mine. But I'm not sure it matters. What matters is what he said as he slid the gifts across the table, looking at each of us in turn. 'Love each other. Look after each other. Promise me?'

Acknowledgements

I have been a freelancer for over ten years now, bobbing about in a karmic soup of kind and supportive creatives. Without their honesty, encouragement and occasional kick up the bum, I would not have even started writing this book, let alone completed it. So thank you to Adam ('just write the damn thing') Cumiskey, Philly Beaumont, Alexandra Quinn, Anya Spence, Kate Taylor, Natalie Steed, Annalisa Barbieri, Kirsty Hunter, Eleanor Garland, Sharmini Selvarajah, Nick Carter and Tony Phillips. I hope I get to pay you all back.

To my agent, Emma Bal from the Madeleine Milburn Literary Agency, you were exactly what the doctor ordered, and I only kept going thanks to your firm but funny approach. Thank you so much. Similarly, to my UK editor Cecilia Stein at Oneworld, a chef's kiss for how skilfully you have guided me to this point, with such a perfect combination of patience and forthrightness. To Karen Rinaldi, my editor at HarperCollins in the US, thank you for your notes and your galvanising enthusiasm for the whole project from day one.

An honourable mention to Jane Garvey, who dropped the whole idea of siblings into my lap, back in 2020. Thank you for that, and for letting me phone you occasionally for no good reason. That the podcast ever got going is in no small part because of Vanessa Neville. She let me bore her on and on and *on* about it, before issuing a very kind ultimatum. Thank you, Ness. I don't think you realise how much you helped. The podcast was pretty much a solo production – although midway through, I was rescued from the admin hell of my own making by producer Rachel Oakes, who then suddenly lost her brother Daniel in 2023, while we were working together. Both of them were on my mind a lot while writing this book.

I am lucky to have amazing friends who live nearby, who are also 'out there' hustling and trying to be brave at the same time. These women and their utter loyalty are the reason I can take the knocks when they come – and have complete permission to celebrate any wins. The deal is that we all do the same for each other and I am so proud of what each of them puts out into the world. I also like drinking beer and eating sweet potato fries with them. To Anna Lawlor, Anna Marsden and Charlotte Griffiths, thank you so much for absolutely everything. D.F., especially. Without your skills and generosity, none of my ideas would ever have made it off the back of envelopes, and out into the world.

To 'Swim Club' – Rebecca Chicot and Ruth Jordan. I am so lucky to have you both in my lane, being so enthusiastic and impressive (professionally, rather than aquatically, I hope you don't mind me clarifying!) as well as taking amazing underwater pictures. Thank you. I hope we swim together for ages to come. To Jack and Jennie Tennant, Tor-tor and Rupert Espley. Tash and Dan Forster and to Sarah Matthews. Thank

ACKNOWLEDGEMENTS

you for topping up my courage by always being so kind and encouraging. To Staci Larkin, who lives far away but who feels very close – thank you for always checking in.

To Greg and Margaret Chapman-Scherkoske and Guy and Cherry Blanchard, whose friendship has been constant in all things. Thank you. And to Locke, the LMG. We will always remember you to everyone, but mostly to your brother and sister, Iris and Thom. To Helen Thompson, I have learned so much from you and will always be very glad we became friends. I cannot wait to read what you write next. To Donna Ferguson, who directed me to Wordsworth and his poem about his little brother. To Cathy Moore, who has kindly talked about this as 'a book' when it was just a set of anxiety dreams. And to the team at Loftus Media.

In a book about siblings, it's fitting to include my 'sisters from other mothers': Helen (Brewer) Parker, Cat Morris, Louise (Bousie) Halling and Mary Cusack. I don't like to imagine a world in which we are not in almost daily contact, urging each other to just Keep Going, come what may. You are Titans. Thank you for always being there.

When I moved back to the UK as a teen, I became friends with Hannah Ashton. She, her mum Gill, dad James and brother Robert were a refuge for me during the years that much of this book stems from. I even got to see what having an older brother was like (sorry, Bobert). Writing this book has reminded me again of just how much I owe them, for keeping me grounded and letting me stay for tea, when I was lingering hopefully in the kitchen *again*. God bless *Ready Steady Cook*. I loved being with you all. Thank you so much.

WHO'S THE FAVOURITE?

At university, some lucky stars ensured that I met Hester (Williams) Stevns in the first minute of freshers' week. Throughout everything – between that first cup of tea and now – I am so grateful to have had your friendship. Thank you for also gifting me your mum, 'Hils Wils', as a loyal first listener and critic to all of my projects. (I am slightly nervous to think about her review of this.) Your sibling relationships are gold standard and it's one of the best feelings in the world to be somewhere in the orbit of the Williams clan.

I obviously owe an enormous debt of thanks to everyone I spoke to for the podcast and this book: all of the seventy or so pairs of brothers and sisters who let me peek into their relationships, or shared about a sibling they care for now, or have loved and now lost. I tried my best to capture your stories in the episodes and these chapters. From car journeys to sibling separation, to competition, estrangement and protection, they all felt very precious and I hope I have done them justice. Thank you, too, to all the experts who patiently talked me through their research and helped me to understand siblinghood better. You were all very generous with your time.

To my dad Paul and mum Jane, to my stepmum Christine and my stepdad BP/Gerald: even when it was rough, I held on to the knowledge that out of the mess I was gaining two people who really cared about me. It has always felt like that, and it's a big win. Thank you for always cheering me on and telling people at ping pong, book club, tennis, golf, the WI, the National Trust, yoga, art class and photography club (am

ACKNOWLEDGEMENTS

I missing any?) about the things I am up to. It means such a lot to have your support. I love you.

To Eleanor Mills and Richard Brooks, my stepsister and stepbrother – I am so happy that when the circle of the family widened, it included you. Old friends who become family is a priceless thing. To my Dutch stepsisters, Pam and Fiona Delahunt, you are simply *gezellig*. To my sisters-in-law, Libby Collett and Jo (Larly) Hobbs: being given extra sisters when you get married is a bonus. Being given extra sisters like *you* is the dream. To my brother-in-law Mike Norris, thank you for being so encouraging. I would also like to say thank you to my very lovely mother- and father-in-law, Maggie and John Carr, whose steadfast support over the years has been a gift.

To my actual schwesters, Bex Norris and CJ Jay: I've just written a *whole* book about and for you, which explains just some of the many ways I love you both. I simply couldn't have made it through without you. Thank you for loving me back.

Finally – most importantly – to my family. To Max and Theo, who have been so sweet this year. Despite studying for GCSEs and A Levels, they kept cheering me on. You both make me proud every day – especially in the way you love and support each other. And to Matthew, who I married twenty-five years ago this year, but have loved since I was nineteen. Thank you for being my number one cheerleader and being squarely behind all of my ideas, even when enthusiasm outweighs any logical planning. We make a good team.

♡

Remembering:

Charlie Radha Spearing

Daniel Oakes

David Jay

Elliot Coan

Hannah Timings

Jess Sherlock

Liam Fairhurst

Nicholas Dimbleby

Simon Flynn

Further Reading

Little Women by Louisa May Alcott

The Sister Knot: Why We Fight, Why We're Jealous and Why We'll Love Each Other No Matter What by Terri Apter

Pride and Prejudice by Jane Austen

Sense and Sensibility by Jane Austen

The Sense of an Ending by Julian Barnes

Siblings: How to Handle Sibling Rivalry to Create Strong and Loving Bonds by Linda Blair

Home Truths: The Facts and Fictions of Family Life by Lucy Blake

Superfudge by Judy Blume

Bittersweet: How Sorrow and Longing Make Us Whole by Susan Cain

The Empty Room: Surviving the Loss of a Brother or Sister at Any Age by Elizabeth DeVita-Raeburn

My Naughty Little Sister and Bad Harry by Dorothy Edwards

Kitchen Table Lingo by The English Project (written and edited by Bill Lucas, Edward Fennell and Richard Brooks; Foreword by Melvyn Bragg; Afterword by David Crystal)

Adult Sibling Relationships by Geoffrey L. Greif and Michael E. Woolley

Spare by Prince Harry

WHO'S THE FAVOURITE?

The Little Princess by Frances Hodgson Burnett

The Secret Garden by Frances Hodgson Burnett

Little House on the Prairie by Laura Ingalls Wilder

The Walsh Family series by Marian Keyes

To Kill a Mockingbird by Harper Lee

Marrow: A Love Story by Elizabeth Lesser

The Lion, the Witch and the Wardrobe by C. S. Lewis

Things in Nature Merely Grow by Yiyun Li

Small Pieces: A Book of Lamentations by Joanne Limburg

The Scent of Dried Roses by Tim Lott

Maybe One: A Case for Smaller Families by Bill McKibben

Two Sisters by Blake Morrison

Everything I Never Told You by Celeste Ng

Codebreaking Sisters: Our Secret War by Patricia and Jean Owtram

Wonder by R. J. Palacio

The Dutch House by Ann Patchett

The Future of Your Only Child: How to Guide Your Child to a Happy and Successful Life by Carl E. Pickhardt

Fault Lines: Fractured Families and How to Mend Them by Dr Karl Pillemer

Unspoken Grief: Coping with Childhood Sibling Loss by Helen Rosen

One and Only: The Freedom of Having an Only Child, and the Joy of Being One by Lauren Sandler

Brothers, Sisters, Strangers: Sibling Estrangement and the Road to Reconciliation by Fern Schumer Chapman

FURTHER READING

Where'd You Go, Bernadette? by Maria Semple

The Red of My Blood: A Death and Life Story by Clover Stroud

Olive, Again by Elizabeth Strout

Born to Rebel: Birth Order, Family Dynamics, and Creative Lives by Frank J. Sulloway

Step Up: Step-Parenting and the Art of Creating a Happy, Healthy, Blended Family by Katherine Walker

She Has Her Mother's Laugh: The Powers, Perversions, and Potential of Heredity by Carl Zimmer